Talking with the Children of God

Talking with the
Children
of God

Prophecy and Transformation
in a Radical Religious Group

GORDON SHEPHERD AND GARY SHEPHERD

University of Illinois Press
Urbana, Chicago, and Springfield

Library of Congress Cataloging-in-Publication Data
Shepherd, Gordon, 1943–
Talking with the Children of God : prophecy and transformation
in a radical religious group / Gordon Shepherd and Gary Shepherd.
p.   cm.
Includes bibliographical references and index.
ISBN 978-0-252-03534-0 (cloth : alk. paper)
ISBN 978-0-252-07721-0 (pbk. : alk. paper)
1. Family International (Organization)
2. Prophecy—Family International (Organization)
3. Family International (Organization)—Interviews.
I. Shepherd, Gary, 1943– II. Title.
BP605.C38S54   2010
289.9—dc22   2010007693

Contents

Preface

Jumping up from her front-row seat, "Mama" assumed the role of master of ceremonies and addressed the informal gathering in quick, animated tones: "Hi, everybody! We're so glad to see you all. It's almost like one of our monthly parties. In fact, it's better than our monthly parties—isn't it?—because we've got Gary and Gordon here. Not only are we fellowshipping, but we have distinguished guests. We're going to see slides and hear news of our wonderful Family all over the world from Gary's trip. Thank You Jesus!"

Distinguished or otherwise, it was nice to be spoken of so generously and, for four days, the two of us certainly had been treated with great courtesy and candor by our hosts. The place where we were assembled was called the community center, which served as a fellowship hall for social and recreational activities. The gathering consisted of a sizeable number of "World Services" staff members of the Family International—or Family for short—a novel religious organization founded by itinerant Christian evangelist David Berg and notoriously known in the 1970s as the Children of God. World Services is the Family International's central headquarters unit, and "Mama" is the affectionate nickname bestowed by devotees upon Berg's consort and spiritual successor, Maria, whose name prior to joining up with Berg and the Children of God was Karen Zerby. (Prior to his death in 1994, Berg was known by his followers as Father David, or even more familiarly as Dad. Members typically use only first names, and most converts adopt a new name when they join the group.)

Mama (or Maria) continued speaking in her breezy, spontaneous style: "Some of you, we know, were not able to talk with Gary and Gordon, and that's because they're so thorough in their work! Originally they were going to just take a tour of the offices. You know, go room by room to greet people and say 'hi' and 'how are you' and 'bye.' Well, Gary and Gordon don't work that way. Ha! They can't meet you without talking to you for at least a half an hour, or maybe an hour. So if you want to know why some of you didn't get a visit, that's why. They just got stuck! You all had so much to say, they couldn't get away. But I think they've gotten a pretty good overview of everything. If you haven't met them, at the end of this meeting, please do go up and introduce yourselves and tell them who you are and any interesting facts about yourselves. They do their job well. They're conscientious. They have a job to do as social scientists of new religions, and they want to find the truth. And in talking to all of you I hope they have found the truth about us, as much as possible. I hope that you told them about the problems, too, that you encounter, and didn't just gloss things over and tell them everything is great, because we know we have lots of problems. But we also know that the Lord works those problems out and we always get the solutions to them through the power of the keys, and our spirit helpers, and our counseling together."

Pausing, Maria turned to us and inquired, "They didn't just tell you good things, did they?" To which Gary responded, "Not at all."

Maria, turning back again to the assembled gathering, exclaimed: "Good! We wanted them to be honest. Because in doing research there is nothing worse than to have things covered up or not be able to get at the facts. So we thank the Lord that they really wanted the truth, that they are thorough, and that they want to find out these things so they can explain to others. We're a complex, complicated, unusual group, and we're a little difficult to understand."

Prior to our visit at World Services we had stayed many times as guests in Family communal Homes around the world, sleeping in whatever facilities were available and eating whatever food was served to Home members themselves during the course of our observational visits—up to a week in a number of different Homes.[1] However, during the 17 years we have been studying the Family International, we have never accepted any payment for our research, nor, indeed, have we ever been offered payment or any other compensation for what we have written. In 1993 and 1995, trip expenses (airfare and lodging) were covered by Family officials when we were specifically invited to engage in interviewing and consulting visits that required travel. However, on all other occasions, we have looked upon our time spent traveling to and observing in Family Homes as a normal cost of carrying out our research as academic scholars. We have successfully applied to various scholarly funding sources to pay for much of our traveling costs. For instance, during the winter, spring, and summer of 2005, Gary's around-the-world trip to visit 23 Family Homes in 16 countries was supported through competitive research grants awarded by Oakland University. This support included the travel costs associated with his trip to World Services, where the material for this book was obtained. Gordon's observational trips to Family Homes during this same time period were much closer to his residence in Arkansas (excepting the trip to World Services) and were paid for as out-of-pocket expenses. We have both paid for a number of other incurred expenses, not covered by research grants, with our own funds.

A disclaimer of this type is necessitated by the level of controversy surrounding the Family International and by accusations of some critics that scholars who have written about the Family and other controversial new religious movements have been compensated for doing so, thus rendering their work mere paid-for propaganda.[2] We cannot speak for other scholars, but we can say for ourselves that seeking financial benefit has not in the least motivated our work or what we have written. We find the Family to be of intrinsic sociological interest and argue both in this volume and elsewhere that the Family International affords scholars a unique case study that provides a variety of valuable insights about the transformational processes that all new religious movements must undergo to survive, let alone be successful in accomplishing at least some of their major organizational goals. Critics of the Family focus almost exclusively on historical issues of sexual deviance and putative child abuse.[3] But in spite of all its problems—past and present—and the horrendous claims leveled against it, the Family International endures, and in many ways thrives, well into its third generation. Why and how such long-term endurance occurs in the face of widespread public opposition are questions that sociologists of religion ought to find important to answer. The bulk of published writing about the Family, however, has not focused on these questions but has continued to rehash accounts and charges of abuse made by disillusioned former members. While these accusations have their own level of significance, they do not advance us very far in understanding the sociological viability of the Family. This latter point is the one on which we focus, and we hope that at least some partial answers emerge from what we report in this book.

In a related vein we believe our investigation of the Family International is particularly timely relative to the dramatic events that took place in the western Texas communities of Yearning for Zion Ranch (YZR), Eldorado, and San Angelo in the spring of 2008. National and international attention was focused for weeks on the state's wholesale removal of 467 children from homes of members of the Fundamentalist Church of Jesus Christ of Latter-day Saints (FLDS) and the huge morass of legal, civil, and social problems this precipitous action immediately created.[4] Though quite different in many ways, the FLDS and the Family International share a widespread public opprobrium whenever their respective presence and activities are brought into headline news, typically related to claims of systematic, group-sanctioned sexual abuse.[5] In the early 1990s, based primarily on the claims of disgruntled former members, police raids of Family Homes in four countries (Australia, Spain, France, and Argentina) resulted in removal of over 600 children from their parents and the internment of hundreds of parents and other adults. All children were eventually returned to their also-released parents when no credible evidence of actual abuse could later be generated by authorities in any of the four countries. In Argentina, the judge who oversaw the case was eventually impeached for improper judicial conduct, and in Australia the Family successfully sued the Province of New South Wales for millions of dollars.[6]

Family International officials have made numerous attempts since the early 1990s to rectify and prevent past abusive practices but have made little headway in public and media perceptions.[7] Thus the Family shares and suffers with the FLDS from the generic ethnocentric attitudes and stereotypes of outsiders that are routinely attached to any socially unconventional groups to which the "cult" label has been successfully attached. Several so-called "cult experts" who commented on the unfolding FLDS situation in the U.S. national media in fact also made reference to the Family International as a parallel case, thus putting Family Homes and their children at risk for future state interventions.[8] We do not directly address these specific issues in this book. But readers of our book will acquire a knowledgeable foundation about both the historical and current functioning of the Family International that is based on direct observation and candid communication with organizational functionaries. Readers can then arrive at their own judgments about the general purposes of the organization, the present processes by which it operates, and the nature and character of its leaders. The level of information and insight obtained from our studies of the Family International is rare for this kind of group and will hopefully fill a gap that is all too often the province of rumor, speculation, and ignorance.

Our descriptions of World Services operations, and the sociologically remarkable process of obtaining and publishing what Family members believe to be God's Word in Family publications, are based on open-ended interviews with Maria, Peter, and a significant portion of the World Services staff. Their willingness to speak candidly in response to our questions is crucial to the validity of our study. These particular individuals are uniquely positioned to provide us with information and insights that are found nowhere else. It may be assumed that their primary motive in meeting with us was to cultivate good public relations for the organization they lead, and that they, like most effective organizational leaders, are skilled at selectively managing the information they provide outsiders in order to project a positive impression of the way they conduct their affairs. None of the people whom we interviewed, however, refused to answer any of the questions we posed, nor were they vague or evasive in their responses.

Many of the WS staff members were young adults and, although they carried out organizational roles of considerable importance with apparent competence, they were not experienced with long, probing interviews by outsiders. Most importantly, on the specific subject of how published prophecies are generated and processed in World Services, and how each of them contribute to this process—a major focus of our research—we have little reason to believe that our informants substantially or intentionally misled us in their accounts. They were perhaps surprised at our interest in the small details of their routine tasks, taking much longer in each interview session than expected to pose follow-up questions rather than merely becoming superficially acquainted with a general overview of their roles. At the same time, they were eager to explain to us what they did, articulating their own understanding of the jobs they perform at World Services, perhaps more clearly in some cases than they had ever had occasion to do before.

In the end, however, the analysis and conclusions we offer in this book concerning what we characterize as the "social construction of prophecy" in official WS publications, are ours, not the Family's. From their perspective of religious faith, what we describe as a complex social interaction process is simply viewed by Family leaders as the realization of God's will and the peculiar modus operandi God chooses in guiding what they believe is their divinely commissioned end-time mission of Christian evangelizing.

THE FAMILY'S WORLD SERVICES ORGANIZATION

Our initial contact with the Family was a byproduct of the aftermath anxiety experienced by Family leaders over the deadly results of the FBI siege and assault on the Branch Davidians at Mt. Carmel, Texas, in the spring of 1993.[9] Fearing a similar fate, Family leaders contacted several scholars of new religious movements, including us, and proposed that we visit and observe patterns of life in Family communal Homes, hoping that our subsequent reports might allay government and public stereotypes of the Family as a dangerous cult meriting suppression. Following these initial observational visits, we continued to observe in an expanding number of Family Homes around the United States. Over the years we also had several lengthy interviews with Maria and her current husband and coleader of the Family, Peter Amsterdam. In 2005, Gary took a sabbatical leave from his university to visit 23 Family Homes in 16 countries to conduct field research on Family Home life and to administer a detailed survey questionnaire to adult members living in the Homes that he visited. Gordon made similar observational visits to communal Homes in Texas and Michigan.[10] All of these various data-gathering activities provided us with a substantial amount of information regarding the contemporary Family International, on the basis of which we have published several academic papers concerning the evolutionary development of the Family as a new religious movement.[11] But we still lacked a clear understanding of the operations of World Services, the Family's central headquarters organization.

Like many other enduring religious movements, the Family International has survived the demise of its charismatic founder, David Berg, by developing an organizational structure that has provided institutional leadership and management of the group's religious mission. The central staff organization that began to emerge in the 1970s, as Berg sequestered himself in a series of secret locations, eventually came to be known as World Services. The chief task of World Services (often referred to simply as "WS") is to publish and disseminate to Family communal Homes Berg's visions and revelations, doctrinal commentaries, ecclesiastical policies, and counsels for everyday living, as well as other religious materials. WS publications not only provide guidance for rank-and-file members but also were and are deemed to be essential tools for both Christian evangelizing (or what the Family calls "litnessing") and fundraising through voluntary donations. By the time of Berg's death in 1994, WS had assumed an increasingly complex set of additional administrative tasks.

One unique facet of Family administration, making it difficult for scholars to study, is that World Services is made up of relatively mobile organizational units that periodically change and keep secret their geographical locations from both outsiders and regular Family members. This mobility and secrecy represent a continuation of Berg's reclusive practices that is justified by current group leaders primarily as a security measure. Based on their history of conflicts with anticult organizations, law enforcement officials, and a number of disgruntled former members, Family leaders are concerned that revelation of their headquarters location would disrupt their administrative and publishing work by mass media searches for sensational news stories about religious "cults," in turn stimulating renewed public opposition to their missionary efforts and, they fear, make them inviting targets for vexatious lawsuits and potential violence.

On several occasions we had intimated to Maria and Peter our interest in the possibility of visiting World Services but, given their insular organizational practices and closely connected security concerns, the prospects of such a visit seemed slim. To our surprise, shortly after we completed our tour of Family communal Homes in spring 2005, Maria and Peter contacted us with an invitation to spend several days at the current WS headquarters to observe their operations and talk with members of the staff organization about their daily work. This was an unprecedented opportunity. While we and other scholars had been given open access to certain Family data sources and Family Homes for field research and interviews, no one, to our knowledge, had ever been allowed to visit World Services to witness the secluded administrative operations of what, in the 21st century, has emerged as an intriguing, transnational religious organization. On our part we agreed not to disclose the current locations of World Service units, neither in subsequent research reports nor in our personal conversations with friends, colleagues, or representatives of the mass media.

We were told that we would have open access to all WS departments and staff personnel and that we were free to ask any questions we wished during our visit with the exception of queries concerning WS finances. In addition to numerous informal conversations and observation, over the span of four days we conducted a total of 21 open-ended interviews, including preliminary overview

Karen Zerby and Stephen Kelly, aka Maria David and Peter Amsterdam, leaders of the Family International, circa 2008. Photograph used by permission of the Family International.

and concluding interviews with Maria and Peter, a round-table interview with Maria and a dozen WS staffers who regularly contribute to "channeling" and editing prophecies for Family publication, and individual staff interviews with a majority of WS department heads.

INTERVIEW METHODOLOGY AND EDITING DECISIONS

All of our interviews were sound-recorded and subsequently transcribed; we have quoted from the interviews at length in this book. In addition, we also took extensive notes of our conversations while at World Services. Perhaps *conversations* rather than *interviews* would, in fact, more accurately describe our methodology for obtaining information from our informants. We debated whether or not to attempt developing some structured interview protocols to follow when meeting with various WS department heads and staff members. But we quickly came to the conclusion that we didn't know enough about our subjects and their specialized work responsibilities to formulate a sequence of precisely focused questions. Instead, we opted for an informal, open-ended approach in which we attempted to put people at their ease while paying careful attention to what was being said so that we could respond with appropriate follow-up questions.

A more-or-less spontaneous method of asking people questions can, of course, lead to lengthy tangents that are not always relevant to the data gathering task at hand. We did our best to avoid too many such digressions while simultaneously maintaining the relaxed ambience of a true conversation. While we did not systematically work from a set of preformulated questions, we did have a specific interest in the way that WS staff utilized prophecy in their work, and this helped us to channel the direction our many conversations took. While there are obvious pitfalls in the methodology of conversational interviews, it is a methodology that facilitates a process of discovery, leading to new insights that might otherwise never come to an outside observer's attention or understanding. And it is through conversational dialogues that we are most likely to obtain some of the rich detail of people's work lives that allows us to comprehend them as human beings, however different their beliefs and practices might be from our own.[12]

In editing these interviews for publication, we had to make decisions about how much to include and what to leave out. There were, in fact, several spontaneous discussions that were not even sound-recorded and others in which there were failures in our recording equipment. We have only included here modified excerpts from interviews for which we have complete verbatim transcripts. Even with editing, as explained below, there is a certain amount of overlap in these interviews and occasional repetitiveness, but we have attempted to include everything that, in our judgment, adds valuable detail and increased insight into WS operations. At the same time, concurrence of responses from numerous interviewees concerning a shared understanding of their interrelated roles validates the conclusions that can be drawn from our interviews.

Occasional ad hoc references to apparently random individuals whose names are included in the context of many of our staff interviews may seem distracting to readers. But these references—many of which are to Family members residing and working outside of World Services—also illustrate the dense network of social ties that unite the Family International as a global evangelical community, and for this reason we decided to include them. In short, the interviews in toto constitute the primary data source from which we draw our conclusions.

We have taken some editorial liberties with the contents of selected interview transcripts. The only interview reproduced more or less in its entirety in this book is the discussion with Maria and other contributors to the Family's *Good News* publication on the nature of prophecy, as the Family understands and employs it (see chapters 2 and 3). The remaining interviews with WS department heads and other staff are condensed and reorganized by thematic content. For the sake of reader clarity and comprehension, we have corrected grammatical errors and garbled syntax of the sort that are common in ordinary, extemporaneous speech. We also trimmed the interviews of any excessively redundant or extraneous comments that were irrelevant to our topics of discussion, and in the WS department interviews we also eliminated the bulk of our own dialogue comments and questions, compressing many of these into summary statements. We inserted additional summary comments into the text as necessary in order to provide clarifying linkages between discussion points. These linking comments typically reflect either our own prior research on the Family or information gleaned from other WS informants outside the interview in question; they serve to anticipate and contextualize points that will be emerging in the subsequent responses given by our interviewees. Furthermore, we have sequenced the interviews by topic rather than chronologically.

We precede each interview with a brief introduction, including information about the person or persons involved in the conversation, their particular WS roles, and a synopsis of salient points that emerged in the discovery process of our conversations. With the exception of references to Peter and Maria, who are publicly known by their Family-adopted names, we employ pseudonyms in reference to all of our many WS informants. Except for briefly in chapters 2 and 5, we identify ourselves simply as "Shepherd," rather than either Gary or Gordon, in those interview narratives selected for full reproduction. Additionally, in each interview there is occasional usage of Family terminology and organizational acronyms, the meaning of which we clarify within brackets in the text or, for longer explanations, in the endnotes; in some places we replaced an acronym in dialogue with the spelled-out term for easier understanding.

Finally, even though these interviews were recorded in 2005, in writing the chapter introductions we speak in present tense to avoid constant disclaimer references to "currently" or "at the present time." One of the dependable facts about Family organization is that both its institutional programs and the individuals assigned to administer them are frequently in flux. Since our visit to World Services in 2005, both the organizational structure and some of the personnel that we identify and describe in our interviews have, in fact, undergone a certain amount of change and transition.

OVERVIEW OF THE BOOK

In chapter 1 we offer our argument for why the Family International has become an especially interesting and important case study in the sociology of religion, and we provide an overview of its history and basic beliefs. In chapter 10 we analyze and summarize what we think we have learned about World Services as the headquarters organization for an innovative and controversial religious faith. In between, we provide the reader with both a mostly verbatim transcription of one key recorded interview and condensed versions of a number of additional interviews conducted with WS staff and administrative personnel over the course of our four-day visit in June 2005. These conversational interviews and interview summaries capture much of what is distinctive and even peculiar about the Family's religious beliefs and practices.

At the same time, many readers should also recognize in the material a certain amount of doctrinal overlap and convergence with more conventional expressions of charismatic Christianity and Protestant evangelicalism. Perhaps most importantly, we trust these interviews portray the deeply human side of the Family International's leadership organization. For the most part they demonstrate that World Service leaders and organizational staff members are ordinary people with ordinary foibles and an ordinary range of talents. Many readers may be surprised at the degree of candor, extent of technical knowledge, and level of articulate expression demonstrated by these typically young, formally untutored, staff personnel.[13] While neither college educated nor seminary trained, they nonetheless are innovative and highly effective at maximizing the human and technological resources at their disposal. Our interviews underline Family members' belief in the value of community organization and their steadfast commitment to teamwork and group cooperation. They reveal the extent to which current Family leaders are open to outside input, self-criticism, and institutional change. While devoutly insistent in proclaiming ultrasupernatural beliefs that emphasize their special standing with God as his anointed end-time servants, WS leaders and staff did not come across in their conversations with us as fanatical nor as smug or self-righteous in performing their organizational duties. To the contrary, most of the people interviewed impressed us as being self-effacing and strongly service-oriented in their personal motives.

Acknowledgments

The debts we have incurred in producing this book are most obviously owed to the Family International. Neither Family leaders nor ordinary members necessarily assume our perspective, as social scientists, on their religious faith. Nor do they agree with all our interpretations of their experience and the meanings of what they do as religious devotees to a missionary cause. Nevertheless, Family coleaders Maria and Peter generously facilitated our unprecedented access to World Services and its daily operations. They have also been exceptionally open and candid in their own personal encounters with us. Claire Borowik and Lonnie Davis, the Family International public relations representatives, have been our primary contacts for a number of years and have been responsible for arranging and coordinating our various visits to Family communal Homes and other operations around the world. We cannot name here all the hundreds of Family members, worldwide and including the World Services staff, whom we have talked to and observed, but we are grateful to all of them for their generous contributions of time and candor. We are also grateful to the highly competent staff of the University of Illinois Press. Kendra Boileau first recognized merit in our manuscript, then assiduously guided it and us through the toils of acquisition and final publication approval. Jennifer Reichlin and Deborah Oliver expertly helped us knead the manuscript into final form, and Copenhaver Cumpston oversaw the striking cover design. Last but not least, we appreciate the ungrudging support of our wives, Faye Shepherd and Lauren Shepherd, who not only tolerated listening to us read rough drafts of our manuscript but also have accompanied and assisted us on many of our trips to visit Family Homes, contributing significantly to the kind of trust and rapport that is essential to authentic ethnographic research.

Talking with the Children of God

CHAPTER 1

Prophecy and Change

The Children of God Become the Family International

Scholars of religion have long focused attention on the emergence and subsequent histories or "careers" of heretical religious groups like the Family.[1] We apply *heretical* to doctrines and their corollary practices that are severely at variance with the authority of established orthodoxies. The term *sect* is usually applied to groups that deliberately split off from an already established parent organization. Such splits typically occur over doctrinal disputes and a desire to return to a former purity of the faith and practice that disgruntled reformers perceive have become diluted over time. Thousands of such schisms have, of course, occurred throughout the history of Christianity alone. The term *cult* has been applied more often to religious innovations—not merely sectarian schisms—that deviate markedly from already existing faiths. Cult organizations typically are founded de novo by prophetic figures who attract followers on the basis of charismatic claims to transcendent insight and instruction, or even a divinely appointed mission.[2] The origin of Christianity in the form of the incipient Jesus Movement serves as a prime example. Formed initially as a heretical Jewish sect, Christian disciples imputed to Jesus the divine status of the messianic Son of God following his death and subsequently transcended the confines of Jewish law to propagate a new religious tradition.[3]

The Family International's emphasis on the Bible, and its attempt to reinstate such early Christian practices as sharing all things in common and dedicating their lives to evangelizing the world for Jesus, are sectarian Christian themes. At the same time, the Family's radical sexual teachings and practices, its origins in the prophetic claims of David Berg, and its continuing dependence on direct revelatory guidance from Jesus (as well as Berg's departed spirit and a host of other supernatural entities) clearly mark the Family as a religious cult in the strict sociological sense. Unfortunately, the sociological concept of a cult, as a certain type of religious innovation, has not retained its morally neutral meaning in the arena of public discourse. Interview a hundred people at random about what the term *cult* conjures for them, and you are likely to hear 98 or 99 allusions to frighteningly bizarre and menacing organizations that are fanatically engaged in fraudulent or immoral activities under the quasi-hypnotic control of a maniacally disturbed leader. Groups approximating such a caricature do, from time to time, emerge, including those that advocate violence.[4]

But the vast majority of new religious movements are nonviolent, legally compliant, and sincere, however strange their beliefs may seem to outsiders. For this reason, the morally neutral term of new religious movements (NRMs) has come to replace the pejorative label of "cults" in the lexicon of most social science scholars of new religions.[5] To the degree that NRMs are able to attract even a small following, a major obstacle to their ultimate survival, let alone widespread growth in their membership, is the concerted public opposition against them that is almost always aroused by discovery of their presence and perceived deviant practices in host communities. How do such heretical groups survive and even prosper in the truly unusual case? The Family International provides us with an exceptionally informative case study for illuminating these questions.

INSTITUTIONAL HISTORY AS A MORAL CAREER

Like individuals, groups may be thought of as having careers. A career entails passage through certain typical stages in one's history.[6] While specific groups, like specific individuals, always display unique and idiosyncratic characteristics, the concept of a career focuses our attention on standard status transitions that are common to the members of certain types of groups or designated social categories. Thus, group careers inform us of institutional histories from which we may hope to form sociological generalizations. A *moral* career involves patterned transitions in the way individuals or groups justify themselves and are correspondingly judged by others over time, either achieving some measure of acceptance or moral censure within the larger communities in which they develop.[7] To study a group's institutional history is also to analyze and interpret its moral career. At the same time, while scholarly researchers are expected to maintain their objectivity in achieving what Max Weber and other German historicists call *verstehen* (subjective understanding by outsiders of the constellation of shared meanings and motives that guide other people's actions within the framework of their society and its history), they are under no personal obligation to either approve of or condemn the moral careers of the groups they study.[8]

A typical career pattern for new religious movements that attempt to live among and convert others is to find ways to gradually modify those beliefs and practices that outsiders find most offensive. One thinks, for example, of late-19th-century Mormonism abandoning polygamy as a requisite for its acceptance into U.S. society.[9] This process of shifting patterns of group conduct and corresponding moral justifications is fraught with risk. To survive and flourish, heretical groups must achieve moral compromises that do not mortally wound the integrity of their central tenets, causing permanent disillusionment and disintegration of the faithful. At the same time, accommodation and compromise must sufficiently mute the condemnation of powerful adversaries who are determined to suppress or destroy what they consider to be a threat to the moral integrity of their own majoritarian institutions. In this process of adjustment and accommodation, the moral careers of both sects and NRMs may take different paths. Failure to make any adjustments typically leads to extinction. This has been the fate of uncounted heretical movements. A different path leads to eventual respectability by shedding what was once most controversial about the group's beliefs and practices to become more or less accepted denominations in the religious economy of the host society.[10] Lutherans, Presbyterians, Methodists, Baptists, and to a lesser degree Mormons (or Latter-day Saints) and the Assemblies of God have followed this path.

Yet other splinter groups or NRMs—such as the Old Order Amish, Jehovah's Witnesses, and Lubavitch Hasidic Jews—make very modest accommodations over time while tenaciously adhering to most of their basic peculiarities or heresies.[11] Such groups maintain a state of relatively high social tension between themselves and the outside world and persist more or less indefinitely on the margins of conventional religion. To remain on the margins of any social order requires learning to manage a deviant status relative to the normative expectations of the dominant culture.[12] While still very much at odds with both orthodox Christians and the institutions of secular society, the Family International, like other heretical groups in the past, has thus far navigated its moral career in the world by making organizational adjustments and occasional modifications of its religious practices. The primary social mechanism for both modifying and sustaining its religious way of life increasingly has been the Family's group practice of channeling messages from the beyond, a practice that is described and explained at length in this book.

REVELATION AND PROPHECY AS A SOCIAL PROCESS

Charismatic claims of spiritual authority and the closely related activity of obtaining and broadcasting revelations attributed to a transcendent source have been fundamental and reoccurring phenomena in the history of religion. Whatever personal qualities prophetic religious founders may possess, sociologists of religion since Max Weber have emphasized that it is the group process in which prophetic charisma is attributed to leaders by followers that most deserves social science attention and study.[13] Rodney Stark, however, points out that while the scriptures of the major Western faiths—Judaism, Christianity, and Islam—are all believed by their followers to be based on divine revelation, the question "How do revelations actually occur?" has seldom been studied empirically. This, he argues, is a sadly neglected area of analysis in the sociology of religion: "To the extent that we cannot answer this question, we remain ignorant of the origins of our basic subject matter: religious culture."[14] Stark emphasizes that, by revelation, he is referring not merely to personal insight or belief in inspiration but to reported messages that are believed to be literal communications from a divine being. When recorded, such communications often have become the transcendent scriptural foundation for the subsequent doctrines and practices of new religions.

Criticizing his own earlier work on this topic, Stark concludes that the psychopathology, entrepreneurial, and subcultural-evolution models of revelation, which he and William Bainbridge proposed in earlier studies, do not account adequately for the most significant revelations that have inaugurated major religious movements historically.[15] He subsequently formulates a set of theoretical propositions to explain how revelations occur that come to be accepted as the word of God by a community of believers. Stark's propositions emphasize the social dynamics between the charismatic claims of exceptionally creative individuals whose heretical thinking is nurtured through close ties with intense primary groups in the context of a supportive religious culture, especially in historical periods of uncertainty and crisis.

In his analysis, Stark clearly affirms that revelation needs to be understood and studied as a social process, as a form of human interaction that occurs in particular kinds of social and historical contexts. Reflecting on the supportive cultural and familial contexts out of which prophetic Jewish, Christian, Muslim, and Latter-day Saints faiths originated, Stark identifies what he calls the importance of the founders' "Holy Families," who "not only reinforce the founder's confidence [but], more importantly, their testimony generates faith among potential new converts. Followers effectively attribute charisma to their leader, and this can, to a considerable extent, be independent of the actual traits or behaviors of the leader."[16] Congruent with Weber's analysis of the routinization of charisma, Stark concludes that religious movements founded on revelation eventually will attempt to curtail the proliferation of more revelations, or at least prevent novel, heretical revelations from occurring as disciples seek stability and accommodation with other groups.[17] This latter conclusion is one that is profoundly challenged by the prophetic moral career of the Family International.

Over the past several years we have been guided in our research on the Family by the basic proposition that prophecy and religious revelations, of the type analyzed through historical examples by Weber and Stark, need to be understood and studied more systematically as a social process in contemporary religious groups. Ideally, to carry out such studies, researchers would have regular access to the key actors—religious seers or revelators and their primary groups of core disciples—in order to observe and record directly the process of formulating and publicizing revelations for the guidance of religious believers. This, of course, is what makes the empirical study of revelation so difficult. Seldom can researchers expect to obtain unfettered access to the interaction of religious principals involved in the social settings and sequences of events in which revelations are produced. Skeptical outsiders or nonbelievers typically are viewed with suspicion by religious devotees and may expect to be barred from observing either the private or organizational conduct of group leaders. Furthermore, the formulation and announcement of guiding revelations are relatively rare events in the history of most religious movements and are not easily anticipated in advance of their occurrence. Consequently, the study of revelation has depended for the most part on the inspection of historical documents—the revelations themselves if and when recorded, diaries, letters, minutes of meetings, autobiographical accounts, interviews, and secondhand reports—rather than through the careful observation of field researchers.

These methodological limitations not withstanding, the Family International represents an exceptionally inviting case study for scholars interested in the sociology of prophecy and revelation. The Family is a mature religious movement that already has received considerable scholarly attention since its founding in the late 1960s.[18] What we find most inviting about the Family is that it is a religious group that continues to be led by belief in direct, continuous revelation channeled from the spirit world. Rather than rare occurrences, official revelations or "prophecies" are regularly published in the group's literature as God's latest word on doctrinal and policy issues. And unlike most prophetic religions that curtail the dissemination of fresh revelations once they become institutionalized, promulgation of prophecy remains the essential mechanism for directing the contemporary Family's communal way of life and end-time evangelical mission. Furthermore, Family leaders have been relatively open to scholars interested in studying them and their religious institutions.[19] Thus we have a group in which the process of producing guiding revelations believed to be literal communications from a divine source is not rare or concealed, and whose leadership by and large welcomes legitimate scholarly study by outside observers. For us, the question to be addressed in the case of the Family International is not merely how do we explain the construction of the original revelations that set the course for a new religious movement (Stark's propositions work well for that); but how do we account for the generational persistence of purported prophecies through multiple channels in such a way that the religious group is not fractured into warring factions, all claiming God's ultimate truth on the basis of their own, contradictory revelations?

In the remainder of this chapter, we outline some of the salient turning points in the Family's prophetically guided moral career. This is a career that covers the transition of the Children of God from the stage of incipient religious ferment and agitation to the rapid coalescence of a new religious community, with an urgent evangelical mandate for saving souls, to what it has become today: an organizationally complex, transnational missionary society that has produced a controversial religious culture for its members that continues to put them at odds with conventional religious denominations and, occasionally, with public officials around the world. In order to better understand the pathway of the Family's moral career, and its relatively stabilized but still marginal position vis-à-vis establishment Christianity, we must also review the Family's most fundamental teachings and religious values—especially those associated with belief in divine guidance through daily revelation.

SYNOPSIS OF FAMILY HISTORY

The Children of God (COG) gained notoriety as the most controversial group emerging from the Jesus People movement of the late 1960s.[20] Its founder, David Berg, was a middle-aged, self-proclaimed Christian missionary and itinerant preacher who dramatically reignited his career by focusing conversion efforts on "hippies" and other youthful dropouts from the counterculture of that era, first in Southern California and then throughout the United States and Canada. COG was quickly characterized in the mass media as one of a number of menacing, contemporary cults of the time (including the International Society for Krishna Consciousness, the Unification Church and, later, the People's Temple), became embroiled in the brainwashing-deprogramming controversy of the 1970s and 1980s,[21] and was later the target of several severely condemnatory exposés by former members.[22]

Within two years of founding COG, Berg (for a time dubbed Moses David in the media and lightheartedly as "Mo" by his early followers) and his four energetic children had attracted several hundred young, devoted disciples, who began dispersing all over the world as missionaries to save souls for Jesus in the end-time of human history. While carrying out their evangelizing activities, COG also attempted (and Berg's adherents have continued ever since) to emulate the perceived lifestyle of primitive Christianity. This included forsaking secular occupations and living communally in what, at the time, were called COG colonies.

Significantly, the contemporary Family has important biographical links to the post–World War II Pentecostal revival.[23] Both Berg and his second wife and eventual successor, Karen Zerby, grew up in evangelical Pentecostal ministries. Berg's mother was an itinerant revivalist preacher for the Christian Missionary Alliance, whom Berg assisted as a young man and remained close to while pursuing his own evangelical ministries as an adult. Zerby's father was a Nazarene minister, for whom she performed secretarial duties prior to meeting Berg and converting to the Children of God, where other Family disciples came to know her as Maria and eventually as Mama. Berg, in his prophetic role as founder and religious mentor to the Children of God and then to the Family, strongly emphasized the fundamental Pentecostal principle of being "spirit-led" in every aspect of daily living. Maria's major contribution to the Family's continued development has been to stress even more emphatically than Berg the need "to hear from the Lord" in all matters large and small, in order to exercise and develop the gift of prophecy in the form of directly channeled messages from the spirit world as the essential mode of action for every Family disciple.

Berg's Pentecostal taproots as a self-appointed evangelist to the 1960s counterculture notwithstanding, the early Children of God rapidly congealed into an insular new religion that cut itself off from any continuing theological influences or institutional constraints emanating from the worldwide Pentecostal and Charismatic movements of the 1970s, 1980s, and 1990s. Consequently, what is now the Family International has developed and currently implements a radical conception of both personal and corporate prophecy that in key respects is arguably unique in the long history of charismatic Christianity.

The Family's early history is replete with the kinds of internal upheavals and conflicts with outsiders and legal authorities that have been common to heretical religious movements founded on charismatic claims of prophetic guidance.[24] Two years after the inception of COG, Berg announced in 1970 a vision that prefigured a new mode of prophetic leadership. Feeling overburdened by the sharply increasing demands for counsel and supervision required by his rapidly growing flock of untutored adherents, and perhaps anticipating the later emergence of vexatious lawsuits and threat of criminal prosecution that would be initiated by anticult groups, Berg determined that God wanted him to withdraw his personal contact from the individual concerns of rank-and-file converts and, instead, provide a more Olympian form of organizational guidance through his prophetic writings and correspondence. Sequestered and protected from public scrutiny by a small, devoted staff in a series of secret locations, Berg commenced a prolific writing career. Thereafter, very few Family members ever saw or knew Father David personally. He communicated through a series of epistles or *MO Letters*, which were distributed to Family members worldwide through the mail. Over the next twenty years, hundreds of *MO Letters* were published and distributed. To detractors, Berg epitomizes the malevolent religious autocrat who obtains abusive control over the lives and material resources of his followers. To his devout disciples, however, Berg was and is God's anointed end-time prophet. To them, the *MO Letters* were often believed to contain the Word of God and were sometimes, depending on their content claims, accorded the status of holy writ.

Berg's withdrawal from direct contact with his followers contributed greatly to the consolidation and preservation of his charismatic authority. In seclusion he was able to assume the role of a fabled prophet figure whose personal foibles and eccentricities could be minimized or portrayed in such a way as to enhance his image as God's anointed spokesman. New converts and their children would know "Dad" or "Grandpa" only through the power of his emphatic writing and authoritatively published proclamations. The charismatic authority attributed to him by believers was channeled through the *MO Letters*, in which the idealized image of a stern but loving father was institutionalized and preserved for future generations. Loyal Family members shared the belief that Father David's policy edicts and doctrinal statements in the *MO Letters* were divinely inspired. But Berg did not, as a rule, write as though he were channeling the verbatim words of God. Although the gift of revelation was upheld from the outset as a fundamental principle in Family teachings, many of the doctrinal innovations, moral admonitions, and policy "revolutions" contained in the *MO Letters* were written in colloquial form as Berg's own exposition of Bible verses, anecdotes, parables, and his occasional interpretation of dreams and visions.

From 1969 through 1974, governance of the Children of God's communal lifestyle practices and evangelizing mission was essentially ad hoc and featured Berg's children in various leadership and supervisory roles. Following Berg's directions, hundreds of communal colonies were established in scores of countries. Membership numbers initially grew quickly into the thousands, although dropout rates were also high. Eventually growth through conversion tapered considerably but was compensated by the rising number of children born to member couples, who subsequently were raised to become a new generation of Family missionaries.

Having to assume long-term parenting responsibilities was not something Berg's disciples had realistically contemplated. For most of them, their youthful attraction to the Children of God had been fired by Berg's end-time preaching and the urgent mission to save souls before the imminent destruction of the world. Now, with the largely unanticipated emergence of a veritable baby boom, their attention increasingly became centered on the nurturance and educational needs of a second generation. Emphasis increasingly shifted to domestic concerns. The focus of evangelizing activities began to change from recruiting new disciples as full-time Family members to simply bearing Christian witness, persuading listeners and other contacts to accept Jesus as their personal savior, and modeling what they considered to be a Christian lifestyle while awaiting Christ's return.

At the same time, COG was going through a period of organizational upheaval and change. In 1975, Berg proclaimed an organizational revolution called the Chain of Cooperation, which consisted of a pyramid of colony shepherds and district, regional, national, and international heads who served as intermediaries between Berg and disciples' communal Homes.[25] It was a top-down authoritarian structure that, as it turned out, was susceptible to abuses of power on the part of Berg's appointed intermediaries. When Berg finally acknowledged the extent to which abuses were occurring in the Chain of Cooperation, he impetuously "fired" the group's entire leadership. New leaders were appointed, colonies were renamed as "Homes," and, for the first time, individual communal Homes were allowed to elect their own shepherds. But, by 1979, the old COG organization was effectively disbanded. Those followers who remained loyal to Berg began calling themselves the Family of Love and, soon thereafter, simply the Family.[26]

Beginning in the mid-1970s, Berg also introduced several sexual themes into his teachings that were subsequently implemented in practice, causing enormous controversy that has plagued the Family ever since. These themes were derived from the primacy of what became known in the Family as the Law of Love, including the One Wife doctrine, which in effect removed the requirement of fidelity within marriage. "Sexual sharing" between unmarried individuals was defined as appropriate if carried out in a loving way and with mutual consent or to serve higher, God-sanctioned purposes. Berg parted company with his first wife (Jane Miller Berg, known in the Family as Mother Eve), began living intimately with Maria, and engaged in sexual relations with a number of other women, as well. He sometimes arranged or sanctioned the abandonment of an established marriage with the "re-mating" of particular couples who he (or his authorized representatives) felt would constitute a more effective working team to carry out various organizational tasks.

Another application of the Law of Love was the practice of "flirty fishing," which subsequently became the group's most notorious heresy. Publicly proclaimed in 1976, flirty fishing was legitimized by Berg as a witnessing tool for bringing spiritual comfort and Christian salvation to ostensibly unloved and lonely souls through loving sexual encounters.[27] Since COG women who engaged in flirty fishing not only witnessed to the men whom they offered sex but also accepted monetary donations, flirty fishing was viewed by outsiders as blasphemous humbug that rationalized prostitution in the name of God. Berg argued, however, that sex is a highly positive and essential aspect of God's creation and, among consenting adults, is intrinsically good for human happiness, especially when engaged in with loving, sacrificial intent. In addition to adult sexuality, Berg also discoursed on the natural sexuality of children and carelessly inveighed against suppressing their intrinsic sexual curiosity and masturbatory experiences as an aspect of healthy child development.[28] These teachings were intertwined with marriage and child-rearing issues for novice Family parents. One highly regrettable consequence was a certain amount of adult-minor sexual contact occurring in a number of Family homes, especially at World Services and other leader residences, during the late 1970s and early 1980s that, along with the practice of flirty fishing, would indelibly stigmatize the Family as a religious "sex cult" in the decades to follow.

In the meantime, Berg instituted the Fellowship Revolution in 1981 to reestablish an organizational foundation to support the Family's continuing evangelical agenda as God's chosen end-time disciples. The Fellowship Revolution organized communal homes into Local Fellowship Areas that would meet weekly with other nearby homes. Local fellowships were connected with district fellowships for monthly meetings and, in turn, each district fellowship was part of a national area fellowship that was to meet on an annual basis for socializing, unification, and instructional purposes. At each fellowship level, leaders were elected instead of appointed from the top down. According to Gordon Melton's historical assessment of Family governance practices, the democratizing aspects of the Fellowship Revolution created for the first time a more responsive national and international leadership in a position to effectively monitor and assess Family life and the emerging problems associated with having and raising a second generation of children.[29] Venereal disease concerns and the explosion of the worldwide AIDS epidemic prompted a more judicious assessment by Family leaders of the group's open sexual mores. Consequently, in 1983 a *MO Letter* was published titled "Ban the Bomb!" which ordered a stop to sexual sharing at fellowship meetings. While still advocated as a Family disciple norm, sexual sharing among consenting adults was limited to members' residential communal Homes. Any adult-minor sexual contact was abolished and, in 1987, more than a decade after it had been introduced, the practice of flirty fishing as an evangelical tool was officially discontinued. On the threat of excommunication and banishment from the Family, sexual contacts with minors were now strictly prohibited.[30]

These highly charged sexual images, however, have remained firmly planted in public consciousness and have been at the heart of subsequent criminal charges and prosecutions levied against the Family in countries around the world. The most serious instances of actual police action (see the preface) took place in several commando-style raids of communal Family homes from 1991 to 1993 in Spain, Australia, France, and Argentina on the basis of child abuse charges made by embittered former members and anticult organizations.

Hundreds of adult Family members were arrested or otherwise detained, and approximately 600 children were examined by authorities. Eventually in all of these cases, all detainees, including children, were released when no evidence was found to sustain the charges.[31]

However, a tragic spin-off from the sexual abuse charges of the 1980s and early 1990s having major internal Family ramifications was the 2005 murder-suicide case involving Maria's estranged son, Ricky Rodriguez, and Angela Smith, a former member of World Services who had also been outside the Family for several years. Rodriguez, Maria's only son—known as Davidito until his departure from the Family as a young man in the early 2000s—had been lionized in Family literature as a child and was projected as the eventual leader of the Family. However, Rodriguez became increasingly disillusioned and bitter as he attained adulthood, and he began making public charges that David Berg, his mother (Maria), Peter, and other Family leaders had sexually and physically abused him and other children growing up in WS. He became obsessed with finding and killing his mother and Peter to avenge himself and other putative victims, but was frustrated by the changed and secret whereabouts of WS. When Ricky learned that Angela Smith was visiting in Tucson, Arizona, where he was residing, he contacted her and persuaded her to meet with him, hoping she might know Maria and Peter's location. Smith either did not know or refused to say if she did. Ricky slit her throat and inflicted other knife wounds on her body in his apartment, then began driving to California with the apparent intention of killing other Family members at a Family center located near San Diego. However, he was apparently overcome with remorse en route and fatally shot himself at a road stop near the California–Arizona border.[32]

In 1994, at the height of anti-Family publicity around the world, David Berg died. But by then his support staff had evolved into a talented and highly effective organizational headquarters unit called World Services. WS increasingly had become responsible for oversight and management of a complex international publishing, educational, humanitarian, and missionary enterprise. By 2005, in order to highlight its contemporary international mission and membership composition, the Family's official name was expanded to the Family International. Today the Family International has a global presence in 90 countries, and its missionary agenda is spearheaded by the daily efforts of approximately 5,000 core members (including children) who live communally in what are designated as Family disciple (FD) Homes—Homes that are in compliance with all disciple standards.[33] These Homes overwhelmingly are rented or leased in urban areas to maximize access to the countless millions of "unsaved" souls who are the target constituency of the Family's evangelizing efforts. Among other things, FD Homes are required to homeschool their children and sustain a minimum of six adults, 18 years of age or older, living communally, with a maximum residential membership of 35 people. FD Home members do not earn a living through employment outside of the Family. Rather, they are engaged in full-time evangelizing, humanitarian outreach, and domestic activities within the urban communities in which their Homes are located. FD members typically cultivate networks of local "friends"—that is, people sympathetic with the Family's teachings and missionary work who contribute financial and other material aid. FD Family members own very little real estate or taxable assets. They subsist primarily from what they call provisioning (i.e., obtaining donations of both goods and services) and through the sale of various religious materials and educational products produced by World Services. As a result, Family disciples typically live frugal but relatively comfortable lives.

FD Homes also are partially supported by members who chose lesser levels of commitment. These include member missionaries (MMs), who currently number approximately 2,500, and another 2,000 or so fellow members (FMs). Thus, the Family's current total membership is around 10,500, a figure that has remained relatively stable for the past decade.[34] Missionary members and fellow members may be employed in secular jobs, are not required to live communally, and may send their children to secular schools rather than homeschooling them. At the same time, MM Homes are expected to be engaged in various missionary activities and to pay tithes to World Services. In contrast, FM Homes are expected to be supportive of Family programs and pay regular tithes but are not required to be active missionaries. Since only disciple members are required to live communally and dedicate their lives as full-time missionaries, missionary members and fellow members are allowed to become more integrated into the larger societies in which they live. MM status in particular represents an appealing option to first-generation Family members who, as they age and begin to experience health problems and a decline in their former, youthful enthusiasm for daily evangelizing, find ways to continue serving at a lower level of personal investment and sacrifice. Family adults who have already raised their children can, if they so choose, step back and let a new generation of disciples carry the burden of full-time proselytizing and communal living that ultimately depends on the generosity and goodwill of people outside the Family.

Authority and policies governing disciple Home activities continue to emanate from World Services. Prior to his death, David Berg designated Maria as his successor. He also sanctioned a coleadership role for Peter, who subsequently married Maria. Maria and Peter's status as "Dad's" heirs was bolstered by receipt and publication of additional revelatory messages claimed to come from Jesus and from Dad's departed spirit. After a period of doubt and apostasy on the part of some members during this transition period, Maria and Peter have consolidated the support and faith of active Family members, and they now jointly direct all WS activities.[35] The year following Berg's death, a key benchmark achievement of the new leadership was *The Family Charter*, published and disseminated to all disciple Homes in 1995. It is in the charter and current board organization that we most clearly see the Family's contemporary movement in the direction of becoming a more democratic and responsive communitarian religion.[36]

The charter is now the Family's basic governing document. It is a detailed exposition of Family members' rights, responsibilities, and membership requirements. It goes to great lengths to specify, among other things, how a child's educational, physical, and mental health needs are to be met and protected. It systematically regulates sexual contact between Family members based on age categories and proscribes sexual relations with nonmembers. It also details a system of governance for individual Homes organized around the concepts of team leadership and democratic participation in decision making. While bolstered throughout with selected statements from Father David's previously published *MO Letters*, the charter is a legal-rational, statutory document. The charter was a collaborative project, drafted by WS staff members in consultation with legal counsel and in response to input solicited from a series of grassroots workshops conducted by members worldwide. The initial draft was subsequently revised, edited, and finally voted on at a lengthy summit meeting of the Family's worldwide continental officers—the then-designated top rung of field leadership. Periodic summit conferences of the group's leading officers subsequently have become an established forum for deliberating organizational problems and advocating or changing Family policies. The charter itself has been updated several times since 1995 in response to new issues that have emerged over time, including tightening of commitment rules for homes to maintain their disciple status and for individuals to be classified as full-fledged disciple members (see chapter 9 for an elaboration of details).

The process by which the charter was produced and implemented and the new operating modes and living standards that it specifies are sociologically significant in comprehending the Family's moral career. They represent adaptive responsiveness to both external and internal pressures for change. From without, the Family has had to comply with the demands of courts, welfare agencies, and other secular authorities. From within, equity issues, educational concerns, the rebellion of second-generation youth, the aging and disillusionment of first-generation adults, and a host of other internal organizational problems all have had to be addressed. The charter modeled an expansion of shared governance through consultation, establishment of a responsible and representative officialdom, voting, and other democratic principles.

Issued in 1995, the charter foreshadowed the emergence in 2001 of another significant organizational development, namely the establishment of international, regional, and national boards that innovate and implement policies in areas that are now considered essential for the Family's continued vitality:

parenting of young children, guiding teenagers, homeschooling for children and teens, missionary and outreach programs, supervision of Family homes, and public relations.[37] These boards are staffed by approximately 500 appointed disciple members, both male and female; they have greatly expanded organizational participation and leadership opportunities, especially for young adults of the second generation. They also have increased input from local Homes and national boards with regard to unique problems confronting them in their particular parts of the world. All of these developments support the conclusion that the contemporary Family International's moral career has evolved in the direction of a much more responsive religious community as compared to its initial authoritarian incarnation as the Children of God.

SYNOPSIS OF CORE FAMILY BELIEFS

From its inception as the Children of God, the Family International has been remarkably flexible in adjusting its policies to historical exigencies and developing innovative ideas and programs that supersede previous modes of action. The Family's core beliefs and practices, however, while susceptible to modifications in interpretation or emphasis (and they are certainly susceptible to the elaboration of esoteric details), have remained relatively stable and resistant to significant change. Indeed, in recent years, several of these interrelated core beliefs have been reemphasized and implemented even more forcefully as Family leadership has pursued a deliberate course of retrenchment and purification to heighten commitment and to resist compromising fundamental standards. Core Family beliefs include the following:

1. *Witnessing for Jesus.* The Family was founded as a religious calling to witness and save souls for Jesus throughout the world. The organization's mission ever since has been to carry out this basic Christian duty with urgency and total dedication as God's elect "Endtime Army."
2. *The End-time.* The imminent apocalyptic conclusion of human history, including the temporary emergence of satanic earthly control through the prophesied ascendance of the "Anti-Christ," was and remains the second intertwined foundational belief in Family history.
3. *Father David as the End-time Prophet.* As the group's founder and guiding light for quarter of a century, David Berg is believed by the Family to have been specifically chosen by God as his prophet to lay the necessary groundwork for the end-time through direct revelations and guidance from Jesus and other spiritual entities. These inspirations and revelations were complied as "the Word" in hundreds of *MO Letters* and, subsequently, in thousands of other Family publications.

4. *Revelation that is direct and ongoing.* From its Holiness and Pentecostal roots, the Family has elevated emphasis on personal contact with God's spirit, especially in the form of prophecy, channeled through verbatim conversations with Jesus and other supernatural personages that provide concrete guidance for both daily life and the formulation of authoritative Family policies. Revelations authorized by Maria are disseminated in current publications as a continuation of the Word and represent official faith and practice directives for the Family as a whole.

5. *Rejection of the World.* Drawing on Christian fundamentalist notions of worldly wickedness, David Berg's contempt for established churches and from the countercultural attitudes of the group's initial converts, the Family sees itself as separated from and at odds with both secular society ("the System") and Churchianity, its term for established Christian churches.

6. *Anti-Materialism.* Greed and love of material things, selfishness, and seeking competitive advantage to obtain wealth, power, and social acclaim are condemned as snares that corrupt individual souls, making people susceptible to satanic control instead of the "saving love of Jesus," and therefore hinder the great end-time work that the Family believes must be speedily accomplished.

7. *Communalism.* Living communally and "sharing all things in common" is taken to be the true mode of Christian living, modeled by Jesus' early apostles, and serving as the social mechanism by which Family members can stay apart from the world, develop loving qualities, and collectively concentrate their energy and resources to fulfill their end-time mission.

8. *The Law of Love.* Experiencing and sharing God's love is believed to be the single greatest end of human existence. This law is extended, most controversially in the view of outsiders, to the arena of sexual relationships among believers and with Jesus himself.

While their millenarian expectations and belief in spiritual gifts are shared with other Christian groups—especially Pentecostals and charismatic fundamentalists—the Family's insistence on David Berg's role as an end-time prophet, their prolific channeling of God's Word that carries them far past the religious strictures of Biblical literalists, their urban communal living, and especially their radical sexual interpretation of the Law of Love, are core beliefs that continue to position the Family International beyond the pale of mainstream, contemporary Christianity. Throughout the book we use the term *ultrasupernaturalism* in reference to the underlying metaphysical character of the Family's core beliefs.[38] Ultrasupernatural beliefs not only posit the existence of supernatural entities and a spirit world that transcends mundane human existence, they are, most importantly, beliefs that promote a miraculous rather than a naturalistic worldview by emphasizing the permeability of the boundary separating the spirit world from the natural world; they are beliefs that serve to explain virtually every aspect of daily life as the result of supernatural intervention in human affairs. Typically this supernatural intervention is seen as an integral element in the struggle between good and evil—literalized in ultrasupernatural beliefs as a ferocious spiritual clash between the evil forces of the devil and the Godly forces of heaven. Ultrasupernatural beliefs are used to interpret specific human events as the dramatic unfolding of this cosmic clash by anthropomorphizing specific spirit entities, both good and evil, who relentlessly labor to achieve their conflicting ends by deploying miraculous powers and recruiting human agents into the struggle.

When ultrasupernatural beliefs are linked to a religious culture like the Family's that *democratizes* prophetic gifts to sponsor, rather than curtail, the ongoing proliferation of official revelations channeled from the spirit world, we should expect to see the steady supernatural elaboration of a theological system that takes it far beyond the orthodoxy of conventional religion. This is precisely what has occurred in the Family International. Our interviews with World Services staff members are not only laced with references to God and Jesus but also to Satan, the "Enemy"; to "spiritual warfare" with specifically identified demons commissioned by Satan to interrupt and interfere with the Family's end-time mission; and to numerous "spirit helpers," who are commissioned by Jesus and also identified by name, as well as to specific "keys" of spiritual power granted to assist World Services and Family missionaries in realizing God's great work of ultimate redemption. Virtually every Family "victory" or organizational success, however large or small, in pursuit of its evangelical mission is seen to be the miraculous realization of God's power. Correspondingly, every setback or organizational problem, however major or minor, is considered to be the result of satanic opposition.[39] Rather than modifying or toning down their core beliefs, the elaboration and embellishment of an ultrasupernatural worldview has been one of the major consequences of World Services' emphasis on corporate prophecy through multiple prophetic channels.

INVITATION TO WORLD SERVICES

As already indicated, World Services evolved from Father David's personal staff in the early days of the Children of God to become the headquarters organization of the Family International. One general conclusion confirmed by our visit and interviews at World Services concerns Maria's and Peter's respective roles in building the Family International since the death of David Berg. Peter clearly has been central in the development and administration of Family organization, while Maria has been the key figure in promoting the use of prophecy in planning and decision making at all levels of Family organization.[40] Both the conceptual distinction between administration and prophecy and the essential integration of these two institutional aspects of current WS operations should become apparent as we describe and discuss in later chapters what we learned through our observations and interviews at World Services. In general, WS has become organizationally much more complex over the past decade. There has been much greater delegation of authority and responsibility to WS staff members and a corresponding emphasis placed on staff training. For the most part, Maria's and Peter's roles have shifted from the iconic oracular status enjoyed by David Berg to overseeing and giving approval to the work done by others at World Services.

We spent a total of four nights and four days at WS headquarters, which, for want of a better term, may be described as a residential work complex. There were not, however, any visible signs or barriers that separated WS operations from the surrounding environment. There was nothing to indicate to neighbors or outsiders that within their midst was situated the communal headquarters of a transnational religious organization. Each work space was equipped with one or more computers linked to the World Services server. In the particular unit where we stayed, there was a communal kitchen, a space set aside for the children's school, and a large room that accommodated weekly staff devotionals. Although tidy and serviceable, WS quarters were relatively Spartan. Most living quarters and offices (or work areas) were outfitted with secondhand furnishings. Walls were occasionally decorated with reproductions of religious art produced by the Family; these prominently featured pictures of Jesus and Bible verses or quotations from various family publications.

All WS staff members are expected to put in a five-day work week, plus an additional four hours on Saturday. The minimum work standard is 46 hours per week—a standard typically exceeded, we were told, by most staffers. In addition to their regular staff assignments, what was described to us as the "WS work ethic" also requires daily prayer, prophecy, and study time for all WS staff, "ministry" hours, community service hours, and "parent time" of one hour for parents to spend with their children every evening before dinner. Parents may also spend time with children after dinner, have nap time with very young children, and spend time together in the mornings before children join their child-care group and adults begin their workday. Parents also are allowed a free day on Saturday to spend with their children. Family leaders emphasize the importance of what they call "a balanced life" for WS personnel. Family leadership recognizes that people can't just work for WS without providing other outlets. According to Peter, "they need recreation, social activities, and vacations from their work." Consequently, a social activities center is part of the WS complex, including outdoor recreational and sporting facilities, and all WS staffers are given 14 vacation days annually to spend as they choose. Every WS staff member is allocated a scant $25 a month for personal spending; basic material needs such as food and household utilities are supplied and managed communally.

Simplicity and egalitarian sharing are basic values practiced at World Services, as well as in Family disciple Homes located throughout the world. A conscious effort is made at WS to model Family principles and practices associated with communal living and to minimize invidious comparisons with disciple Homes in the field. In fact, working at WS is considered to be a personal sacrifice. Unlike ordinary Family members in the field, staffers are not allowed to witness or "provision" their material needs—two fundamental aspects of Family life for disciple members worldwide. Rather, staffers must concentrate solely on their WS office tasks and cannot engage directly in the missionary activities so strongly idealized for disciple members in Family beliefs and prophetic literature. As far as we could discern, only a modest fraction of the tithes sent to WS from local Family Homes around the world appear to be used in supporting the material needs and personal living expenses of the WS community. Most tithing income is invested in a variety of WS production costs and organizational technology, and some is reallocated to support missionary projects initiated by Family members in the field. At the same time, as in ordinary Family Homes, daily life in the WS complex is supervised by both "Home shepherds" and "Home managers." Those assigned as shepherds concentrate on "spiritual concerns," which include monitoring both group and personal morale and maintaining disciple standards. Managers, on the other hand, oversee the Home's temporal concerns, including grocery shopping, food preparation, vehicle and home maintenance, equipment purchases, and utility payments.

At the time of our visit, World Services was administratively divided into nine departments (or teams), including the GN Department, Maria's Secretaries, General Public Department, Art and Text, Layout, and the Web Department. Each department has its own head and assistant head. Department heads exercise relatively autonomous decision-making authority within their own departments. This increasingly has become the case since the death of David Berg in 1994. At the same time, each department's work and direction is periodically evaluated by WS oversight committees, and Peter meets collectively with all department heads every two to three months to review their operational and personnel concerns. In addition to WS department oversight committees, there are a number of ad hoc committees (such as the Security Committee, the Inspiration Committee, and the Events Committee) that address on-site problems and concerns that arise at World Services as a communal-living work organization.

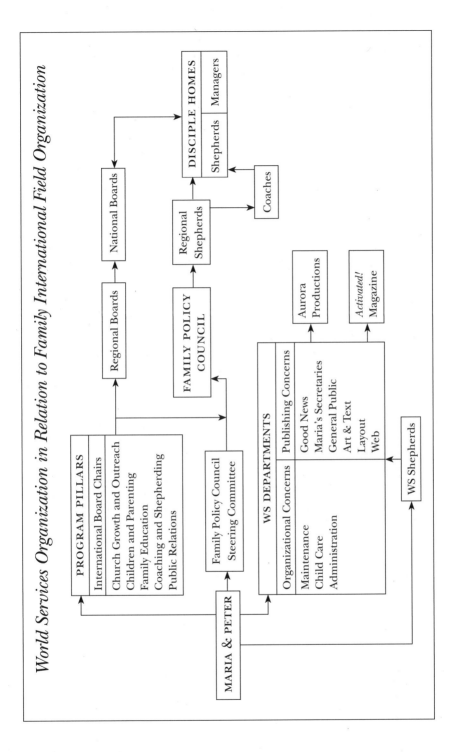

World Services Organization in Relation to Family International Field Organization

PROGRAM PILLARS

International Board Chairs

Church Growth and Outreach
Children and Parenting
Family Education
Coaching and Shepherding
Public Relations

Regional Boards

National Boards

DISCIPLE HOMES

Shepherds | Managers

Coaches

Regional Shepherds

FAMILY POLICY COUNCIL

Family Policy Council Steering Committee

MARIA & PETER

WS DEPARTMENTS

Organizational Concerns | Publishing Concerns

Maintenance
Child Care
Administration

Good News
Maria's Secretaries
General Public
Art & Text
Layout
Web

Aurora Productions

Activated! Magazine

WS Shepherds

Finally, the Family Policy Council Steering Committee, consisting of Peter and all international board chairs, also operates out of WS. International board chairs supervise the Family's system of both regional and national boards, which, as previously mentioned, are organized worldwide to provide grassroots input for Family leaders in developing policies and programs with respect to parenting and children, teenagers, Family homeschooling curricula, supervision of individual Home units in conformity with Family Home standards, church growth and outreach strategies, and public relations. The FPC Steering Committee advises the Family Policy Council—an international organization that consists of all (approximately 40 in number at the time of our visit) the Family's worldwide regional shepherds, and is the most important and powerful oversight committee for the entire, worldwide Family.

The chart on page 19 summarizes the basic organizational structure of World Services operations and the Family International's field organization in relationship to each other. Arrows indicate primary authority lines and oversight responsibilities. WS departments are schematically identified by their primary function, in either publishing "the Word," or maintaining and administering World Services as a communal living organization. At the same time, our interviews also contain numerous references to Family disciple Homes in the field, the governing Family Policy Council, the board structure, the new "coaches" program under the supervision of Regional Shepherds, and Aurora Productions and the *Activated!* magazine. The latter two entities are within the purview of the General Public Department and orient themselves to producing publications and religious products for non-Family members.

It is the Family's organizational structure and prophetic modes of functioning that are at the center of the interviews we have transcribed and edited in the chapters to follow. Information gleaned from these interviews provides unprecedented insight into the routine operations and assumptions of a highly complex religious community, which, following decades of hostile attacks from opponents and attendant secrecy and inaccessibility to outsiders, has been much maligned, often mischaracterized, and little understood.

CHAPTER 2

The Practice of Prophecy in the Family

*A Roundtable Discussion
with the GN Team, Part I*

In this and the following chapter, we report the dialogue exchanged during what turned out to be a daylong discussion with Maria and the GN Team on what Maria referred to as "this complicated subject of prophecy that even *we* don't understand."

"GN" in the Family International is simply an abbreviation for "the Good News"—the term most Christians understand as referring to the salvation offered to humankind through the atoning sacrifice made by Jesus through his death and presumed resurrection. This term is used as the title of the Family International's most important prophetic periodical, distributed to Family Homes worldwide.[1] As summarized in chapter 1, Family missionary programs are founded on ultrasupernatural beliefs that emphasize the principle of continuous revelation through direct, personal contact with the spirit world. Verbatim messages (that Family members call prophecies) are "channeled" from Jesus or, on occasion, other spirit entities, including the departed spirit of David Berg. According to the Family, the *Good News* (or simply *GNs*) contain "the Word"; that is to say, the Word of God, which, in addition to Bible scripture, most importantly refers to contemporary doctrinal and policy pronouncements attributed to Jesus or his spirit agents through channeled prophecies. The central tasks of the GN Department at World Services include determining which topics should be addressed for publication, obtaining and verifying prophecies that will serve as the basic content for selected topics, and organizing and editing the obtained prophecies into coherent articles for publication.

Publishing "the Word" is Maria's primary responsibility, and the GN Department ultimately functions under her direction. In previous studies of the Family we have characterized the complex process of putting *GN* issues together as "the social construction of prophecy."[2] By this we mean that official Family prophecies today are never the result of a single oracle. Rather, in final form they are the interactive product of a relatively large number of contributors from within the GN Department, as well as outside channels (individuals who receive prophecies) and editorial readers referred to in Family terminology as "locals."[3] Over the course of our four days of interviews, we discovered that editorial locals are used to review and refine virtually every item that is published or produced at World Services. In particular, all prophecies published in the *GN*s have been proofread, elaborated, or specified and validated as the collective result of numerous prayer sequences and "channeled" prophecy confirmations. In conventional publishing terms, official prophecies obtained for *GN* publication as the contemporary Word of God go through a number of editing stages, and Maria is the editor-in-chief. Nothing is published in *GN* without her final approval.

Published prophecies typically are formulated in response to prior deliberation about emerging group issues and concerns. Various WS staff may be involved in initial discussions depending on the topics under consideration. In particular, Peter and the Family Policy Council Steering Committee (see chapter 1) now play a key role in many preliminary discussions of subjects to be expounded on in *GN*s, especially those issues with policy implications. At the same time, Maria often receives personal inspiration for a particular topic, in which case further discussion is not undertaken. Typically the latter are "spiritual" topics—such as how to claim and use the "power of the keys" in spiritual warfare against the forces of evil, or the existence and function of various "spirit helpers," etc.— rather than policy *GN*s that outline organizational reforms or initiate new action programs. We should note here that the "power of the keys" is believed to be a miraculous gift democratically available to all Family members for obtaining righteous ends. It is also believed, however, that specific "keys" must be named and called upon to be efficacious. Similarly, "spirit helpers" are believed to be specific spirit entities that specialize in providing different types of supernatural aid; like the power of the keys, they too must be identified and called upon in order for Family members to benefit from their services. These are all prime examples of what we refer to as the Family's ultrasupernatural beliefs.

Once particular topics and questions are identified, Maria assigns individuals to channel prophecies addressing them and subsequently reviews what is submitted by her staff. From these preliminary submissions she identifies what she perceives to be most appropriate for the Family as a whole and then requests specific follow-up prophecies. Maria (or "Mama") is credited by her staff as having a spiritual gift for asking questions, reviewing and selecting initial prophecies, and asking more clarifying questions in order to obtain "complete" versus "incomplete prophecies." Complete prophecies, in their final form for publication, are typically the product of numerous contributors.

Though Maria herself does not channel prophecies for publication, she has great faith in her *GN* staff channels and feels free to request them to "take questions to the Lord" on virtually any topic imaginable. In turn, designated WS channels are inspired by and have faith in Maria's faith. The operations of the GN Department are, in fact, predicated on the dynamics of these mutually reinforcing components of Family faith regarding revelations from the spirit world: Maria has unwavering faith in her designated staff members' "gift of prophecy" and, reciprocally, their faith in channeling prophecies is based on belief in "Mama's anointing" as the Family's "Winetaster." For Family members—as well as for Pentecostal or Charismatic congregations outside the Family—to be anointed means to be empowered or gifted of God. Maria's anointed designation as the Winetaster signifies a spiritual status that Family members believe betokens the ultimate gift of prophetic discernment. Reinforced in their own prophetic abilities through faith in Maria's gift of discernment, individuals who are assigned to receive prophecies for publication are relieved of the burden of having to judge what constitutes God's final Word on a particular question or issue. Consequently, WS staff members who submit prophecies for the *GN*s feel more free to open themselves up and express whatever revelatory ideas comes to them without exercising a great deal of internal censorship. They understand that whatever prophetic messages they submit for publication will, through the *GN* editing process, be scrutinized, modified, abbreviated, expanded, or perhaps merely filed rather than incorporated into the final version of a particular *GN* issue.

We should point out that all of the many WS staffers with whom we spoke about channeling prophecies believed that the messages they record are not merely their own thoughts or words but are instead spiritually dictated. They also believe that God speaks to different individuals in different ways; that human channels of God's will are imperfect; that individuals' personalities and personal attitudes always, to some extent, shape or "flavor" channeled messages; that absolute humility and "yieldedness" to God's will is essential for valid prophetic channeling, and that the degree of yieldedness varies from time to time and person to person; that even those whose "gift of prophecy" is exceptional must struggle with their faith; and that, in fact, God wants his disciples to struggle collectively in coming to a consensus as to the proper interpretation of his Word in resolving questions and problems. Thus, one of the unique characteristics of Family oracular guidance is an institutional commitment to "teamwork prophecies" and, accordingly, one of the major "pitfalls" in producing prophecies, we were told, is losing faith in other Family members' prophecy channels. It is these beliefs about prophecy—how it is collectively obtained and used—that justify the *GN* assignment and editing process that has become institutionalized at World Services for publishing God's

Word. Perhaps what is most important sociologically about Family prophecy is the way that organizational norms have been developed to guide and control prophecy construction so that democratic consensus, rather than division, is the typical outcome.

Because prophecy plays such a central role in the work of WS and is the primary focus of both this book and the discussion that immediately follows here, we have elected to reproduce a larger volume of the verbatim transcripts from our interview with Maria and selected staff in this and in chapter 3 than we have done in our other interviews. In attendance at our roundtable meeting with Maria were a number of WS staff members who regularly channel messages from the spirit world or, as "locals," help edit *GN* prophecies. These staffers included the following individuals (to whom we have assigned pseudonyms per our anonymity agreements with all WS personnel who participated in the interviews):

Alecia: Department head of Maria's secretaries. At age 26, Alecia is a second-generation member with eight years' experience working in WS.

Barbara: Department head of general public publications. At age 29, Barbara is a second-generation member with nine years' experience working in WS.

Chuck: Contributor to the *Endtime News Digest* (a Family publication) and *GN* "pipeline" work. At age 53, Chuck is a first-generation convert with 23 years of experience working in WS.

Frank: International board chair of Church Growth and Outreach and overseer of Aurora Productions. At age 36, Frank is a second-generation member with 11 years' experience working in WS.

Jack: Part-time aid to Maria and Peter and part-time worker in the Child Care Department. At age 52, Jack is a first-generation convert with 26 years of experience working in WS.

Julie: International board chair of Coaching and Shepherding. At age 30, Julie is a second-generation member with nine years' experience working in WS.

Keri: One of Maria's Secretaries. At age 53, Keri is a first-generation convert with 11 years of experience working in WS.

Melody: International board chair for Coaching and Shepherding. At age 52, Melody is a first-generation convert with 16 years of experience working in WS.

Rachael: Department head of the GN Department. At age 31, Rachael is a second-generation member with nine years' experience working in WS.

Viola: One of Maria's Secretaries. At age 54, Viola is a first-generation convert with 10 years of experience working in WS.

SHEPHERD: Is everyone here in one way or another associated with the prophecies published in the *GNs*?

MARIA: They all have worked closely with me at one time or another with *GN* work, or MPL work—that's the ministry of answering the Family's letters—but mostly *GNs*, I think, and getting prophecies. We had a list of about 30 people that we would have liked to have at this meeting, but as you can tell, we couldn't fit them all; we had to make the dividing line somewhere. So we made it a group of people who had at some time or other helped me put together *GNs*. These are the ones who usually work more with the prophecies in putting together the *GNs*, than with just getting the prophecies. So they come up more with so-called problems, which are actually challenges—that's what we call them—to get solutions. But also in this group, if you would like, we wanted to also explore some of the benefits of prophecy and the things we use prophecy for in our lives—not just in the *GNs*, but a broader prophecy study. But having said that, you can ask whatever questions you want. Did you have any other questions before we go ahead and have prayer?

SHEPHERD: No, we think a lot of things are just going to emerge through an interactive process.

MARIA: So we're going to ask for the Lord's help, and our spirit helpers' help, and the keys' help to explain this very mysterious, complicated subject of prophecy that even *we* don't really understand sometimes, to you, in a sufficiently clear manner, so that you can go and explain it to others. How's that for a challenge?

MARIA PRAYS: Thank You Jesus! Thank You so much our dear, wonderful Husband![4] Thank You for this opportunity to gather together, to celebrate this wonderful gift that You have given us. To celebrate our love for You, our intimacy with You, this love-link with You that You've given us, our communication channel, our survival in the days to come. We praise You and thank You for it, Jesus. It's our survival even now, and the way we can manage to do *anything* for You, the way we can do our ministry, and without which we would be severely hampered and disadvantaged.

So we do thank You and praise You for this tremendous gift that You've poured out upon us, Lord, that You've given us as a weapon as well.[5] We just want You to speak through us today and help us to explain clearly, Lord, things that we don't even sometimes understand as clearly as we should, or are able to articulate as well as we should. So we ask You to make this a good time of learning for us too, as well as for Gary and Gordon. We call on Your keys of clarity and articulation and communication, good interaction with each other. We ask You for the keys of understanding for Gary and Gordon and that they'll be able to ask the right questions to get the answers that they're seeking. We call on our spirit helpers, Michael and the Chiefs, and we call on Dad [David Berg], who said he would be here at this meeting, because of course he's very interested also, and all those, Lord, who can help us to express our thoughts and feelings and the things that we've learned about the amazing gift that You, the great God of the universe, ordained to pour through our weak little channels [claimed capacity by Family members to receive verbatim messages from the spirit world].[6]

We know it is sometimes difficult. But we thank You that we're in the school of the prophets, and that's what schools are for—to learn—and to have our mistakes corrected, and to go further and have more mistakes corrected, and to learn more and go to higher levels, and we thank You for this wonderful school that You've put us in. And Lord, do speak to us now, sweet Love, thank You, dear Love. Praise You Jesus!

SHEPHERD: We don't have a formal list of questions. We weren't sure exactly what the arrangements were going to be, so we thought we'd just let things emerge. We've already learned quite a bit from Mama and Peter. A couple of years ago we had several conversations in terms of an overview of prophecy through WS as it comes out in the GNs, and we hope we got that more or less right. But we probably got some things wrong, and we didn't get all the details we'd like to have. We're interested in religion in general, and what sociologists call new religious movements in particular. The Family has served as a model and key study for the emergence and development of a successful new religious movement.

MARIA: Not one that doesn't have problems, ha![7]

SHEPHERD: That's part of the process—these challenges and how they are responded to. There are many beginning movements that don't survive because they don't respond to the challenges. And what's very clear about the Family is that you do respond in creative, innovative ways; what has emerged in the last eight or nine years in particular is the expansion of the role of prophecy at the WS level. The extent to which prophecy has now become the primary content of the GNs, not to mention its importance for guidance of Family Homes, is really quite remarkable. Also, any Family member now routinely obtains prophecies for personal guidance. These three levels at which prophecy is now employed is something that we think is essential for understanding the Family as a successful religious movement. It sets you apart, makes you unique, as far as we know, from any other religious group in the world. So for us this is an extraordinary opportunity to be allowed to come into your Homes, and now here at WS, to try to get some insight into how this works—this mechanism of prophecy—that gives you the direction you depend on at these three levels. As we heard you say just a few minutes ago, no one quite understands all of it, and of course we're never going to understand all of it either. We're only trying to understand the sociological aspects. To the extent that we can grasp the social elements involved in prophecy at the individual level, the Home level, and the level of World Services, then we think we'll gain some insight that has never been available to anyone else.

MARIA: I believe you're right, ha! We don't know of any other group. Some of the charismatic evangelical groups use prophecy to some extent but nothing like we do.

SHEPHERD: Not in this complex, interactional way that's associated with daily guidance of an institution, if we can use that term. Maybe this is not a word you apply to yourselves, but by "institution" we simply mean practices that are maintained over time so that they in fact are established practices; they become normative; this is the way you do things. It becomes an institutional practice, especially, if you have succeeding generations who perpetuate it. You've got a second generation, and now a third generation, and the practices that you've already established and are now pursuing, are going to be pursued in the future. That's an institution.

And it's remarkable how quickly this has become the taken-for-granted reality, not just for second-generation adults [SGAs], but for first-generation adults [FGAs] as well. Because there was a time not so long ago in the Family when prophecy was not emphasized as much and not practiced the way it is now. And yet, in a very short time, it has become pervasive throughout the Family; members simply take it for granted the way we now take for granted the use of equipment like digital voice recorders, or cell phones, even though these are all relatively new mechanisms as well. For the SGAs, this simply is the way their world is, and that's further evidence of an institutionalized culture.

You might find it interesting from our perspective, since we have been around the world now, that in every Family Home, in every country, regardless of the particular ethnic culture in which those Homes are embedded, there is a standard Family culture. Our anthropology colleagues tell us that it is rare to find a standard culture that can be followed in a variety of countries without becoming notably changed. There are small variations around the world that reflect the adaptations that Family members have to make in different places, but the basic routines of Family life are essentially the same worldwide. You can go to a Family Home no matter where, and even though they may be complete strangers, you could fit right in, and you wouldn't feel lost or like you had to learn the ropes. You could immediately become functional as a full-time, participating Home member. This is something that anthropologists would find fascinating and want to study too.

So, maybe what we ought to do is just go around the room and focus discussion on the *GN*s. You're all contributing to the editing process, or whatever you want to call it—the production of Family *GN*s. You're collectively involved in producing what you believe is God's Word. In our academic work we would call it "the social construction of prophecy," and you're all part of it. So what's your part?

MELODY: Let's see, Lord help me here. Usually there's a general process. For example, we may have a meeting with a small group or a large group, or with Mama and Peter. We talk about situations, problems, and directions. Or sometimes concerns come from the field via communications with the Boards or with the leadership of the field.[8] So, there's usually some sort of a discussion process to try to get as big a picture of a problem as possible. And the reason that's so important is because then you have a much better question to bring to the Lord. The question you bring to the Lord is extremely important.

So we talk about the problems or the issues, and we'll come up with a question. And then Mama and Peter will ask one of the people participating to try to summarize it. Then it goes back to Mama to go over it and to amplify and to pray further about, and then various people pray about it—the question, or many questions—for publication in the *GN*. Depending on the nature of the problem it can be very complex, lots of angles. So, usually there are many channels involved in hearing from the Lord on these questions. Then Mama goes over the received prophecies, and the process begins of putting them together or praying further about them. Or *she'll* have more questions and say, "Well, what about this, or what about that?" That's sort of how it starts.

SHEPHERD: It's interesting that you've put so much importance here on formulating the right questions, and by that you mean being as focused and clear as you can?

MELODY: Yes, the question is written out in detail, and sometimes several people will go over the question before even sending it back to Mama and Peter to see, "Did we get everything, all sides—the pros and cons?" The question can be *long*.

FRANK: Or several questions. Or it's broken down into several subquestions.

MARIA: We've learned through experience, for example, to ask a specific question. Earlier you referred to Uganda and the road trip you took. If a channel had the question, "Should Gary go on the road trip, because it may waste his time?"

SHEPHERD: Or it may be dangerous for his well-being. (Smiles.)

MARIA: Yes, but see, *if* they were just asking, "Should he go, because he might have more important things to do," they might have gotten "no," that you shouldn't, because you do have more important things to do. But if they were asking should you go on the road trip because of safety, they might get a different answer. So you wouldn't just say, "Should Gary go on this road trip?" If you ask if it's going to be a waste of his time, the Lord might say, yes, it is. In other words, you might have more important things to do. But on the other hand, He might say yes, you should go, because it will be very inspirational for you and it won't be a safety problem. So the question is very important.

SHEPHERD: Who formulates your discussion questions that will lead to prophecies for *GN*s? Is there a group or a committee who are assigned to do this?

MELODY: Well, there are quite a number of us all sitting here that work on that.

FRANK: It often depends on the subject as to who's involved or where the questions are coming from. If they're questions that come up primarily as a result of one particular facet of Family life—let's say one of the Boards [boards are policy advising groups, see chapter 1]—then the people involved with that Board are more likely to be the ones who might be formulating the questions, because they're the ones most involved. They've gotten the most data, you might say, or are more familiar with the issues involved.

MARIA: Remember we told you about the Family Policy Steering Council, made up of the International Board Chairmen, and how Peter said he had to get together with them periodically to hash out these huge, overall worldwide Family situations? When they get together, it's very complicated. They are really the only ones who, at the end of the day, know what the issues are. So they usually formulate the questions after much discussion, and then members of the Family Policy Steering Council are usually the ones who ask the Lord about them. Because otherwise, if they gave them to somebody else—even with the questions formulated—others don't know all that's gone before and all the background and all the discussion. So it's actually better that they do it themselves to get clearer, better answers than if somebody else tried to get in on it at the last minute.

MELODY: Plus, if you have the question, it provides a record for what the prophecy is answering, which is extremely important for the interpretation of the prophecy. Because after hundreds and thousands of prophecies, a year later you may pull up a prophecy you need to read for some reason, and if the question is not there in detail, it's very hard to know what exactly it was about.

Even if you're praying about it, it's good to have a detailed question for the record. And if you want to share the prophecy with someone, then they're much more prone to understand where you're coming from.

MARIA: Well, if we didn't have the Steering Council members, and all we had was Jason [a randomly identified staff member], for example, we could give it to him, and he could get it. But the Lord usually works through the process of understanding through discussion; that's what He *prefers* to do. He prefers to do it through the organization of different groups and through discussion.

MELODY: The process is pretty much standard. We put our various hats on— whether it's the discussion hat, or the writing-the-question-hat, or the channel hat. And often, in complex situations, you have to then get more counsel, usually by getting back together with whoever was meeting after you've all read and studied the prophecies for further discussion. Or sometimes Mama and Peter will send out the prophecies to the field Regional Shepherds [who have supervising responsibility for the performance of Family Homes in designated world regions] or various Boards to get more input, to make sure that the counsel is well-rounded. Because when it goes in a *GN*, it affects the whole Family.

Then it becomes the process, as you call it, of "editing," in which we're sort of adjusting or clarifying the channeled messages. So, with new questions or more input it's a process of going back to the Lord numerous times, and that's the process that we all use no matter what the question is, no matter what the field or department. Depending on the complexity of the problem, the process is longer. A simple personal prophecy on whether or not you should go to a movie may be pretty straightforward.

MARIA: She asked if she should go to a movie one time—I don't know if we should get off on this!

MELODY: Oh yeah, it's not always real simple.

MARIA: She had to get two or three confirmations.

MELODY: Clarifications on why my first prophecy told me to go to this movie that turned out to be an absolute *horror* film, when the Lord told me it was going to be edifying, and I should go, and it would be a good investment of my time. It was one of the oddest personal experiences, because it was such a bad, clearly evil movie. It was called *Final Destination*.

SHEPHERD: You didn't look at the subtitle, *Final Destination—The Evil Movie!* (Smiles.)

MELODY: I don't know what I read, I mean I did read the write-ups on it, and we prayed. But it was one of the worst, freakiest, most evil, demonic movies I ever saw. And I came back and I said, "Lord, why did You allow that?" I felt like I'd polluted my spirit and my channel, and it was horrible; I had these thoughts and pictures. It was really a bad movie. But the Lord said that He had allowed us to go see it because He wanted to show the input the world is getting on the fear of death, which was the full thrust of the movie—how powerful the Enemy's message is, and why there's so much fear. He said that it was a topic He wanted us to address in a tract. It glorified the Devil, like you have no power over the Enemy. So that was the reason. That was a little sideline on how even those little "should we go to a movie?" questions can be complicated.

RACHAEL: I just thought of two small things to add. Like Melody said, the process is the same regardless of whoever is doing it. She explained the process for when there are problems that need to be addressed. But sometimes Mama will also receive from the Lord that there's a topic more inspirational or devotional that needs to be addressed, like praise, for example. And then it's a lot less complicated, I think, because she just has these little points that she thought of, and we [the *GN* staff] put those points into a question. Often it's assigned to the channels, like "ask the Lord what He wants to tell us about praise," or "how can we be using praise more effectively in our daily lives?" or "what are the benefits of praise?" So there isn't so much discussion or brainstorming or figuring it all out; it's more start-to-finish gotten from the Lord. Then the prophecies, of course, go back to Mama, and she's like, "Oh that little phrase is interesting, let's ask the Lord more about that." And from that, the content of the *GN* grows.

MARIA: But those are the more spiritual things usually, inspirational or devotional. They don't have a lot of controversy attached, or how we are going to fix things in the worldwide Family. It's more from the Lord on how to strengthen us spiritually.

RACHAEL: My other point was—and I hope it's okay to say this—Mama doesn't like us to give her a lot of credit, but from working with her these past years, you really see the anointing that she has for asking questions. It's a special anointing that I've never seen anybody else have. She'll call you in the morning and say, "Last night I was thinking about this," or "Peter and I were talking, and. . . ." Sometimes she's reading this long file of prophecies—everybody here sends in their prophecies on a certain topic—and one little phrase just catches her attention, and it's like the Lord telling her that the Family needs something on this.

And then it starts the whole process of asking questions. Or when she's going over something that the Lord has given an answer on, there's just one little thing, and she'll say, "This part isn't complete; we need to ask the Lord more about this." It's her spirit helpers, and it's the Lord's anointing, but it's very special, and that's why the *GN*s are the way they are, because Mama has the faith to keep getting more and more until the topic is complete.

SHEPHERD: That reminds me of another little story. We met Peter in Annapolis, in 1995. We had several days of conversation, and he was telling us about the *Charter* [the Family's governing document], which was just coming out. We asked Peter about his prophecies, because at that time Peter was getting a lot of prophecies for the *GNs*, and he described the process. He said, "Well, we start off, and then Mama has a *zillion* questions." (Laughter.)

MARIA: I have to constrain myself every day and only ask the Lord one or two questions, because I know Peter, I don't want to give him my whole list. (More laughter.)

MELODY: The whole notebook, ha! When the notebook comes out, oh boy!

MARIA: Well, about that, I agree it's probably my best talent. I was bemoaning the fact one time that "Lord, I don't have any special talents or gifts." I regularly say this, I said it to Jack. And then I said, "Jack, could you ask the Lord?" I think I was discouraged that I didn't have anything special, any talents or gifts, and he got a prophecy and the Lord said, "Your best talent is asking questions!" Ha! So I agree, Rachael.

KERI: Sometimes a *GN* will be generated just because someone got a prophecy, and Mama will be led to put it in a *GN*. It could be from the field—the MPL ministry—do you know what that is?

MARIA: It stands for "Mama's personal letters," or "Mama and Peter's letters." We have many Family members who write to us, to Peter and me, and we answer all of them, each one—we and my helpers [see chapter 9]. I guess many here sort of got their training through working on the MPLs.

SHEPHERD: So everybody here, except us, is a channel, or has channeled prophecies for the *GN*?

MARIA: Me, me! I've only had one little thing one time.

KERI: Mama, you got a prophecy for me one time.

MARIA: I know, I get a few prophecies, but normally mine are not used in a *GN*. Mine's still a baby stage gift. Sometimes I'll say, "Well, Lord, why don't I have a better gift of prophecy?" and the Lord always reminds me that "If you did, you would feel the responsibility to do every single prophecy." I would feel bad if I gave something to Melody and said, "Could you get this?" And someone might think "What's wrong with *your* channel? You have it, you can do it," ha. The Lord keeps me from feeling so guilty, I think, by not allowing me to be able to do it. Then I have all these wonderful channels, so I don't have to.

KERI: I don't know if this is really pertinent, but every once in a while, if you don't know the question, then Mama will say, "Well, just ask the Lord the question," and the Lord will give the question. A lot of times she says to ask the Lord to formulate the question exactly.

MARIA: You have a general idea sometimes. You want an answer. There's a problem or a challenge or something, but you don't know exactly what to ask.

SHEPHERD: Jesse [Alecia's husband] was saying this morning that sometimes people who have particular areas of interest, or are knowledgeable in certain areas, may be specifically asked to get particular types of prophecies; it's kind of their specialty area. So if you're concerned about an issue that falls within that area, you might specifically go to this person and say, "This is the issue, can you get something on that?"

MARIA: It seems like it's particular gifts the Lord gives people. Sometimes it has to do with interests, but other times it's that some people have a gift for stories, whereas other channels haven't been practiced in that and they don't have the faith for it. Maybe they could get them, but the Lord hasn't really given them that particular gift. But some people get stories, and not just stories, but things from actual spirit helpers. Sometimes people have a special link with Dad, and their prophecies are more from him.

FRANK: Some people have a gift for getting lots of practical points on a particular issue. Some people have a gift for getting longer prophecies, and other people just don't last as long—their prophecies tend to be shorter, or more concise. Some people also have a gift for getting prophecies that are more geared toward the general public, whereas others get the same message, but it's not as relatable to the general public.

SHEPHERD: Good sociologists would ask if there are gender differences in prophetic styles. So I guess we'd better ask that question. In talking to Jesse [chapter 4] earlier, he likes to get straight to the point, and his own approach is one where, as he put it, he doesn't like a lot of fluff in it, or poetic expression. These are different communication styles, whatever the content might be. Are these different styles related to gender? Do women employ different styles of prophecy on average compared to men?

BARBARA: I think so.

FRANK: I think so too.

JACK: I think there's a tendency, but I don't think it's across the board, because there are personalities too. A person that is very direct and straightforward is going to naturally be more receptive to that type of approach. Whereas someone who is more sensitive and needs the other kind of thing, they're naturally going to be a lot more receptive to it, so it would be easier for them to get it. But I think you can get both.

SHEPHERD: Jack, you're absolutely right; you always end up with individual preferences and variations regardless of people's gender. But at the same time, we are interested in making sociological generalizations. What is most typical? Over the long run, is there a distinctive tendency for certain types of prophecies to be given by men compared to women?

JACK: Well, another aspect of that are the types of prophecies. Some people get prophecies that are expressed as speech. Others get ones that involve visions. Some people get things in poetic forms, or they get impressions of things, rather than specific words.

SHEPHERD: You know what's interesting about this in comparison to other religious groups that believe in prophecy, is that you've got all these different variations that are not only tolerated but *encouraged*. If there was just one style—say, a stereotypically male style—"Thus saith the Lord, thou shalt not . . ." and that's all there was; but you don't do that. You've got a community of different personalities and what appeals to some people doesn't appeal to others, so you offer a range and variety of prophecies in different styles that appeal to different people within the community. You believe you're all hearing from the Lord but in different ways. So, as a group, you've got a way of communicating prophecy that involves everybody—or at least all these different types of styles—and that seems to have something to do with how and why prophecy works the way it does in the Family.

ALECIA: Another thing that I was thinking is that although we all have our different personalities, the Lord is not limited by that. And if we ask Him specifically for a certain kind of prophecy, He always gives it. For example, even if I don't like to receive stories, I've asked Him for them, and He's given them to me. If I ask Him for an analogy or Word picture, He'll give it, even if it's not maybe my preference.

SHEPHERD: Why would you do that, if it's not your preference?

ALECIA: Why? Because . . .

STAFF IN UNISON: Mama asked her to! (Loud laughter.)

ALECIA: Or if you want to receive a song, the Lord can give it to you. Or if you want to receive a fluffy, flowery encouragement message, you ask the Lord for that. If you want a straight-to-the-point, you ask for that.

SHEPHERD: Have you ever received a straight-talk, straight-to-the-point message?

ALECIA: Oh, I like those.

KERI: But you know there might be a reason for that too. Maybe somebody desperately needs an encouragement prophecy, and you don't like to do those, but what are you going to do? Say, "No, I'm not going to help you, I'm not going to do it." Maybe people are going through things; they've lost a loved one, so these are situations you can't ignore. You get the assignment, and there's nobody else to do it.

FRANK: I think that in regard to the diversity of styles of prophecies, as opposed to let's say another religious organization where it might always be a certain way, I think that's come about much more in the last 10 years. If you go back and read prophecies in older Family publications from 15, 20 years ago, you'll notice that almost all of the prophecies are very similar.

SHEPHERD: And they were expressed in King James English.

FRANK: Yes. I don't know why it is, maybe that's another question to ask the Lord: why it has developed. But I think it could partly be because we've all become a lot more practiced, and a lot more comfortable in getting prophecies and talking with the Lord, and it's just become more of a conversational thing. And I think the Lord likes to work through us as channels in different ways, because we're all different, and there are different things that speak to our hearts. A certain style might really speak to one person's heart. Whereas, for someone else, it's another style that speaks to their heart. And since it's all from the Spirit, we're translating something that's spiritual into human language, you might say, so the translation can always be a little bit different. Just like if you have five different people translating something from English to Russian, they might all write it in five different ways even though they're translating the same thing. It all means the same, but perhaps in a slightly different style.

MARIA: We deliberately asked the Lord if we could change that Old English style. Probably we started getting it that way, and the Lord gave it that way, because we'd never known anything else. It was from the old school, and I don't think anybody had ever had any prophecies that were so intimate and familiar with the God of the Universe talking to us in this way. But the Lord wanted to bring us into that more and more—that intimacy and that friendship—and you don't do it in this day and age with a lot of "thee's" and "thou's." So we asked the Lord if it was okay to change it, and He said "yes," and we did start changing. Even for people who for awhile continued to get prophecies in that Old English, we changed it in all our publications.

Another thing about styles: Sometimes what we've done is actually ask the Lord for different styles for different people. We've done it for the young people where we've wanted Loving Jesus words. We've had Loving Jesus words that were given through the channels of older folks—or anybody for that matter. If you want a publication for young people, there's been a case or two where they've asked the Lord, "Could you give something in new, fresh language that appeals more to young people?" and the Lord does that. We've done that with other things too.

ALECIA: For the young people's publications, like the *Xn* [illustrated stories for youth], we asked the Lord specifically for messages that will appeal to the JETTs [Junior Endtime Teens, 12- to 13-year-olds] and junior teens [14- to 15-year-olds] in the Family.

MARIA: It's the same type of content, but it's in young people's language. And the Lord gives that whenever you ask. Even if people aren't used to getting that, when you ask, He gives it in that way. So He does give it in different styles if you want them, or different kinds of prophecies.

JACK: It seems socially our whole foundation is built that way. From the beginning Dad taught us to become one with whom ever we're reaching, and that's been the key to how the Lord's used us in a lot of situations. And by giving a variety and diversity, it relates to each person. So it seems like it would be the logical evolution of what the Lord's doing in our lives. He gets us built into it until we're comfortable, then He starts adding all the angles and different approaches so we can reach other people beyond ourselves.

MELODY: Back to the question about men and women. I think a lot of whether there's a pattern between men and women depends on how much experience the channel has. Experience is not usually the word we use, but how *exercised* the channel is. Let's say in WS, there are male channels who are very exercised; they have a wide range, and they have the aspects of women as well. You would normally think that men would not be giving gushy sort of encouragement messages, or the long ones, or the detailed ones. But if you work with prophecies a lot from a variety of people, there are male channels that can receive long—not that long is so important—soft and tender encouragement, as well as something strong, like a warning or a spiritual leading that stirs you, or a practical message or something related to loving the Lord intimately that's very sexy.[9]

So in my opinion, I don't think it's a male/female thing, because it's a spiritual thing. I mean, I do agree, as the Lord said in the Understanding Prophecy series [a series of *GN*s that explored all aspects of the methodology and group practice of channeling prophecies] that it has to do with your personality, it has to do with your education—that's what the Lord calls the "color" of the channel. Some people naturally have very beautiful vocabulary, even when they're just talking, very rich, and so the color of their prophecies is very rich in that way. But I feel that if a channel is very exercised, it doesn't necessarily have to be that it's a male and female thing.

SHEPHERD: It's interesting that in this small subgroup, we've got three males and seven females. Is that a representative ratio in terms of people involved in prophecies for *GN*s? In other words, is there a higher proportion of women than men?

ALECIA: Well, as far as who in WS actually receives prophecies, I think it's pretty even. I think there are maybe a few more women in this room because we've been more involved with the grammar and punctuation, the secretarial side.

SHEPHERD: Women can spell! (Laughter.)

ALECIA: A lot of the men are more involved with the Web work or the programming, because that's their talent, but they still have excellent channels.

VIOLA: One point I thought of as far as style and variety of prophecy goes, is how the Lord has told us that if we have faith, we should be able to receive anything on any topic in any way. And that can be a big challenge, but it does work if you ask. Plus, now we have spirit helpers. Years ago I don't know that we had so many spirit helpers, but now we have so many, that maybe they just have an influence on us that we're not even aware of. If you ask for a message and you ask the Lord to give the tone of it, sometimes messages are totally different from what you would normally speak, and the channel personally would just never talk that way. But the message will come out in a certain way that's different from their personality.

SHEPHERD: Did I hear you correctly just say that sometimes you will pray to get a certain tone of prophecy? So you say, "I want this particular tone . . ."

VIOLA: Well, no, we'd ask the *Lord* what the tone should be.

SHEPHERD: But in prayer you could say, "When I hear from You, please make this tone a loving, consoling and comforting tone," or "I want this to be a stirring call to repentance type tone?"

VIOLA: Sometimes that could be the case, if we know that's what the Lord intends, and we're pretty sure of the message that was needed. We could ask Him to confirm if indeed He wants the tone to be very encouraging or comforting, if that's the need. Or if not, to give it in the tone that He knows is best. Or if it's a different type of question or message that is needed, asking the Lord what the tone should be is really a big and good step.

CHUCK: A lot depends too on both the purpose of the message and the audience. If you're going to give a message for the general public, of course, you'd give it a certain way. And you'd expect the Lord to give it in a certain way. Or if you're going to give a message about current events, for example, you'd give it in another way.

MARIA: For example, Chuck gets things for the *Endtime News Digest* [a Family periodical specializing in prophecy and current events signaling the last days], which is more geared to the general public—in other words, to outsiders. We give it to Active Members now too. [Active Members subscribe to Family periodicals and are studying Family teachings.] With some of those messages the Lord has told you, "Well, if I were giving them just to the Family, I would give them a little differently. But for the *Endtime News* I'm doing it this way."

FRANK: Sometimes in preparing publications for the general public, there might be a message that the Lord gave for the Family on a particular topic, but it's very much geared toward the Family in the way it's expressed, and so a non-Family member reading it might not really grasp what it's saying, whereas of course we read it and we understand it right away. The culture is a little different, you might say. So what we'll do sometimes when preparing publications for the general public is take that prophecy, and we'll ask the Lord to give this message again, but in a way that's going to be relatable to the general public. And then He gives it again. And that's what you might say is setting the tone, or the audience.

SHEPHERD: Well, that's closely related to a question we have regarding the role that those of you who are involved in what we've called the editing process. You get prophecies and those who are reviewing and editing perhaps are sensitized—because this is what you do—to the audience and to the purpose, and you are sensitized to the tone. Is that something that is included regularly in the editing process? You're getting a certain message, but it's not the right tone, so that's what you work on?

MELODY: Well, the editing process is for many things. It's for clarity: Is the message well-rounded; are there portions that will be easily misunderstood? That would cause a problem if they're misunderstood. Not just because people didn't read it carefully, but actually drew the wrong conclusion. Or especially if the tone is harsh. That is especially dangerous, because prophecy reflects the Lord's love. Even with instruction, it reflects the Lord's love. So if the tone is harsh, then that's something that would be particularly damaging to an individual or in the *GN*s, because it causes people to feel condemned or distant from the Lord, or to feel that the Lord is unhappy with them, which is not the way that the Lord wants to give instruction. But as Francis brought up, the audience, and what you're trying to accomplish, are certainly what you bear in mind.

VIOLA: Sometimes the Lord does give what you could call harsh, direct prophecies, right?

MELODY: Well, He gives strong prophecies.

FRANK: The Lord may have given a prophecy for an individual that is very strong. Someone may have gotten a personal prophecy for themselves that was deliberately very strong simply because, as Alecia mentioned earlier, some people prefer it that way. I like it that way. And maybe that prophecy would be good to share with the Family. Mama might read it and say, "This is great to share with the Family, but maybe not expressed in that way." Well, the Lord wasn't talking to the whole Family.

MARIA: They don't all need it that strong.

FRANK: So maybe you ask the Lord, "Can You give this part again?" or "How would You say this if You were saying this to the whole Family?" And He might say it differently, maybe a little bit smoother.

MELODY: Or give an additional prophecy, or cover another angle to *balance* it.

SHEPHERD: A lot of what you're saying here strikes us that this is what you have learned through practical experience. It's not as though you went to school and learned all these things as part of the curriculum. This is the result of your collective work experience.

MARIA: This is the way the school of the prophets works.

RACHAEL: I don't know that it's so much of our personal experience, as much as it is training from Mama. She worked and lived with Dad for all those years.

For instance, she reads a prophecy, and she just knows "this isn't appropriate for the Family; we need to ask the Lord to give this again." And then, through the years that we've worked with Mama, of course we've learned to recognize that. We can read a prophecy and say, "Mama, I think we need to get this again, because it's a good point, but probably not the right tone," and she'll say, "Yes, you're right." So we've learned, but from that. It's not like prophecies have gone out to the Family and people have written and said, "Oh, I've really been hurt," and we're like "Oops, that's wrong," because thankfully we've had that training from Mama, and she's caught it before it's gone out.

MARIA: With all of you guys it was more like informally discussing the work that we were working on, and going over it, and asking people. I don't usually know much either, so my standard line for everybody is, "Could you ask the Lord about it?" So then we get another question, and we're discussing it, and we don't quite know what to do, so, again, "Could you ask the Lord about it?" And that's how they learn.

SHEPHERD: But each time you do that it throws up a signal—there's something problematic about what we have right now. So the rest of you eventually learn to recognize what's problematic.

BARBARA: We think of it before she has to tell us, ha.

MARIA: Well, it's delegating. That's why now we have so many people that can work on these things, because they've learned and gone to the Lord about it themselves.

KERI: Something else we've learned from Mama that I think all the channels do in WS is that, after you receive a message from the Lord, you should always ask the Lord if that's all; is there anything else; is it complete enough? So that's a practice that we've learned.

MARIA: You can misinterpret prophecies just because they're incomplete, and you didn't get some of what the Lord wanted to give you. Maybe you don't wait long enough, or you're in too big a hurry, you can miss something. Sometimes I think the Lord uses that as a test and gives you some of the most important things at the end. So if you don't wait long enough to get the whole thing from your audience with the King, and instead just say "bye" and run out the door, they can be incomplete prophecies, and we can misinterpret them. Or it can seem contradictory to some other prophecy because you don't have the whole picture.

MELODY: On what Rachael said about working with Mama: We've been working with prophecy for so long that it's really become sort of second nature to us. We have a common foundation that we've learned from Mama. I've told Mama often that her best training is on the "beeper." We're all very privileged, we talk to Mama for many hours on the beeper, and that's how the training has been passed on.

SHEPHERD: All of the rooms are wired to Mama's bedroom?

MARIA: They used to be.

FRANK: We had an intercom system.

MARIA: That's why they call it the beeper—that's the old terminology. Now it's the Voice Chat.

MELODY: I came to work with Mama shortly after Dad went to be with the Lord, and learning to use prophecy—even Mama's learning to use prophecy—was very elementary in comparison to things that we are now so familiar with, that are a part of the way we work and live and our mindsets. I remember so many times, and you all probably feel the same, that you'd be talking to Mama in the early days on the beeper—and now on Chat—and she'll ask you to do something that's so zingy! (Laughter.)

MARIA: Ha, I didn't realize that Melody, you never told me that before, ha!

MELODY: It happened so often in those first years. She would come out of the blue and say something like, "I think we should just ask the Lord to give the stories in prophecy." Now we're very comfortable with it. But at first there were so many things like that—getting stories in prophecy, getting the question in prophecy. Sometimes she'd call up and say, "I need an answer, and I'm not going to tell you the question." Just all kinds of experimenting. Things would come up and she'd say, "Find out why."

MARIA: I wasn't as dramatic as she is, ha!

RACHAEL: Or, "I forgot something important, can you ask the Lord to remind me of what it was?"

JULIE: "Ask the Lord right now, on the beeper please."

MELODY: Or we're on the beeper and she says, "I just got an idea from the Lord!" And she'll talk about it, and you're all enthusiastic, "Oh, that's really cool." And she'll say, "Can you just confirm that?" We were talking on the beeper, and Mama said, "So now can you just get a message right now from somebody, on the beeper?" And you're like, okay!

ALECIA: In those days, if you were going to watch a movie, Mama might say, "Oh, why don't you ask the Lord, before you watch, what it's like." And it was so good for us, because it was so hard for us and took so much faith. But the Lord always did it.

MELODY: Or she'd say, "Could you ask the Lord to tell me about my childhood, because I don't have a good memory—you know, anecdotes about when I was with my parents."

MARIA: A lot of that little book [a biographical profile of Maria that was produced in 1995] is made up from that. It rings true, you know. I get little things, but I couldn't tell you the whole story.

SHEPHERD: You could use your parents as "locals" [editorial readers] (Laughter.)

MELODY: Sometimes I've heard that people would say, "Well, Mama, I don't have the faith for that particular question." And she'd say, "Well, it doesn't matter, I have the faith for it," ha!

MARIA: But if you really didn't, I didn't force you.

MELODY: No, no, but it did *stretch* us, it exercised us. Often my personal experience is that I went on the faith that she had asked me. I figure that the Lord will not fail Mama; He wants to give her what she needs—she's the prophetess and the Winetaster. So if Mama asks me to pray about something, that just increases my faith immensely. I figure she needs it, and the Lord's going to give her the answer. So it's irrelevant how I really felt about it. But I think it's a growing, stretching process. And now the things that we talk about that we're so comfortable with, like asking for the tone, or getting it again, or rewording—we're very comfortable with it.

SHEPHERD: This all has become the norm.

MARIA: They all have great faith. It just came to me now. I think one reason the Lord didn't allow me to have a very practiced gift is because then I might not have had the faith to ask them to do something. I mean, if I had had a channel equal to yours, Melody, I might not have had the faith to do all those zingy things, but I had the faith for *you*. I could just ask you, and you had to endure the hardness, but it didn't affect me so much. If it had been a real stretch for me, I might have felt like, "If it's so difficult for me, and such a stretch for me, how can I ask you guys to do it?" But because I didn't have the gift at all, I could just ask you, and I believed the Lord could give it.

ALECIA: And He always did.

FRANK: When questions would come up, I'd be like, "Wow, can you really ask the Lord this question?" Heavy questions, not so much along the lines of zingy things, but *weighty* questions that affected the Family. I was like, "I don't want to ask the Lord this." But it helped to think, "Well, okay, I don't have to worry about it, I just have to give what I get, and then it's up to Mama and Peter to figure out what they're going to do with it, how they're going to use it." Not having that responsibility kind of made it easier too, because I think if I'd had the responsibility, then it would have been a freak out.

JULIE: Just a comment on that time when everybody was really getting stretched in our gifts and growing, and Mama was asking us to do things that were very scary or that took a big step of faith—it wasn't just all about that. To me there was another very important side of her encouragement afterwards through her *commenting* on the prophecies. Of course when I came to WS there were only four of us young people—so she was able to call us all. I remember every time I got my first assignments from her, I'd send in my prophecies and just be on eggshells waiting to see if they were tainted or false or whatever, because I just had no clue!

And for many months, Mama would call me back instantly. She'd get it, she'd listen to it, and within 30 minutes she'd be calling me and saying, "I listened to your prophecy, it was good, I want to let you know this . . ." and commenting on various parts. And then always in the course of that she would say, "I thought that was interesting, could you ask the Lord this as well?" So then it was a little tougher question, and you'd grow like that. But because you had that feedback spurring you on and giving you faith and confidence, it didn't only stretch you, but it built your faith, and I think that was really key for a lot of the channels who have been exercised the most, that we not only had the training, not only the stretching, but also the encouragement and the input.

And that's what we have to turn around and do with other people who are just coming into using their gift. You can't just give them the question and get the prophecy and let them just go back and wonder what happened. That took a lot of time on Mama's part, I'm sure, just to drop what she was doing and listen to my very unimportant prophecy and then call to comment. But to me it was probably one of those foundation stones that gave me the faith to keep progressing.

MARIA: I think because I couldn't do it myself, I sort of put myself in their place. I was asking them to do something that was very difficult, and I thought, "Well, I certainly need to give them the encouragement, because I'm not doing it, and they're doing it for me." I needed to encourage them. I learned that from Dad.

RACHAEL: And even if you don't comment on every prophecy, if we ever have a question, we can say, "Mama, I got this prophecy, and I'm really not sure about it," and then as soon as she listens to it she'll write you back or call you back.

MARIA: Once in awhile, in the early days, there would be somebody's prophecy that Dad didn't really know about, so he'd say, "Praise the Lord, thank You Jesus." But he never discouraged anyone; he never came right out about it, unless it was obviously a false prophecy. People were just learning to prophesy, so if it was a little questionable, he was very encouraging about it, and he didn't want to highlight it before a whole group. If it had just been him and them, he might have said, "Well, maybe you should pray again." But he'd just say, "Praise the Lord, thank You Jesus." And you sort of knew after awhile that there might be a little question about it when he said that; but he was very sweet.

FRANK: Just a comment on that. It ties in I think with how central Mama's role as the Winetaster is to prophecy in the Family, and particularly in the GNs. That was the topic that started this. Without that, we wouldn't have it. Because at least for me, and probably others here, we wouldn't have had the faith to give prophecies that were going to go out to the whole Family. I don't know that I have so much faith in my own channel, although the Lord's been increasing my faith over the years—but I do have faith in Mama and Peter. I have faith that the Lord is anointing them or guiding them to lead the Family, so I have the faith to get things from the Lord and then pass them on. And that if something's wrong, or if something needs to be clarified, that the Lord's going to show them, and that what's going to go out to the Family is going to be right because of the anointing that He's given them, and not because I'm such a good channel.

But because we have Mama and Peter, and Mama is wine tasting the prophecies that go out to the Family, then that gives me—and I think that gives all of us—the faith to be able to do this. And it gives the Family the faith to be able to believe it too, because they know that Mama and Peter didn't receive all those prophecies. So, "Who are these people who receive these prophecies; we don't know them, and what are they like?" But it's not an issue so much with the Family, because of the fact that they also have faith in Mama and her guidance and anointing. That is what I think is so central to the whole ministry of prophecy.

MARIA: I'd better add to his thoughts. We confirm everything too. It's not like we get one prophecy and say, "Well, that sounds good." Maybe we do say that sounds good, but if it's anything in the form of a revelation or something that we haven't heard before in the Word, we get confirmations, so that is a double check on us. We don't just go, "Oh, that sounds really far out, let's use that. That's great. We know God is going to do great things in the future, so here's one of these events" and just pop it in the *GN*. That's not our gift. It's not Peter's gift either. We still have to confirm any revelations, anything that's out of the ordinary, anything that's different than what the Lord has shown on a consistent basis through the months and years.

SHEPHERD: Why have you become so cautious? Or why are you so cautious about publishing the Word? And by cautious I mean doing exactly what you're saying, going through this process of confirmation, which again is highly unusual compared to other prophetic religions historically. Moses, for example, comes down with the tablets and that's it. The general conception of prophetic religion is that you don't go through this checking process, which really reflects a concern that you are getting it right. It's very unusual, as far as we know, in most prophetic religions historically that proclaim and publish revelations. Normally they don't say, "Wait a minute, is this right?"

MARIA: Not only do we get a lot of confirmatory prophecies for revelations, but as we explained to you before, then when we finally put it into the *GN*, it goes through the process again—more confirmation through locals. I think we have to do that, because biblically it says "in the mouth of two or three witnesses." Way back then the Lord was laying down the rule that we needed more voices heard from, more channels. Because, as we've been talking about, sometimes prophecies can be incomplete, or tainted, colored, lacking information, disconnected, or unbalanced.

ALECIA: Also, sometimes the Lord might give a message, and it's true and good revelation, but now is not the time to get it out.

SHEPHERD: One thing that we've heard continually since we began talking is that it's a great burden of responsibility to receive prophecies for the Family as a whole. Because you know that once this finally comes out, it's going to be read all around the world, it's going to be taken with the utmost seriousness, and people are going to guide their lives by what is said. That weighs heavily—you've all expressed this concern—and we see it as a very admirable thing that you want to be careful and cautious if it's a reflection of the degree to which you feel responsible.

GARY: Gordon, you should be taking notes now, because I just looked down and I see that I have filled my little recorder. Is this going to be transcribed eventually?

MARIA: Yes.

RACHAEL: We could take a break, and you could download your recorder.

GORDON: How long is it going to take?

GARY: I don't know. Get a prophecy on that, somebody! I'm one of these straight-to-the-point people. (Laughter.)

MARIA: We could take a short, ten-minute break. [The interview picks up in chapter 3.]

CHAPTER 3

The Role of
Prophecy in the Family

*A Roundtable Discussion
with the GN Team, Part II*

In this portion of our discussion with Maria and the *GN* staff, focus shifts from more personal experience and individual variation in the expression of prophecy to such topics as: why the use of prophecy has increased so dramatically in the Family in recent years; more on what Maria's role is in training her staff to use prophecy; how conflicting prophecies are avoided and consensus is achieved; how prophecy appeals to outsiders; how Family prophecy contrasts with standard Pentecostalism; how the Family avoids routinization of the religious experience involved in receiving prophecy; and more on how the exercise of prophecy stretches and strengthens faith. The second round of discussion began with a prayer by Maria.

MARIA: Thank You Jesus! We love You, Lord. Thank You for this wonderful opportunity. Thank You for the good fellowship we're having. Thank You for the ideas You're giving us. We thank You for our Spirit Helpers too that we know are jogging our memories and bringing things to us that are important points and facts. We ask You, Jesus, to help us to continue to be tuned into them in our comments and thoughts that we can get as well-rounded a picture of what happens in this complicated process of prophecy as possible. Do help us, Lord. We thank You for how You have been. We claim Your keys of continued wisdom and articulation and communication, and continued help for Gary and Gordon in asking the questions that are important and to get the right answers."

FRANK: You were asking about why we're so cautious as far as what is put out to the Family, and how in other religious groups it tends to be more like, "This is the prophecy and that's it," and just send it out. It's the difference between Dad's style, or the anointing that Dad had, and the anointing that Mama has—and the Lord has explained this too even in prophecies that we've received. With Dad, he was more that way. He'd just get the revelation, put it out there, let the chips fall where they may, "if the truth kills, let it kill," and then often he'd come out with another Letter later saying, "Hey, everyone, don't go to such an extreme just because I said this."

MARIA: After we'd seen all the repercussions.

FRANK: Because the Family would tend to do that. Dad would come out with one Letter, and we'd all just go to one extreme and take it really literally, and we didn't always have the wisdom to be able to realize that, "Oh, he's saying this, but you know, he also said something different before, maybe we should balance it out." We'd just kind of go with whatever the latest was.

MARIA: And we didn't use the gift of prophecy either.

FRANK: Yes, we didn't use the gift of prophecy at the Home level so much. And the Lord has explained that that was good, because we needed that to start the revolution [the Family's term for the group's inception as the Children of God[1]]; it had to be radical and dramatic, and it couldn't be just part way. But now the movement has matured, and Mama has a different anointing—that of giving the counsel from the Lord in a more rounded way. So rather than writing one Letter now, and another Letter six months later that balances it out, we try to put it all in one, so the Family gets a little bit more of a complete package and can interpret it correctly and move in the direction that the Lord wants us to go.

SHEPHERD: Talking about changes in the way prophecy is given and received in the Family, comparing now to during Dad's time: until now messages have been channeled primarily through, at most, a handful of voices at any given time. But now there are hundreds of channels, thousands of channels, and this is something unique. As we said before, we don't know of any other religious group either now or in the past that is doing what you're doing. On reflection, what do you think that means? Why at this particular point would there suddenly be what we have called in one of our articles, a "profusion of prophecy" in the Family?

FRANK: I thought of a verse that says, "And it shall come to pass in the last days, saith God, that I will pour out My Spirit upon all flesh. And your sons and your daughters shall prophesy" (Acts 2:17). So it would make sense, since we're living in the Last Days, that the Lord is pouring out His Spirit in more abundance and speaking through more people than He did before.

SHEPHERD: That says it's going to happen, but the question is, *why* is it going to happen? What's the explanation for this happening in these times? Why is there a need for a profusion, for a "pouring out on all flesh," as compared to the rest of human history?

JACK: It does say that one of the conditions for the End is that the Gospel is going to have to be preached in all the world.

SHEPHERD: Christians have been doing that for two thousand years.

JACK: Yes, but not to the extent of reaching everybody, because there are a lot of peripheral groups that never even hear the Gospel. So perhaps that has something to do with it, just the sheer magnitude of it.

SHEPHERD: But you'd be able to preach the Gospel without having to prophesy, wouldn't you?

FRANK: Just one thought on that, and this is something that Dad emphasized in the beginning, and that Mama emphasized even more through prophecy, is that the Lord wants us all to be able to establish our own personal link with the Lord—to be able to get instructions from the Lord so that we're not dependent on so-and-so leader having to tell us what to do, because we can't hear from the Lord ourselves. In the Endtime events to come, we're going to be scattered, and we're not going to be able to call up our leader and say, "Hey, what do I do about this?" We're going to have to hear from the Lord ourselves in order to be able to effectively operate in the future. We already have to do that now, anyway. Say you have a Home in Fiji and you have a problem, you need answers. You're not going to be able to call halfway around the world and ask someone; you're going to have to ask the Lord and get the answers yourself.

MARIA: We used to do that [World Services making calls to Homes], but we don't anymore. The Lord said personal prophecy is going to be our survival.

BARBARA: To me, a simple explanation might be that we believe that in our lifetime we'll go through the Great Tribulation, which will be the worst period ever that God's people have had to go through. And therefore it stands to reason that we would need the most spiritual input, the most spiritual assistance to get us through that time. The Lord said that about the power of the keys, and that is also a reason for the outpouring of prophecy at this time, that we need more help. Maybe we don't need it all right now, but we need to get used to it, because in the future we're really going to need it, since it's going to be the worst time of trouble in the world.

VIOLA: To build on what Barbara was saying, we will probably teach other people, and maybe in those days other people will see the need for using prophecy. It'll become a personal thing, a reality. Right now they hear about "some weird sect that uses prophecy," and what does that mean? But maybe in the times of the Great Tribulation, when the signs come to pass, some people are going to have their eyes opened to what a useful gift it will be.

CHUCK: The Lord's also said it's going to help us to preach the Gospel, because as time goes on, people are a little more hardened to ordinary religion. Whereas, "Oh, you can get a prophecy about this, God speaks to you?" That is something new and different. It really helps to catch people's interest, and it helps them to receive the Lord. So besides personal guidance, it also helps you to preach the Lord's message.

SHEPHERD: We've seen examples of your "Activated" membership, that is, people who receive the *Activated!* magazines and get regular visitations, who ask for prophecies when they have problems. They feel a need for some guidance, and they've discovered that Family members claim that gift; they take it seriously, and they'll come to them and ask for prophetic help.

JACK: Just another example of that, my cousin: she's quite a young Christian, and when her husband died, I channeled her a few prophecies from him. The result was really dramatic in her own life. Now she's started trying to get prophecies herself for people. She's really working at it. But it inspired her to want to step out and try as well. So maybe it's a step in our whole stretching of other Christians' faith, drawing them into it.

SHEPHERD: For those of you here who are first-generation adults [FGAs], we're guessing that the prime attraction and appeal for you when you encountered the Family was exactly what you're talking about—this idea that there are revelations, prophecy, and that you're not just going to church. You FGAs were seekers, apparently, of something, and that's part of what you were seeking. There are still people like that, and as you said, it appeals to them when you say, "Yes, we get regular prophecies and communications with the spirit world, and that's how we function, that's what we believe."

But there are a lot of other people, maybe even more, that are not looking for that and, as a matter of fact, find that very off-putting—the idea that you claim to be getting the Word of God. You get a very strong reaction from fundamentalist Christians—Southern Baptists, for example—who base everything on the Bible, and to them there can't be any other Word of God. What you're calling appealing is, to many people, an occasion for them to dismiss you as a crazy cult, because normal people don't get prophecies.

FRANK: But we're not trying to reach the fundamentalists. We're trying to reach the people who don't know the Lord. We're trying to reach the people who are turned off by the traditional religions.

SHEPHERD: The unchurched and the seekers?

FRANK: Yes, that's who the Lord wants us to reach.

CHRIS: The people Southern Baptists couldn't possibly reach, because they couldn't relate to them.

RACHAEL: I was just going to give another reason for maybe why we have to use prophecy now, or why the Lord has given so many of us the gift of prophecy.

I think it ties into what the Lord has said about how we're going to have a miracle ministry with so many people, where the Lord is going to give people the gift of healing, or the gift of doing really obvious miracles, as part of our witness and part of helping people to be attracted to our message, and also just out of sheer necessity, like what Barbara was saying about going through the worst time the world's ever known. We're going to obviously have to have some miracles to get any of us through that time alive.

And prophecy, I think, is a sort of preparation for that. Because in order to receive those gifts of miracles, we have to be humble enough to ask the Lord everything. We have to know how to find His will. We have to know when it's time to call for an out-and-out miracle, and when it's time to run—those kinds of things. Otherwise we'll miss it too often, and we wouldn't survive. So besides it helping us to survive, I think it's a prerequisite to the gifts the Lord wants to give us in the future as well, our being willing to ask Him. And not just ask Him ourselves, but to do the whole teamwork process of getting confirmations and working through prophecy and really finding the Lord's will above our own, and then we'll be at the stage where He can give us those gifts, that miracle ministry.

MELODY: Also about our witness, I think it has to do with what it says in that cool *GN*, "Endtime Prophecy Power." I love that *GN* issue; it's about the role of prophecy in the Endtime. I think besides using the gift of prophecy to hear from the Lord for people, that *GN* says that people will come to us to hear from their departed loved ones. And that's where we really go over the top as far as blowing away the traditional Christians. Getting the Word of God, that's pretty presumptuous, but when you start hearing from spirit helpers that have never been to Earth, or you hear from people from the Other Side who have gone to be with the Lord, it's very radical.

I think in this day and age and going into the Endtime, with the movies and video games and everything, the mindset of the people is very much towards the supernatural, and it's gotta be pretty far out there to get their attention. It can't be ordinary. Ordinary's not good enough, it's boring. So I think, as the Lord says, when we become known as the prophets who can communicate with their loved ones, it's really going to cause no small stir. People are going to come to us because they're so desperate to make amends, or to say they're sorry, or to hear from their departed loved ones. I mean, there are lots of things you'd want to hear from your loved ones. Even now we've had times where we've heard from people's loved ones on the other side. Often when somebody goes to be with the Lord in the Family, one of Mama's first tacks is to hear from that person on the other side so they can comfort their loved ones, or comfort those who are grieving, or who maybe feel responsible.

It's prophecy, but a different sort of prophecy; it's really channeling more psychic style. And then sometimes Mama will say, "When you hear from this particular person, ask them to say something that will prove to the person receiving the prophecy that it truly is them speaking, to encourage their faith, to give them peace." So that, I think, is pretty non–Southern Baptist like.

SHEPHERD: Yep.

MARIA: People pay thousands of dollars in the world to certain channels for that kind of thing. There are a few you hear of once in awhile who are very popular and hold seminars and meetings where people come. People give anything to relieve that burden or to know what their loved ones are thinking. It's very important.

FRANK: It's a bit sad that many of the churches have divorced that from the Lord and feel that all that is not godly or is non-Christian. It just pushes people to go to others who do hear from the other side, but maybe they're not so in tune with the right spirits, because there's the good spirit world and the bad spirit world. I think the Lord is trying to use us to help to show people that you can believe in the Lord and love Jesus, and you can also hear from the spirit world—to show that it's something that can be done. There is bad stuff too, but it's not all bad, like many churches say. That's a message that doesn't really get out there very much, and the Lord is using us to get it out.

SHEPHERD: There's another question related to what we've been talking about. This is primarily a question for scholars who have studied religions historically, especially new religions, and how they go through a process of change over time in order to make the necessary kinds of adjustments and accommodations to survive as new religions—especially new religions that are based on revelation and prophecy. And the overwhelming consensus is that new religions that get started this way have to impose institutional controls on revelation and prophecy, as part of this process of surviving.

The primary problems are the disagreements that are expressed in conflicting revelations, conflicting prophets, rivals within a movement, both or all claiming to be hearing from the Lord. So these become wedges that can split religions apart. The historical record demonstrates that those religions originally based on prophecy that survive and then flourish are precisely those religions that find ways to impose organizational controls on prophecy. Instead of expanding it, they narrow it quite severely. And an important part of that is to limit the number of voices that channel prophecies. Historically, this idea of expanding the number of channels is preposterous. But you are doing it.

So the question shifts to figuring out what makes it possible in your organization. We're trying to make better sense of how you manage this problem of conflicting prophecies. There is not really much of a history in the Family, as far as we know, of this being a constant source of division. To the contrary, this practice of multiple channels of prophecy appears to be a major source of bringing people together and achieving consensus rather than division. Our colleagues, if we submit something to them and say, "This Family group is very interesting because they do this," they say, "Yeah, but those conflicting prophecies, that's going to be their downfall." And we say, "Well, not so far." There's a lot of skepticism about it, because it is so unusual. As we would say, there have emerged norms in WS and in the Family generally—in Family culture—that appear to control and regulate this process in such a way that it produces consensus rather than division. We're interested in these norms and how you manage the potential problem of conflicting prophecies. Whew! That was a very long statement of a question.

BARBARA: I feel that in part it's because of the Family's very high respect for the Lord's Word as given through Dad and then Mama, and in adhering to the standard put out in the GNs. And while Mama has totally encouraged everyone in the Family to hear from the Lord for oneself, it's also been fairly clear that the vision is to hear from the Lord as to how to apply the direction that He's already given through the GNs, or how to fulfill what He's already expressed as the Family's calling. It's not control, but there's a standard, there's a respect that this is what we're following, and our own personal prophecies and revelations will support that.

FRANK: Along those lines I would also say that in the Family we have a little bit of both. We have the expansion, as far as everyone hearing from the Lord. And then there is—I hate to call it institutionalized control, because that's a word that goes against my grain . . .

SHEPHERD: How about sensible regulation?

FRANK: When it comes to feeding the Family, we're all encouraged to hear from the Lord for ourselves, but it's not like I'm going to get a prophecy to send out to the whole Family and say, "This is what God told me; everybody do this."[2] Because we believe that the Lord is giving the direction for the Family through Dad, and now Mama and Peter. So if something is going to go out in a GN, it's going to go through them. It's not really control, it's that we believe that they have the anointing to govern and direct the Family. I have the anointing to govern my own life in hearing from the Lord. I might have the anointing to govern my home in consultation with other members who hear from the Lord about those things. But every Family member doesn't think, "I should hear from the Lord what the latest revelation is for what the Family should do next year," because that's not the calling He's given us. We all abide in our own calling.

SHEPHERD: But you do have this discussion process, which is an important part of the overall procedure, and there may be in principle—I don't know about practice—sharply disagreeing views.

FRANK: Yes, sometimes there are.

SHEPHERD: But again, we have a process that ends up producing consensus rather than more deeply dividing people based on these disagreements.

KERI: I think that part of the answer might be something that the Lord has told us to do, and Mama repeatedly reminds us of and makes sure that we do, and that is continually going back to the Lord. We have a whole *GN* issue called "Ask Me Everything." If people don't agree, or if there are what seem like conflicting prophecies, we just keep going back to the Lord as many times as we need to go back. The whole Family is taught to do this.

SHEPHERD: So, to use our language, the norm appears to be: Keep at it until you agree. Is that a norm?

ALL: Yes.

BARBARA: About people discussing things and there's disagreement, and then you go to the Lord: sometimes, from my observation, no matter how many times you go back, He keeps saying the same thing. But meanwhile, He gives all the people involved a chance to meditate on it, digest it, absorb it, and come around to where they do agree. Maybe I have one opinion, and someone has another, and we don't agree. Somebody gets a prophecy, and it's my side and not his, and then there's another one that does that. Eventually after numerous explanations, someone will get to where they say, "Okay, I accept the Lord's answer." And it seems to me that's often one of the ways prophecy is eventually resolved.

SHEPHERD: If you're going to reach a consensus, you actually have to listen to and take seriously what other people are saying. And that's something I think you have to learn. We assume that's part of what you've gone through here. It seems to us that part of the Family culture that children acquire is the idea that in living communally you have to be respectful of other people's feelings, you have to take into account other people's wishes, you have to be sacrificial, and that carries over in a lot of ways, including listening to someone else's opinion. So it's a basic orientation that can apply in many areas, and one of them happens to be prophecy.

FRANK: There's a key quote from Dad, from an old Letter, that says, "The only way to find the will of God is to have no will of your own." And that is a real key to prophecy. I think that's why prophecy works in the Family, because we've learned that if you're going to hear from the Lord, if you're going to get it right, you can't go into it with your own will, with your own ideas, and try to get God to rubber-stamp your idea. "Here, I'll write out my prophecy, God, can You just put Your little stamp on it?" But you've really got to go into it like, "Lord, I may have my own thoughts about this and what I think, but ultimately I just want to find Your will."

If everybody involved is truly seeking the Lord's will, then they'll all get the same answer in the end. It's only when we're trying to hold on to our own will and ideas, and we're not yielded, that our own spirit ends up coming through. And that yieldedness is something that the Lord has taught us over many years. The Lord has had us go through things in our lives, or teaches us through reading the Word as we're living together, and we learn yieldedness. It's a prerequisite to being able to use prophecy.

RACHAEL: We do still have problems, and we have to take things back to the Lord, and we do hear from the field sometimes that people have a difficult time when someone gets something for them that they don't agree with. It still happens occasionally, and Mama wants to get more encouragement and instruction to the Family about prophecy. But one thing that's really helped is the "Understanding Prophecy" series in the *GN*. Mama really studied prophecy and asked the Lord a lot of questions about how we should use prophecy. I know that in the Bible there were people who just got something, and it went straight into the Bible, and they didn't have locals and teamwork and all that.

But that's not the gift of prophecy that the Lord has given us in the Family. He's made it almost like a science. That if we don't do it right, if we don't follow these steps, if we're not willing to work in teamwork, if we're not willing to keep going back to Him, if we're not willing to really look at the questions, then we don't wind up with the right answers. Because Mama articulated all that in the "Understanding Prophecy" series, it's helped people not just to have more faith, but also to be willing to do it and not to feel so bad if there are problems at first.

If you get a prophecy that's conflicting, it says very clearly in "Understanding Prophecy" that it's not that you're hearing from the Devil, and it's not that you're really out of it, it's not that you're wrong. It just means that God probably has more to say, so go back to Him and find out what else He wants to tell you. Or, maybe you both asked different questions, so sync up [i.e., make sure the same question is asked of God by all participating channels] your question and ask again. There are all these things that you can fall back on that really show you how to get it right without feeling like, "I'm right, and you're wrong, sorry we can't agree, and that's the end of it." You can just keep working through it in a peaceful, loving manner.

JULIE: Also, as you have more experience with prophecy, when it comes to the discussions and all those different opposing opinions, or really strong viewpoints, even personal feelings and deep concerns, of which there are many, you realize that when your fellow disciples are fulfilling the requirements for being reliable channels—they're humble, they're desperate, they're yielded—even though you know you have a strong opinion, you're willing when you pray to say, "Lord, clear my channel, I don't want my opinion, I want what You have." You see there's not one prophet who confirms every Home decision. So you learn to respect everybody's gifts.

The day before, you sit in a room, and you're really bashing it out with someone, and it can even get a little heated. Then you pass out the prayer and prophecy questions—same questions—those four people, two on one side, two on the other. The prophecies come back, and those who have such strong opinions get the opposite of what they had argued. The fact that they get something different than what they felt or what they hoped for just reinforces your faith in the Lord and your admiration for them. If you use prophecy, and you use it right, it works. And over the months and the years, all of this gives you a strong sense that the Lord's in control, and that you can trust the channels of your fellow disciples. You know that you're all fallible, weak human vessels, but if you are following the requirements, then the Lord punches through.

SHEPHERD: One thing that we observed at the Home level, when there was decision making that would affect the Home as a whole: there might be a difficult issue, but usually the prophecies that were received, and that were in consensus, involved taking relatively small steps toward resolving whatever the issue or the goal was. It wasn't an overall, "This is the whole plan from A to Z," but it was from A to just B. "So this is the first step to take"—everybody would agree on that. Then they come back and ask again, this time to go from B to C. So it worked step by step, if it was the kind of issue that required a process over time, rather than the whole thing having to be decided upon immediately.

JULIE: I think another important part has been Mama's training to the Family on the spiritual side of prophecy, like the pitfalls. For example, in a Home, you've got your highly opinionated people, and when those kinds of conflicts come up, or the person gets a prophecy that supports their viewpoint, well, if that happens once or twice or repeatedly, you can get critical of that person, or you can start doubting or lose faith in their channel. Throughout all the Letters since prophecy started, Mama has spiritually shepherded the Family, not just in the encouragement to use it, but also in the pitfalls. If it had just been encouragement and "here's how you do it," but never pointing out or correction for pitfalls, or even giving examples of where things have gone wrong, then the Family probably would have veered off, and there would be a lot more contention or negative offshoots from prophecy.

MARIA: Well, I give the credit back to the Lord, because when we ask Him "what do we say, what do we tell the Family?" we have been given those cautions and the pitfalls of prophecy.

BARBARA: The way decisions are made in the Family is in itself somewhat of a safeguard against someone saying, "I am the prophet, follow me!" Because if you're in a Home, whatever decisions are made, the Home has to agree to it. Or if you're on a Family board, whatever decision you want to make, the board has to agree to it. Same if you're on the Family Policy Council. So at every level there is a body that must agree before things are implemented, which serves as a very big safeguard.

SHEPHERD: We have used another phrase to describe what you just said. We call it the "democratization of prophecy"—another distinctive way in which prophecy works in the Family. The idea that prophecy is a democratic process would strike most religious people as being kind of nutty.

JACK: But really it's been Dad's setup from the very beginning. Over and over in the prophecies, he'd do studies, and he'd present what he felt the Lord was showing, and he'd always say, "You go back, you study, you research, you see if this is really right." And Mama has followed in that same principle. It's never been "Thus saith the Lord, you do it, no questions asked." It's like what you said: democratization, really.

FRANK: As far as everyone being able to hear from the Lord, expanding it, like you said, is actually a really important safeguard for helping the Family stay on track. Because, otherwise in the Home you wind up with the type of scenario where, "Oh, he's the one who can hear from the Lord; I can't hear from the Lord because my channel's not so good." So one person becomes the person who can hear from the Lord; everything goes through him or her, and then the others lose their own personal connection with the Lord. Secondly, and more importantly, what if that person goes off on a tangent, or gets lifted up in pride? The minute you start acting like that, that's when you lose the anointing. So the fact that everyone can hear from the Lord means that no one person is the prophet. We're all hearing from the Lord, and we're all seeking the Lord together, and hopefully between all of us we can stay on track if we're following the Word.

CHUCK: Dad would often go back to the Word, too, and he would point out, "Well, even the Lord will counsel with His counselors in Heaven. He would gather His counselors and different spirits, and He'd say, 'What do you think we should do about the situation?' It's not that He didn't know the answer, but He wanted to see what they'd say. And someone would come up with the right answer, and He'd say, 'Yes, go do that!'"

ALECIA: Also, the Lord works so much with our choices. Often He'll say something, but we'll be like, "Oh, I really want to do this other thing." Or maybe you can't come to an agreement in your Home. The Lord often has a few different options you can choose from that are within His will. So He works with us on it.

MARIA: It's true, sometimes Peter and I will want to know what to do. Say, we're going to take a break, go somewhere and have a rest. We'll have a few choices, but we don't know which one to make, and we'll ask the Lord. And I always think in my heart, "Lord, please definitely say one or the other. Don't say it's up to us. I don't want to make the decision on this. I really want You to tell me, Lord. You must know that one is at least a little better than the other." But the Lord really does want to work with your mind and your decisions.

Sometimes the Lord doesn't want to tell you. Sometimes He wants you to fight and really use your own mind and the wisdom He's given you concerning the different ways to know the will of God. Those other ways to know God's will are very important to use. If we were just going with prophecy by itself, we would be seriously off the track, because the Lord says it's not just prophecy. We have to teamwork with each other, we have to teamwork with the Lord, and we have to teamwork with our spirit helpers, asking over and over.

But even that's not enough. We have to use prophecy in conjunction with the other ways to know God's will. With godly counsel, that's part of team working. And the Lord said that unless we do that, prophecy isn't enough in itself, no matter how good the prophecy process is.

SHEPHERD: As sociologists we would say that teamwork norms serve as a kind of brake on prophecy. If there are conflicting interpretations or "runaway prophecies," teamwork norms minimize or reduce the likelihood that they could carry everybody along in a bad direction.[3]

Let's jump to another point here: Even though you have developed a complex set of procedures and practices that seem to minimize conflicts and produce consensus, you still have had some major divisions within the Family. You've had people leave, you've had apostates, and that obviously has always been a problem. We'd say it's become a major problem currently. We don't know of any new religion, successful or otherwise, that doesn't produce these kinds of divisions—not just people who leave, but some who then attack you, who make that their crusade. It's a very common pattern historically; where you have prophetic religions you get these predictable kinds of division. Those who leave sometimes even claim revelation or guidance. But that doesn't seem to be the case with you or your apostates, most of whom—we're guessing—still seem to maintain a religious faith. They just think *you're* off the beam and need to be called to account.

FRANK: The real apostates, or just the people who leave the Family? Because I'd say the people who leave the Family, who don't turn against the Family, for the most part they do keep their religious faith and connection with God. But the smaller group of people who are fighting us, those *we* call the apostates, I'd say the majority of them have rejected Christian faith pretty much entirely. I can't think of any young people, being as I'm more familiar with them, who have left the Family and are actively fighting the Family, who claim to be Christian or to believe in God or to hear from the Lord. They've just basically rejected it all.

SHEPHERD: That would explain why claims of divine guidance are not a part of these kinds of splinter movements out of the Family.

MARIA: A lot of times they leave the Family and start off saying, "I'm just going to serve the Lord somewhere else," or "I have my own faith." But almost invariably it doesn't take very long before they come out with statements against us. I know Pete did [Maria's estranged son, known as Ricky Rodriquez after his departure from the Family].

SHEPHERD: Especially if they get together with others who have left and are unhappy.

MARIA: Yes, time after time we've seen that.

SHEPHERD: So it's not just that they've come to the conclusion that World Services has fallen off the wagon, but that they've personally lost their religious faith.

FRANK: I don't think anyone's ever tried to establish a new movement: "We'll still serve the Lord, but we'll do it differently." That has never happened, not even close. Joel [a former member] in 1968 or 1969, maybe he tried to do something like that.[4]

SHEPHERD: Have any of your apostates gone to other religious groups, maybe back to being Catholics or Baptists or something else, and then from the perspective of those groups attack you because they see you as a false religion?

FRANK: I think that might be some of the older ones, the first-generation adults. I don't think any second-generation adults have done this.

MARIA: I don't know, but I think there may have been one or two, as I recall, like Samuel Ajemian [a former member]. He professed that he was called to be some kind of preacher or something. There are a few who join other religions.

SHEPHERD: Didn't two of your former members try to take over the Family in the Philippines in the early 1990s? As we recall, they faked their way into the Philippines and stole the "dance videos" that were stored there.[5] Weren't they trying to actually take over the Family, or at least draw a following?

FRANK: I don't think they were trying to take over the Family; I don't know what they were trying to do.

MARIA: I don't think anyone wanted to take the responsibility to try to lead the Family. I think they'd think it's too big a deal to do that.

FRANK: To survive this long in the Family you have to be "sold out" [Family term for being firmly committed] to the Family and to the Family's beliefs; otherwise you just leave. Because living communally is tough, you've got to make sacrifices. And hearing from the Lord, if you're going to be a yielded channel, you've got to be humbled and yielded. The Lord has to work in your life, and these are not easy things. So the people who stay are pretty committed.

MARIA: Most of the people that leave after years in the Family are convinced that the Family is the best way to serve the Lord. They may not like a lot of things about it, but they know it's the best way to serve the Lord, and anything else is a downgrade. So I think that's why they wouldn't even want to try it.

FRANK: Especially second generation. When you grow up and have been raised in the Family, it's all or nothing at all. I know, I've talked with a number of other second-generation adults, and we'd always say, "If I ever left the Family, it's not like I'm going to join some other church group. It's either serving the Lord, or I'm going to go make money," but nothing in between.

MARIA: Usually not even Fellow Members [FM]. Very few of our Family Disciple members [FD], especially the young people, will go to FM status [i.e., downgrade their membership]. Or if they do, it's for a very short time just to save face on their way out of the Family. But we hardly have any FD young people that have become FM and stayed in the Family.

SHEPHERD: Well, here's a question. Historically there have been very few prophetic "channels," or people who have claimed to hear from the Lord. And now here you [the channels] are. You don't see yourselves as prophets in the same vein as these others. You see yourselves as humble, ordinary members of the Family. But you get prophecies on a very regular basis. Instead of feeling like this is an extraordinary thing that you're doing, do you ever get to the point where you take it for granted? Does it leave you with a sense of continual awe and reverence for what you're doing, or does it become another taken-for-granted aspect of your daily routine?

JACK: It is a fight not to slide into that. But at the same time, the fact that we're constantly growing, we're constantly being stretched in our channels and learning new things, I think that helps us. Because it's like every time you take a step, and, wow! the Lord did it, there's always one more thing to stretch your faith a little further, to ask the Lord an even bigger question.

MARIA: He's saying that his faith gets stretched a lot, ha!

SHEPHERD: But there is something very different and unusual about the way that Family members seem to deal with the sacred, the beyond, the spirit world—whatever you choose to call it. The typical way this is reported is that there is a transcendent experience when people come into contact with what they consider to be the sacred, an extraordinary kind of experience that's not routine by definition. It's not ordinary. And yet especially for you here at World Services, it *is* ordinary, it *is* routine, this is your job, this is what you do every day.

So it's a very different kind of collective experience to be in contact with the sacred, compared to virtually any other contemporary religion. There have been scholars who have looked at this and see it as a problem.[6] For example, associated with religious ceremonies that, to a greater or lesser degree, are important in most religions, you get the performance of rituals that symbolically represent coming into contact with God, or the spirit world, or the sacred. And yet precisely because they're rituals, they're performed over and over again the same way, they become routine.

And that's a potential problem for young people growing up, exposed to something that's supposed to be sacred and yet is routine. That's what turned a lot of you first-generation adults off about conventional religion before you joined the Family, because it was "churchy"—going to church and just sitting there—the mechanical recitation or performance of something that was supposed to be sacred. This kind of problem is not unrelated to what you have to deal with in your job now, since your job is to be in contact with the spirit world routinely. Does this somehow routinize your experience, making it mundane rather than the extraordinary sense of being in contact with the sacred?

ALECIA: It happens to me sometimes where I just feel a little bit familiar with it, because we do it so many times. But usually when that happens the Lord will talk to me personally about it and say, "Don't get familiar with this wonderful gift that I've given you." I think it's just an occupational hazard of being a channel, and it's something you have to fight against. Another one is feeling like it's so much work, because it is really hard work, and you can tend to get your mind on, "Oh, it's so hard, I have to stir myself up and pray and praise and get in contact with the Lord," and do all these things to be a clear channel. You can tend to get your mind on the hard work of it rather than the awe and the supernatural side of it.

MARIA: It's like on our prayer mornings. We have prayer mornings every two weeks where everybody has an assignment. And I really pray for everybody on that morning, because you have all these people, and it is hard work, and for some it's very hard because they aren't as practiced, and they aren't as used to doing the things they need to do on prayer morning. And so I think to some extent you all feel it's very hard, and sometimes you groan and say, "Oh, no, not another P&P [prayer and prophecy] request," and "oh, look what it is this time, it's even worse than before."

MELODY: Can we please go do the dishes or something? (Laughter.)

MARIA: I don't know if you all agree, but one thing that helps to minimize that familiarity is that it's not the same thing. It is the same in that it's prophecy, but like Jack said, there are so many different ways the Lord speaks, and on so many different subjects, and so many different angles and revelations, that it is new and it's different. A lot of your work is the same, but there come times in your work that you get something that's exceptional and something that's different. And just hearing the Lord speak, or a departed spirit speak, it's always exciting, so that keeps it from getting to be the same thing over and over.

MELODY: I think it depends on the type of prophecy. There are some prophecies that are really challenging and interesting; it's a spiritual experience, and those are pretty cool. There are some prophecies though, when you're actually working with them, that can be very tedious—especially when you've already gotten the main prophecies, or you're praying about the locals [editorial comments and suggested revisions] for Mama and Peter. The locals are compiled and that entails reading everyone's comments, and it's sometimes very complicated, and there are a lot of comments, and you have to read them and then pray about every comment, asking the Lord how He sees it and what should be done. It's tedious. It's real work, prophecies.

Sometimes a *GN* can be read by 50 people—all the ones that go to the Regional Shepherds—and you've got comments coming in from all angles. Someone sweetly and lovingly and painstakingly compiled all of that, and it can honestly be 40 or 50 pages of it before it's prayed about. And then the prophecies are put in, and then Mama and Peter go over that. It's very complicated. But we call these "work prophecies," where you're working through for hours on end, studying, asking the Lord. That's not so fun.

We all do this, and some people really do it a lot, God bless them. It's not like getting a message that's really interesting. For me personally, when I pray about daily things in my life, I don't do very well at that. We're supposed to be learning to ask the Lord everything, so you try to ask the Lord these little things. I don't find it very challenging. I try to concentrate, but I find that if I'm not focusing and writing my prayer, it's really hard for me to feel like I'm tuning in and getting everything. So I'm not so good at that kind of prophecy.

SHEPHERD: It's hard to feel a sense of awe.

ALECIA: Something that happens to me, when I'm praying about personal things—usually on the weekend—it's like, "This is my time off, and I hear from the Lord all week."

KERI: About the personal prophecies. I can relate to what Melody said about that. Sometimes you don't get so inspired. But on the other side of the coin, what helps me sometimes is when you ask a little thing that seems so mundane to you, the Lord gives you some incredible thing that you just weren't expecting. It can be short, and maybe it's not like lightning bolts from Heaven. But it's like, wow, if I hadn't stopped and asked the Lord about that He never would have been able to punch through to me. So that's one thing that inspires me to keep doing it.

MELODY: She keeps the awe!

SHEPHERD: You have to be practical as well. The day is just so long, and it turns out, if you wanted to break it down, you could make thousands of decisions every day, and if you're going to stop to pray and get a prophecy about everything, you're just mired down in minutia. So you end up having to make practical decisions about "What do I really need to do on my own without having to pray about it, and what is relevant enough or important enough to pray about?" Don't you have to do that?

FRANK: Asking the Lord things doesn't necessarily mean getting a big long prophecy. That's one thing that really makes prophecy for us a little bit different. You have the spiritual experience type prophecy, but then prophecy for us is also a relationship with the Lord. It's like the Lord's sitting there and you say, "You know, I'm about to do this, what do You think?" And He says, "Oh yeah, good." Not that that minimizes it, or that it's disrespectful, it's just that the Lord wants to have that kind of relationship with us. So you're working away, "I wonder what I should do next? Should I work on this or should I work on that? What should I do?" And it's just five seconds, and you go and do it.

I'm not that faithful to do it with everything. I don't think about, "What am I going to do for 'get-out?'" [Family term for daily, outdoor exercise]. I probably should pray more about those kinds of things, but at least in my work I usually do. It's that kind of continual relationship with the Lord. On the one hand you could say, yes, it lessens the awe part, but on the other hand, it keeps it from being a ritual because it's something that affects your life personally in different ways. You're not just reciting a Hail Mary that doesn't really affect your life, that doesn't tell you to do anything, or what to do, or how to do it.

Another thing that helps us keep it from being mundane, hopefully, is that in order to be a good channel the Lord has told us that we have certain spiritual requirements we have to meet. It's not as though you do whatever you want and you can hear from the Lord. The Lord wants you to be humble, yielded, reading the Word, really trying to grow spiritually as a Disciple, and following Jesus the best you can. And doing that is not routine; it is not a ritual.

Being forced to do that, knowing that you need to keep that up if you're going to be a good channel, it can't become routine. You know that if you don't, you're not going to be a good channel, and that's a scary thing. If you're going to use prophecy, you want to have the faith and confidence that you're getting it right. Because one of the worst things is to be so lacking in faith that it invalidates what you receive. You have to be making progress spiritually so you can have the faith to hear from the Lord.

MELODY: Like Frank said earlier about the responsibility that we feel when Mama gives us prayer and prophecy assignments, if you're not following the requirements to be a reliable channel, it really takes away your faith. When you know you have unconfessed sin in your life, or you're drifting in your discipleship standard,[7] or you haven't been getting Wordtime[8]—things that really affect your spiritual life—it takes away your faith.

Because we all know—it's throughout the Word and the *GNs* so strongly— that there are very specific requirements and you can't get away with not doing them. They're very real requirements. You go into prayer morning, and you know you have things to pray about, and you want to know you're right with the Lord. You're obedient; you're trying your best to be yielded, to not have pride, because things like that can really kill the reliability of your channel.

FRANK: Not that you have to be perfect, though.

MELODY: No, not at all, but you have to do your best. Some things happened in my personal life along those lines not too long ago. I shared the lessons with some of the guys here, where I got off track spiritually, and it affected my channel in some important prophecies that I had been asked to get. Mama and Peter corrected me—that my prophecies were influenced by my personal opinions. And that is a really bad experience. They were very sweet and loving and kind, but it was very eye-opening for me.

When something like that happens, the first thing you have to do is find out why. Because if you can't find out why it happened, you will never have the same faith again. You can't just think, "Oh, it's a fluke. I guess I didn't pray hard enough." I mean, there's a reason. If you have been a reliable channel over years, and all of a sudden something goes wrong, it's a serious problem. I had gotten correction from Mama and Peter at that time on other things in my life. I was off track in many ways. But that correction wasn't as devastating; we all get off track at times. But the thing about my prophecies being off was what really rattled me. It was so hard to deal with that.

So I asked the Lord about it, and He said it was because I hadn't been keeping the requirements. Over a period of time I hadn't been faithfully taking quality Wordtime, I hadn't been taking conference days, which are like extended Word and prayer days. I had allowed pride to come into my life, and criticalness, things that are actual sins that pollute and taint your channel. So that was a lesson for me. And when you get it wrong, that really helps to bring the awe back!

MARIA: It really helps you, and that's why the Lord allows it.

MELODY: And the Lord just makes it so clear. He said, "Don't think you can disobey and it won't affect your channel." So, boy, I tell you, it really got me in the fear of the Lord. It's been about a year since that happened, but it's been a real touchstone for me. If you think you're going to skip your Wordtime, or you're not going to have prayer time, or whatever, it just doesn't work. It's very humbling, but it's good for us. I mean we're just people, and we have certain training. But even more than that, it's the anointing. We have the anointing because we live here. If any one of us went out to the field to live, we wouldn't have the same anointing, and we wouldn't get the same kind of prophecies. We would never be expected to, because we wouldn't be here as one of Mama's channels.

MARIA: Well, you might, if you went out in the Lord's will [called and sent by God to undertake a particular ministry].

MELODY: Oh yes, if you went out in a certain position where you're given that anointing, that would be different. But if we went out to the field in a Home, to be a missionary, it would be real different, I would think.

MARIA: A lot of you, probably all of you, have had things like that happen, and it helped you, right? It was something that the Lord used. He allows us to make mistakes. We have this little Family motto: Mistakes are good! Mistakes are good if you learn from them, that's the thing, and that's what you're supposed to do. The Lord wants to help us to become desperate and to learn in our school of prophets. I think all of you have. You've grown from any mistakes you've made.

But in talking about mistakes, there are very few, really, in World Services. There are little mistakes here and there that the Lord will allow to make people desperate, so they end up with a better channel in every way. But most of our "contradictory" prophecies are not because somebody got it wrong, not in WS anyway. It might be more that way in Family field Homes. I know because we have people writing us from the field. Just lately we've encouraged people more to send in their revelations, and if they have spirit helpers that they think might be accessible by the entire Family, to send them in, because we want to keep tabs on what's going on, and we also want to know if there's something that would be good for everyone.

We do have a number of people in the field that write in with different revelations they've gotten. Six people lately wrote in and said they thought they were the two Endtime Witnesses [as identified in the New Testament,

Revelation 11:1–13]. But that didn't go very far. It's somebody's private little thing, and we usually write them back, and the Lord has given very sweet response prophecies saying, "Yes, you are one of the witnesses of the Endtime, but probably not one of the two." The way the Lord handles it is very sweet.

But all that is to say, in the field we do have some of those problematic prophecies. Here at WS, when they're contradictory, we're almost positive that there's a very good reason for them, and we ask the Lord to show the reason. We have quite a few examples. One example is when we were praying about whether to put our pictures up on the Web.[9] It was a big step to put them out for the Family. So first we had one person pray, then we had another confirmation prayer, and it was the opposite. Then we had another confirmation and it was the same as the first one. I thought, "When is this ever going to end?" We had two on either side! Four of our most practiced channels. I thought, "We can't just keep asking the Lord and getting different answers. What are we going to do about this, Lord?" Finally we had a fifth person pray and say, "Let's break the tie, Lord, what is this all about?" And the Lord gave different reasons on this side, and then He'd say, "no, you shouldn't do it, yes you should." I said, "Lord, we have to have a definite answer, we can't just be split like this. What are we going to do? We have to make a decision."

They *were* contradictory. They didn't just *seem* contradictory, they were definitely contradictory. So then we had another practiced channel pray and the Lord said, "I'll tell you now. I want to show you the pros and I want to show you the cons. I want to put everything out clearly for you, what the problems will be if you put your pictures up, what the advantages will be if you put your pictures up." It's very hard for one channel to get one answer from the Lord that says, yes, and another answer from the Lord that says no. You almost need different channels to do that, because we just can't compute. We don't have the faith. One person wouldn't have the faith to get both of those prophecies. I suppose somebody could, if they were asking that question, "What are the pros, what are the cons?" But that wasn't the question at all. So the Lord said, "I just want you to be very sure. Here's what will happen if you do, here's what will happen if you don't. I want to give you all this. I couldn't give it to you through one channel getting both messages, so that's why I did it. So you've just got to go ahead and make the decision."

So this is one of those things where we say, "Please make the decision for us, Lord—I don't want to make the decision!" But we finally made the decision of what we thought was best for the Family, overall, and we put them up. And then we prayed and the Lord said, "You did the right thing." Ha! He said, "You'll be happy you did."

SHEPHERD: Let us ask you in this same vein: How much conflict was there in allowing us to come visit at WS?

MARIA: Actually, Peter and I prayed. I don't remember exactly, but we didn't have much conflict. The Lord said from the beginning it would be good. I think Peter might have explained this, but we had talked about it earlier that we might be able to invite you sometime, so we had sort of thought about it. That was a couple of years ago. But then when you decided to make your worldwide tour [of Family Homes], and you went around, Peter and I started thinking about it. Here you're studying the subject of prophecy, you're researching it, but we knew that on the Home level you wouldn't have the same input as you would get here. You'd have good input, but you wouldn't be able to get the same thing as you would here, and some of your questions that you might have run across out there, you could get answered here, really discuss it in depth.

And that's what first made us very seriously decide to ask the Lord about it. Because to us it seemed that in order to complete your research, you needed to see people in WS and how they use prophecy, because we're the ones that are feeding the Family and teaching them to get it for themselves. We thought it just wouldn't be rounded out unless you could come. So we prayed several times about it. I think we did talk to the teamwork [i.e., WS staff] about it, and we had their approval too. So there weren't any conflicting prophecies on you.

MELODY: You probably asked for the pros and cons in the first message: "Lord, give us the pros and cons."

MARIA: And if you were going to be able to maintain our security and all those things. We asked the Lord, but there wasn't any kind of conflicting answer.

SHEPHERD: We know most of you are probably tired of sitting here, but we have one more observation to make. It's an observation about Family spirituality, in contrast to other religious groups, especially those groups who believe that they have fairly close contact with the spirit world and talk about, teach, and emphasize receiving spiritual gifts. Our observation has been that there's not a lot of emotional expression in the Family. We sat here with you today, and you prayed and have expressed yourselves without a great deal of emotion. We've never observed a Family group in which there was a lot of strong emotional expression. It seems like your style, your mode of expressing what you communicate as spiritual gifts or contact with the spirit world is quite different than what one would expect to see, for example, in a Pentecostal religious service. You seem a lot more laid-back.

It seems to us that in Pentecostal and Charismatic groups often it is the emotion itself that is being sought, and that emotion is interpreted as a manifestation of God's Spirit. It's sought as an end in itself to have an emotional experience, which can then be translated as a spiritual experience. There is not necessarily a particular message or lesson or instruction that derives from that, other than having had the experience and saying "God's Spirit was with me," or "I had that gift touch me for that moment." To us, these kinds of emotional experiences don't always appear compatible with the kind of things that you in WS need to do. You're making organizational decisions, you're trying to get guidance of a very specific kind, with a lot of detail that has great weight in other people's decisions, and it's not emotional. Emotion oftentimes might be counter to your objectives. That's the way we see it, our own on-the-spot interpretation. Maybe you have a different one.

JACK: I think that it depends on the prophecy. A lot of what you are seeing is related to the practical, it's an objective kind of thing; but there are revelatory prophecies and sometimes they are very emotional. Not always. It's not something that the prophecy or the relevance of it is contingent on, but at the same time, there are times when it is emotional. When you're getting something for somebody else, sometimes there can be emotional prophecies, or you're experiencing something in a revelatory way, and it can be emotional.

SHEPHERD: But wouldn't the emotion be a by-product rather than the main thing? Always you are articulating a message, and you may do it tearfully and struggle with your emotions that are inhibiting you from expressing the words, and other people may feel touched and moved. But still, what's important is the message, the content of the message, and not just the expression and display of some unusual kind of emotion or loss of ordinary consciousness, such as being "slain in the spirit" and collapsing in a faint, the way some Pentecostals do.

JACK: Or those that feel that they have to speak in tongues.

SHEPHERD: We've seen a little bit of that, and it's not something that is dismissed in the Family, the gift of tongues. But every time we've seen it—and our personal experience has been limited—it's been low key, and it doesn't dominate what's going on. Maybe it's at the onset of a prayer, somebody else is praying and other people will be in the background speaking quietly in tongues. But that always seems to be preparatory to something else. It doesn't continue. Speaking in tongues is not an end in itself; it seems to be one of many means for arriving at an end. We have seen this, but not often; we wouldn't call it the norm. We've never, for instance, seen a second-generation member speak in tongues. In the Family Homes that we've been to, it was always an older first-generation member.

MARIA: I think that that's a case of not being free enough in the spirit. For me, tongues is not an emotional experience. Like you said, it's a means to an end; it's what the Lord tells us to do. But I don't feel an emotion. Sometimes you need more of what other churches might consider emotionalism. We don't exactly consider it emotionalism. We figure that in some of these cases we should be freer in the spirit, there should be more tongues. But that wouldn't translate into being something emotional for us. (To the group): Is that correct? Would you say that's true?

FRANK: It's a way of priming the pump to connect in the spirit.

SHEPHERD: We've been told by other Family members that speaking in tongues also is a form of praise, whereas in some of the other groups that practice it, first and foremost it's an expression of God's Spirit from within, or a sign that you are saved [i.e., have accepted Jesus as savior and are redeemed from damnation]. And, secondarily, on certain occasions in Charismatic or Pentecostal churches, there is considered to be a specific content or message in one's expression that has to be interpreted by someone else who has the gift for interpreting tongues. That's less frequently done, but it is done. Whereas for you, it seems that the messages are so important that you're not going to look for them in tongues because you're going to get it straight, so that everybody can hear and understand, and not have to rely on someone else to tell you, "Well, this is what that person's vocal expressions meant."

FRANK: We used to have more of that in the Family. But it's sort of like we've grown. I'd say that it's not that we don't have emotion in our life, in our spiritual relationship with the Lord. I think we do; we have an intimate relationship with the Lord. But I think what's different is that that is not the sum total of our relationship, which I think is what it ends up being with some other Christians. We've tried to expand that to include the Lord in everything, in every part of our life, in hearing from Him about everything. In doing that, it might seem to make it less important, because you have it spread out throughout your whole day, your whole life, as opposed to if the only time we spent with the Lord was once a week, it would be a big thing. But we're spending time with the Lord throughout the day. It's like if you only see your lover once a week, or once a month, you might have this big passionate lovemaking. But if you're having sex every day, it's not that it isn't important, but maybe it's not quite as fiery every day.

MARIA: I think for us, the Lord wants us to base our foundation on fact and the Word and not feeling. I think He really tries to play down the kind of emotionalism that you see in other groups. We have a problem in the Family with people thinking that they don't feel enough. They say, "We don't feel all the things the Lord says we should feel when we're loving Him." But on the other hand He repeats over and over, "You don't have to feel it, you just have to obey. You just have to know in your heart that it's true." I don't feel anything. Lots of people don't feel anything. Maybe we will eventually as a reward for our faith and doing it in obedience, but we don't have to. We do it because we know it's the truth, we know the Lord said it, and I think the Lord's trying to deliberately de-emphasize and not let people have those kinds of feelings because He wants us to be grounded in faith and not feeling.

JULIE: I wonder too if it could possibly tie in with the fact that in the Family as compared to regular churches, we give our whole lives to this. It's not just about our personal spiritual life and edification. Our whole take on our lives and receiving prophecy, everything we do here in WS, we're trying to do our job of feeding the Family, to provide them with the tools to do their job, for the eventual goal of reaching the world, giving the message, saving souls.

So for us having those sort of "holy laughter," "slain in the spirit" types of things doesn't really accomplish that goal as much as it does to get a message that we can then give to someone in prophecy, or to get the prophecies for a tract. I think our whole take on it, our whole priority, is a little bit different, and that maybe takes away from the thing that edifies yourself a great deal. We can get very edified with our personal prophecies, we have plenty of that, we can do it as much as we want every day. But I think our bigger vision is much more practical, much more methodical. We have a commission to reach the world, and so everything is more geared to that.

SHEPHERD: Well, we don't think we've exhausted the subject matter, but we may have exhausted your energy reserves. It's five to eight, isn't that dinnertime? Even though we've missed some of our appointments today, everything's been flowing very well, and we wouldn't trade back any of the time that we've spent so far.

MARIA: Well, you're satisfied for now, and we are too. This was very good. Thank you for your encouragement, your education about things, and your observations; they were very interesting. This was good for us too to try to formulate and articulate what we do. Rachael, would you like to close in prayer?

RACHAEL: Sure. Thank You Jesus so much for this time that we've had together. Thank You for bringing Gary and Gordon here; it's been a blessing for us to be able to see them and fellowship with them. So we're just very thankful for this time, and we thank You for working it out, Jesus, and helping us all to be able to be here. We pray for their strength, too, as they do these studies over the next couple of days. There are so many people they probably want to talk to and so little time. So please do give them strength, keep them healthy, and work things out for them so that they are able to get their questions answered, and see everything they need to see, and talk to everyone they need to talk to, without any burden of stress or feeling crammed or worried that they won't fit it all in.

Please continue to protect and keep us all. We commit our security to You. Thank You for watching over us so carefully. We ask that You continue to protect and keep us here as long as we need to stay. And bless our dinner. Thank You for providing for us. And please provide for all of our missionaries around the world. We claim the keys of supply for each Home, for each Family member, that they will have what they need. Thank You Jesus!

CHAPTER 4

Producing Prophecy
for the *Good News*

The preceding two chapters reveal the complex ways in which the Family understands and practices prophecy in general, both at personal and collective levels. In this and the next chapter we elaborate on the specific application of these prophetic principles in four different WS work units or departments: the Good News, Mama's Secretaries, Art and Text, and Layout. These departments are all interconnected in the production of the Family's most important internal publication, the *Good News,* which is available only to Family disciple Homes.

Rather than reproduce verbatim transcripts of the entire set of interviews we conducted with the heads and key personnel of these departments, in these two chapters we summarize what we regard to be key interview points and illustrate these with selected interview comments. Authors' summary informational comments are inserted as necessary and provide clarifying linkages between discussion points; these appear in italic paragraphs.

INTERVIEW WITH GN DEPARTMENT HEAD RACHAEL

As discussed previously, the primary responsibility assumed by World Service staff is to receive and disseminate what they believe is God's word, provide leadership guidance for Family Homes worldwide, and produce the literature and proselytizing tools that Family missionaries feel they need in order to bring Christian salvation to the unredeemed in preparation for the apocalypse. The Good News (or GN) Department in particular concerns itself with the task of publishing God's "Endtime Word" to the Family International. While Maria's special domain is oversight of Family *GN*s, the GN Department is organized like other WS departments with a head and assistant head, who are responsible for the day-to-day operations of the department under Maria's ultimate direction. The GN Department head at the time of our visit was Rachael, a 31-year-old second-generation Family member who had been working at World Services for nine years. To us, Rachael claimed that she is not very good at verbally organizing or explaining things (she is actually quite articulate) and is grateful for prophecy because, as she insists, it allows her to write much better than when she attempts to write without channeling. She does not believe that what she channels for publication are her own thoughts or words.

In 1996 Rachael was among the first cohort of second-generation adults (SGAs) brought into World Services after David Berg's death. Recruited as a traveling secretary for Peter, Rachael soon became indispensable to Maria as one of her secretaries involved in the publication of Family GNs. As Maria pushed for a greater volume of prophecy to meet WS publishing demands, it became Rachael's job to coordinate the assignment of different prophecies. Thus, one of her tasks is to manage other people who work on or contribute to the GNs. This shift to managerial roles is common among current WS staffers. Over the past decade WS has become much more complex as a work organization. Initially, new SGA staffers were underworked, according to Rachael, and found themselves performing mostly domestic chores. Maria and Peter, however, soon began delegating increased authority and responsibility to the new WS staff. Consequently, an emphasis on training also increased. Rather than modeling Father David's autocratic micromanagement style, Maria and Peter's roles have shifted to greater strategic planning and giving approval to the work done by others. This represents an important organizational development that is consistent with Max Weber's analysis of the "routinization of charisma" in heretical new religions that persist beyond the mortal life of the charismatic founder and his initial cohort of disciples.[1]

Selected details from our interview with Rachel are excerpted and summarized below. Our own comments and informational summaries are occasionally inserted and set off in italics from her responses.

Virtually every WS staff member we talked to presented a humble and unassuming persona to us throughout our visit and interviews, attributing any personal skills or achievements as a contingent gift from Jesus, often bolstered by Maria's faith in them. In describing her arrival at WS, Rachael notes her initial poor typing abilities:

RACHAEL: I think the first thing Mama said to me when I got here was, "Please take a typing test and see how fast you can type," because I was not a secretary. I was a field person, and I'd always done child care or was on the Home teamwork.[2] Right before I came to World Services I was a Visiting Shepherd and worked with Alexia [Peter's former wife], so I was just out all the time witnessing [evangelizing non-Family members]. I never did any desk work at all. They brought me to be Peter's secretary and to travel with Peter. That was one of the things they wanted me to do, and Mama was concerned that I couldn't type. And it's true, I couldn't. My score was 27 words per minute. Ha! My mom had taught me to touch-type when I was about nine. We were in this hotel in India. We were in between Homes, staying one night in a hotel, and we all came down with chicken pox. So, of course, no Family Home wanted us to come with the chicken pox. We were in that hotel for about three weeks. We had a manual typewriter, and my mom covered all the keys with little yellow stickers and gave us a chart. All my sisters and I learned to touch-type during those two weeks. So I knew how to type, but I was so slow.

But Mama has so much faith in people. She said, "Okay, just start doing an hour and a half of Typing Tutor every day." Then she started giving me tapes to type, and, of course, typing tapes, if you don't want to be bored and be there all day, you get fast really quick. The last time I checked my typing speed was 127 or something.

According to Rachael the functioning of WS has undergone significant change since Rachael first arrived as a slow-typing secretary in spring of 1996; she provides a little history:

RACHAEL: One thing is that the Family has gotten more complex. When I first came to WS, everything was more relaxed. There was a lot less work to do. There were fewer publications for one thing—a lot fewer publications. There was an Administration Department that basically just communicated with the Continental Officers.[3] Then there were people who worked for Mama. There were the artists and people who did the *Zine* [a publication for Family youth], but even that hadn't started when I first came to World Services. There were the *Family Special Magazine* [irregularly published on designated topics relative to communal living concerns], the *GN*s, and an occasional Christian Leadership Training Program. They had a hard time finding work for us when we got here.

Occasionally we'd get a call from Mama saying, "Can you do this prophecy?" We did a lot of cleaning and cooking. We had just moved to this big, beautiful house up in the north of Portugal that was super run-down and needed a ton of work. So that was a Godsend for us, because we'd all go to the garden and do gardening for about six hours and talk and look at the ocean. Ha! Play volleyball and go to the beach. We wanted work, but there wasn't a lot to give us. I started on MPLs [Mama's Personal Letters], because Peter wasn't traveling all the time. He took maybe one or two trips a year. So

I started helping Mama with answering personal letters, but not that many people were writing in. It wasn't that big of a job; it didn't take all my time. So life was much simpler back then. Not just for us, but for Mama and Peter, too. They had a lot more time to do a few jobs.

But then, as things have gotten busier and busier, and there are more and more things that require their focus and attention, they've had to delegate more. The Lord has told them to train more people, or to take people that have worked with them for years and give them more of the responsibility of thinking and praying about things. And then have staff give it back to Mama and Peter for their approval or their counsel, seeking their input, and then turning it back to their staff to carry out, that kind of thing. They've done that with the Boards and the International Board Chairs, who really run their Boards, and they've done that with the departments in WS, too.

I started working full-time on *GN*s in 1998. At the very beginning of the year there was a Summit in Mexico, and I was supposed to go.[4] But I had some personal problems right before, and they decided to keep me home, because I wasn't being very good. Ha! Anyway, it was good for me. But all the other people who had been helping Mama did go to that Summit, and I was the only one who had been working with her who stayed Home. She also stayed Home. Only Peter went with all the other guys. It was an eight-week Summit with the Continental officers and then four weeks of workshops, which was sort of the beginning idea of the Boards, or the beginning of delegating responsibility to these people in the field who could run these pillars.[5] Mama did 32 *GN*s in that eight-week period. Every morning I would wake up with work to do—Mama does this when Peter goes on a trip—she sort of gets on his schedule, not even consciously. She starts staying up later and later at night, and sometimes sleeping very little, and just working; dictating communications to him, and dictating her corrections on the *GN*s; whatever she's doing, she's fully into it. And every morning I'd wake up, and there'd be like six tapes outside my door. And that's when I really started working with her on the *GN*s. I think when Peter came back from the Summit, she was like, "Sorry, honey, she's not going to work with you anymore." And I just never stopped doing *GN*s after that with Mama. So that's how I got the job.

Rachael told us her responsibilities have evolved significantly: she currently has overall managerial responsibility for GN production and works directly with Maria.

RACHAEL: The *GN*s are Mama's work. Basically, I just help her to manage the people that work for her. She directs the work and the *GN*s. I mean, you understand how departments work here, right? Somebody already explained to you that we have the worth ethic and minimum work hours.[6] People have to have a department head to ask for unscheduled community service or to get permission for their vacation days. Or when someone writes our department and says, "We need you to help with such-and-such," I have to figure out who does it. We have to juggle work. We have to meet deadlines. When all the Boards put their criteria out for the Family late last year, that all came through the GN Department pipeline. So at times like that you do a lot more managing. But in general, it's just helping to manage the people that work for Mama.

Rachael then went on to tell us, however, that only about 30 percent of her time is spent coordinating and managing others' work in the production of GNs. The bulk of her time is responding to various requests from Maria.

RACHAEL: Being a secretary for Mama, I help her with her work: do prophecies for her, or help her as she puts together the *GN*s, or pray about the locals [editorial reviews]. It's reciprocal. Mama gives us the job and says, "We need to do this, and we need to that, and these are the points we need to cover, and ask the Lord this or that." But then after we do it, we give it back to her, and she's the one who goes over it and says, "We need more on this," or "this isn't quite right." So ultimately we're just doing it for her, and it's her responsibility. But we really pray to try to get it right, to save her time, because she and Peter are so busy.

We had previously learned that a number of people at WS serve as channels for prophecies that in various ways go into the GNs, or at least are on file as potential GN material. But because Rachael works so closely with Maria, Rachael has become a particular channel that Maria often relies upon for assigning prophecies to WS staff or to channel herself. Below, she elaborates on these procedures.

RACHAEL: I help her to pass out a lot of the prophecies. Sometimes Mama will call and say, "We need someone to pray about this. Maybe pick five or six people," and she'll list some possibilities. But then we have to go through their department heads and ask if they have the time to do it and can be given the time from their normal work. Also, there are some prophecies that sometimes people will send back and say, "I don't have the faith to do this one," or "I just did something similar for such-and-such, and I'm having a hard time feeling the Lord can give a fresh message. Can somebody else do this one, and I'll take a different one?" And Mama works with people like that, according to their faith. So I would say I help her coordinate a lot of the prophecies.

A lot of prophecies are gotten by weekly channels, which are responses to a note that Mama sent out to all the department heads, saying: "We need people whom we can call on every single week to do one prophecy a week." She has different reasons for asking. Sometimes the people are people she feels could really benefit from stretching their channel every week and having an assigned request. Everybody is supposed to be hearing from the Lord every day in our work and for our personal lives. But getting a specific request, which is usually just a little bit beyond what you are comfortable with, is so good for you. And when you do it regularly enough, your channel gets very good. It's very exercised. So that's one reason she asks for some of them. But also we needed a lot more prophecies for the GNs, for our other publications, like *Xn* and *Blade* [magazines that target Family youth], and for responses to Mama's personal letters.

These weekly channels are all people who have been cleared with their department heads, so that every week we can send them an assignment without checking with the department head. So they do a lot of the prophecies, and then every prayer morning [twice a month for all WS staff], unless you have a special exemption from the teamwork, or from Maria or Peter, you dedicate your full morning to prayer and prophecy time. Each person gets at least one or two or three assignments weekly, depending on how quick they are. That requires a lot of coordination too, figuring out who gets what assignment.

There are people who have a gift that makes it easy to put that message in a *GN*, because it's well-rounded, it's well expressed, it's easy to read, it's enjoyable to read.[7] There are other people who maybe haven't been here as long and haven't practiced their channel enough, or maybe they don't desire to sit there long enough to get the full answer. There are different factors and different cases. Maybe it's just a prophecy they're not so interested in. But when it's experienced channels, we generally just give it to one person unless it's a super big question with big ramifications. We'll just see what that one person gets, and if necessary we'll confirm it or get more with another. But when we are assigning questions to people who are less experienced, we'll often give the same question to two or three of them and then take the composite of all three of their answers—not put it together as one prophecy, but Mama will say, "Here's something the Lord said, and here's something else the Lord said, and here's something else the Lord said." And all together it makes a well-rounded picture.

If there are some assignments that people feel are too hard, usually those of us who assign the prophecies, which is mainly Alecia and myself—we alternate every other week—get the overflow. So we wind up doing a lot of those. But also sometimes there are ones that Mama specifically calls and says, "Please, can you do such-and-such one?" Like she said yesterday, she calls on specific channels. A lot of the people who were in the room yesterday [for the round-table discussion, see chapters 2 and 3] are the people she calls on if she wants a specific person to pray about something.

There are some things that I know she'll ask me, if it has to do with anyone in my department, like a personal shepherding thing [counseling with staff concerning any personal problems]. Or—this is something unique about Mama—if it's something she feels you could really benefit hearing the Lord's counsel from personally, like an area you need to grow in, she'll often assign you a prophecy for the *GN*s on that topic, because she feels it'll benefit you as well as the rest of the Family. Or if it's something you're working on, or if it's something that you've been in a meeting about, and you know the background on, she'll assign it to you. Mama has so much faith, way more than I do, and sometimes she assigns things that, in my mind, I'm like, "Are you sure?" But the Lord answers because of her faith.

For example, Mama's called me a couple of times and said, "There was something really important that I needed to do, and I forgot what it was. Can you ask the Lord to remind me?" And I'm always like, "Oh dear!" There's only one right answer in that case. Ha! No variables. I guess it's not so surprising anymore to get these kinds of requests. The bigger the consequences, the more it really stretches my faith. The bigger the possible repercussions, the more difficult it is for me to block that all out and say, "Lord, just give whatever You want to give," because that's the bottom line. You have to get not what sounds good, not what's politically correct, not what's "safe," but what the Lord wants to say. And that sometimes is one of the hardest things for me.

Not only does Rachael assign prophecies, but she also typically reviews them when returned and then initiates the next round of locals or unique Family prophetic editing process of confirmation, addition, and refinement, as she elaborates.

RACHAEL: All prophecies go straight to Mama. But, if it's a project that I'm helping Mama with, then a copy comes to me. I read them because, if the prophecy is not complete, or it seems like it only covers one angle of the problem or the question, then we'll reassign it. We'll ask someone else to also pray. We usually do that even without Mama reading it, because we just know she's going to say, "Can you ask the Lord for more?" So, usually I'll read those right away, because if it's a project that is in the works, it'll take another week for that next weekly channel to get to it and do it. But then once we have all the prophecies on the topic, and Mama's heard them and wants them to go in a GN, then, we start the process of going over them and praying about any wording changes that need to be made or asking the Lord for more, if there are angles that need to be well-rounded.

Finally, Rachael reiterates the common Family belief that competent performance of her responsibilities is dependent on supernatural assistance rather than her own inherent abilities, which she downplays.

RACHAEL: Let me just say that I'm really bad at putting my thoughts into words. That's why I'm so thankful for the gift of prophecy, because I do have to put things down on paper a lot. But to say it myself is very difficult. It makes my work easier when I ask the Lord to give it to me in prophecy instead of trying to write it myself. For example, if I have to write a note as a department head to someone in my department who did something that they're not supposed to do—and as a department head you're remiss if you don't say it—but of course it's hard to say, or it's delicate, or it's sensitive. I just pray and ask the Lord to word it for me. Of course I don't write it as a prophecy with "Jesus speaking" at the beginning. I'll say, "Dearest So-and-So" and write it as a letter. But the Lord gives it, and I'm done in maybe ten minutes. Then I read it over and check it and maybe add a few little things. But if I were to try to write it myself it'd probably take me a half an hour or more.

Sometimes when I'm going fast, and I kind of forget that prophecy helps me so much, or maybe I'm tired of getting prophecy—I've just done a 40-page locals file [reviewing editorial commentary by other reviewers], and I'm like, "That's enough, it should be Saturday already!" Ha. And I'm like, "Okay, I have to write a note to so-and-so, I'll just do it." I usually wind up saying, "I'm sorry, Lord, can You please fix this for me now?" Because at the end of the day, I still don't have confidence that it sounds good, and it probably doesn't. I've found that if I pray about it, it saves me so much more time. The Lord knows the person's heart and what's going to be sensitive for them or easy for them. So if I just pray about it, the Lord says it in a way that I don't have to clean up or do damage control afterward. They don't know that I got it in prophecy, or that I didn't get it in prophecy, but it makes it easier for me if I do, and easier for them, too.

INTERVIEW WITH MAMA'S SECRETARIES DEPARTMENT HEAD ALECIA AND HER HUSBAND, JESSE

Department head of Mama's secretaries, Alecia is a 26-year-old second-generation adult who has worked at WS for eight years. Maria has six secretaries, two of whom work on her correspondence while the others concentrate on potential prophetic material for *Good News* publications. Maria's secretaries are considered to be reliable prophecy channels, and Alecia is considered by other WS staff to be an especially gifted channel. She claims that Maria's faith and encouragement have greatly increased her confidence as a channel of God's word. But like other staffers with whom we spoke, she disclaims any personal credit for her ability. For Alecia and other Family channelers, the spiritual principles on which prophecy depend are their shared humility and faith. At the same time, as important as their group faith is to the channeling practices employed at World Services (a faith that may be characterized as collective confidence imputed to a supernatural source of guidance[8]), our previous research supports the conclusion that prophetic channeling ability is closely correlated with the ability to speak or write fluently and extemporaneously.[9] The latter are ordinary language skills that can be polished and greatly improved through persistent practice. We would argue that imaginative and persuasive writing skills in particular are more prevalent in most groups than the relatively rare talent of cogent extemporaneous speaking. Official encouragement of Family members to record personal prophecies through writing and keyboarding has aided dramatically in the profusion of Family prophecy.

One of Maria's secretaries has the specific assignment of keeping track of all prophecies that are submitted and archives them electronically by designated topics for future reference. Subsequently, parts of a particular prophecy may be selected for publication rather than including the entire message. At the same time, all submitted prophecies are electronically filed, not just those that are assigned by Maria through the *GN* staff for publication. Maria, who takes seriously her role as the Family's Winetaster, listens to virtually everything designated for her by her secretarial staff as a prophecy. According to Alecia, Peter and Maria jointly receive at least one prophecy every day as a result of their daily prophecy time together; the resulting prophecies are archived with all other prophecies.

As with several of our other interviews, we were accompanied in our interview with Alecia by WS shepherds Thomas and Vivian, who served as escorts as we went from one meeting to the next to be introduced to additional staff members. Alecia's husband, Jesse, was also present and contributed to our conversation. Jesse, 32 years old, is another second-generation Family member who has been at World Services for six years as a Web programmer and serves on the Church Growth and Outreach Board. Jesse also channels prophecies for WS publications and typically is assigned "shooting-straight" topics (as described in our interview below). In contrast to his own approach to writing, Jesse claims that when he receives prophecy he writes quickly and spontaneously. He doesn't stop to edit content. If initial prophecy messages don't seem to make sense, he asks Jesus for a "clarifying prophecy" rather than attempt to edit or correct his original words. Using a "spiritual force field" analogy, our informants explained that in their prayer petitions they claim the "keys" of spiritual protection to ward off any demonic influence that might corrupt their attempts to channel God's word. They strongly believe that Maria ultimately will judge correctly if their or other channelers' prophecies are valid expressions of God's will.

In this interview we became more fully cognizant of the astonishing extent to which the practice of channeling and recording personal prophecies is a fundamental part of daily life for disciple Family members, both in and out of World Services. From the descriptions of Family prophetic practices provided here, we are reinforced in our conclusion that the dissemination and sharing of prophecies in the Family are an important group mechanism through which community norms and guidelines are established and socially supported. And we are again forcefully reminded of the ultrasupernatural character of the Family's core beliefs that underlie and legitimize the group's programs and organizational practices.

Selected details from our interview are excerpted and summarized below. Author's summary informational comments are inserted where appropriate.

Alecia is supervisor of Mama's secretaries, excluding Rachael, who is GN Department head in addition to doing secretarial work for Maria. In fact, Alecia and Rachael work closely together, since their responsibilities overlap significantly. Counting Alecia and Rachael, there are eight secretaries who work for Maria on various prophecy-related tasks. Alecia had been elevated to supervisor of secretaries a little more than a year prior to our visit. We were told by two of the accompanying World Services shepherds—Vivian and Thomas—that Alecia is particularly gifted in prophecy, something that was noted at the outset of her arrival at WS eight years earlier as an 18-year-old.

VIVIAN: Before Alecia came to WS, when she thought she had a lousy channel, she used it to encourage people. That was one thing that stood out to us in her questionnaire, her evaluation, before coming: she used her gift. If someone was having a battle about something, she would get a prophecy for them and give it to them.[10]

ALECIA: You knew that?

VIVIAN: Yes! That was an outstanding thing on your evaluation, that you were humble enough to do that and to use it.

ALECIA: Well, that's one of the things I personally appreciate about the gift of prophecy; sometimes your friend is having a really rough time with things, and there's nothing you can do. But you can get something from the Lord for them that says everything that they need, or it's something that is going to encourage them. Sometimes you feel so helpless, but that is always something that you can do. So I'm thankful for that.

I did get my gift of prophecy before I came to WS. I was on partial excommunication—because I tried marijuana.[11] In those days, about nine years ago, when you were on partial excommunication you didn't get to read any of the new *GN*s that were coming out, and you couldn't have sex. So it was kind of a bad time in my life, and I was pretty down. And that was the time when I started using my gift of prophecy and exercising it. It wasn't so developed at first, and then when I came to WS, of course, Mama really encouraged me by giving me things to pray about. I think it just grew over time, because the more you pray and hear from the Lord, the more faith you get. At first, you're very scared to pray about anything; even the smallest thing just freaks you out. But then with time, you see that the Lord answers and that it works. Then you're willing to ask Him for something that seems a little scarier, for bigger things, or you're willing to ask Him about something for somebody else and not just yourself. It's because your faith grows with time the more you exercise it. I don't think that I have a special gift or anything, but I think that over time it has grown, just because I use it a lot. I've used it every day for eight years.

The way prophecy is conceived of, received, experienced, and expressed by individual Family members varies a great deal, something we had already learned. Our discussion with Alecia, Jesse, Vivian, and Thomas provides further striking illustration of some of these variations. At the same time, certain constant principles, such as exercise of faith and humility and confirmation through multiple channels, are universally agreed to be necessary prophetic ingredients.

ALECIA: If it's a major prophecy, I like to have confirmation. It's scriptural that it's good to have other channels confirm: "In the mouth of two or three witnesses." You do gain faith because you've seen the Lord come through for you so much, but still, when you're hearing from the Lord about anything that is going to affect anybody or anything that's going to go to the Family, it's a super big responsibility. You're just desperate, and you want to be as clear a channel as you can and not let your own thoughts get in. So even if you're an exercised channel, I don't think that worry goes away, because it's always going to be a heavy responsibility. If I'm proud, or I think it's me, or my gift, then that's one of the things that can hinder my channel.

JESSE: I guess what is unique to our method of prophecy is that, though we have faith in it, at the same time we don't just take it at face value. We realize prophecy can be quite complicated. Interpreting can be complicated; getting it can be complicated. As scary as it is to get a prophecy for a *GN*, at the same there is a bit of confidence in that you know that if it's something major, it's going to be in the mouth of several witnesses; it's going to be confirmed. Some may consider that a lack of faith, but I consider it more wisdom.

I regard my approach to prophecy to be a little bit unique. The thing is, I'm analytical by nature, so probably more than the average Family member, I don't necessarily take prophecy at face value. I sometimes tend to analyze them and wonder if they're right. At the same time I have faith that, in general, prophecy really is the way to go. It works. I don't necessarily feel it always is absolutely the Lord's words every single time. But I have faith enough to personally practice it on a daily basis, to believe what I read in the *GN*s, to make it a major part of my life, and that is how it works for me personally. I receive a prophecy, and I will take it under serious consideration. As far as my gift, as far as being asked to receive prophecies, most of us here are given prophecy requests by Mama on prayer mornings, twice a month. Often there will be a major request that's given to everyone, and pretty much everyone will ask the Lord about it. And then certain people will be asked to receive more specialized prophecies. Alecia is actually one of the ones who dishes them out, sometimes in counsel with Mama, and I've found that prophecies that I am asked to do tend to be a little bit specialized. I'm not sure how to explain them, sort of very factual, like, "This is what you need to do," no beating around the bush.

Even in the personal prophecies I receive, I don't find there is a lot of, "I love you, my dear love, my flower, etc.," which I think is great for people who need that sort of thing. I don't mean to make fun of anyone by saying that at all, because some people need that. I personally don't. It almost bothers me when I read it if it's too much of what I call "fluff." But the core message is what is important to me. And when I receive a prophecy, that's often how it comes out, because that's what I'm used to. That's how I exercise my gift, because that's what appeals to me the most.

VIVIAN: You know, you'll probably find that most people will tell you they don't think they're a very good channel, and they don't think they get very good answers. I think that about myself. I read everyone else's prophecies, and I think, "Wow, they have such a good channel. They get such good things from the Lord." But I would say that most people feel just the opposite about themselves. I think that's the spiritual principle that keeps people being prepared to hear from the Lord, their utter dependence on the Lord. It's that desperation that keeps people connected to the Lord. Like Alecia is always thinking she has a lousy channel. Ha! And I think she has one of the most beautiful channels, because she has faith for things that a lot of people would not have faith to ask. She just sits down, and it doesn't matter how big the issue is, or what it's about. You pray about it because you're desperate, and you don't feel capable, and that's the very quality that gives you the anointing for your gift.

How Family members actually receive and record prophetic messages is a question of considerable curiosity for outsiders. We asked the staff if there is a standard way of doing this for most members. Is it typical to hear distinct voices or see visions? Does the channel usually slip into a trance state or at least feel the presence of a supernatural force? Or is the process more mundane and similar to writing or speaking in general, including such elements as establishment of a mental focus, production of a written or oral statement to capture an emergent idea, and reviewing and editing of the statement to achieve greater clarity?

JESSE: I'm a writer, too. When I'm just writing something, I'll write and look over it, to make corrections as I go along. But when I'm getting a prophecy it's a different thing. I'm almost afraid that my writing abilities are going to sneak in there and be a little bit of myself. So I generally will just sit there, close my eyes if possible, if I'm typing, and receive what comes. That's it.

ALECIA: What I do is just close my eyes and receive the whole thing, and then I go back over it, and of course there are typos galore; I fix those up and do the paragraphing. But I don't stop to think when receiving the prophecy, because if I were to do that it would distract me. I don't know how it works for everyone, but that's how it works for me.

THOMAS: For me, when it comes to typing, I'd be distracted. So the best messages that I receive, I record on a Dictaphone, and someone else will type them for me. I'll go right through just saying it as it comes, and then someone else will type it. But I would say not many people do it that way.[12]

JESSE: Let's say it's a prophecy for myself, and I go back, read it, and something doesn't make sense. I don't get it, and it doesn't flow. Rather than going in and editing it to what I think it should say, I usually ask the Lord for another prophecy to clarify it.

ALECIA: I do that too. Because sometimes there'll be a sentence, and I'll think, "What does that mean?" And I'll ask the Lord to clarify it. But you're still in the prophecy mode, and you're asking the Lord. I don't think anyone goes in and changes anything unless the Lord tells them to.

I don't personally ever have any feelings while writing prophecies. I'm not one for seeing visions or having big spiritual feelings. So usually it doesn't feel like anything. But with some prophecies I feel a little bit more like I'm "out of this world," or not really "here." I don't know if that makes sense. I don't even comprehend what I'm getting. And then I reread it over, and it's like, "Wow!" Other times it feels like I'm understanding it as it's coming out, but not with big spiritual tingles. Other people tell me that they see things and have these really awesome visions.

THOMAS: Sometimes messages are a real struggle for me, but other times it's to the point where you feel like "that's not really me" for it to flow so well.

I was never very intellectual, because I was just into sports as a youth, and it was very difficult for me to express myself or articulate. And when I was living with Dad, he even asked me one time, he said, "Son, where did you learn your English, from your baseball coach?"[13] So I definitely know when a prophecy is inspired. But at other times I feel "it's just not coming."

ALECIA: I agree with that. That happens to me, feeling sometimes that it's much more of a struggle in the spirit to get the message. Sometimes that happens when it's a very important prophecy. Or maybe you don't even think it's so important, but it actually is; or just because the Enemy likes to attack us from time to time and make it difficult.

From previous conversations we knew that some concern used to exist in the Family about the possibility of unknowingly receiving deceptive messages from evil rather than good spirits. But, according to Vivian, this concern has decreased with more frequent practice and with more recent emphasis on use of spiritual keys.

VIVIAN: I think because we have become, in recent times, a little bit more aware of the spirit world and the hinderers and spirit helpers there, we're a little more aware of praying for spiritual protection. So I think there's a lot less possibility, I would say, of anything evil coming through like that, simply because we're aware, and we put up our spiritual force fields, and we get on our armor before we go into what we know is going to be a spiritual battle. We read a lot of people's personal prophecies. And it's very, very rare that I can remember anything like that happening. Some people are a little more spiritually sensitive, and they can go into the spirit world and see things and hear things. I think with those people, their frequency is so fine-tuned, that they can get other frequencies that most of us aren't tuned into. But I'd say, for the most part, as people exercise their gift, they know what to pray for before they start and to get up their spiritual force fields. There are certain keys you can claim. We do claim certain keys for spiritual protection, certain promises from the Lord to give us that protection

THOMAS: I can't think of any prophecies we've received that were negatively influenced, but sometimes it might have been flavored by people's personal feelings, or emotions, or what they were going through at the time.

We already learned from Rachael that Maria's secretaries both process prophecies solicited from others for GN and other uses, as well as generate a large number of prophecies themselves. Alecia provides us with additional details about these activities.

ALECIA: When they are received, prophecies are filed under different topic categories. The person who's filing prophecies looks them over for the topics in the prophecy so she can slot it in the filing system under certain categories. So then when Mama says, "Can you find all the prophecies on the topic of healing," for example, the secretary will be able to find them.

Often, Mama will say, "Oh, I remember this prophecy so many years ago, and it was talking about such and such." She doesn't have a super great memory, but she'll remember these specific things, and then she'll give you one word or one topic, and the secretary will have to try to find that prophecy. So that does take a bit of time, especially since in the beginning, when we were first categorizing them, we didn't realize that we'd have so many over the years.

We learned that, to keep up with the growing demand for more prophecy to guide both WS and the Family at large, Maria initiated the practice of specific prophecy assignments to WS staff at bimonthly prayer meetings.

THOMAS: Several years ago Mama instituted prayer mornings for the whole Family around the world. It's one day a month. But the way we've done it here at WS is two half days per month, so people can do their work in the afternoons. We'll get together and have a united meeting at 9:00 A.M. with an hour of praying on prayer requests having to do with our whole Family.[14] Then we'll disperse, and people will either do personal prayer vigil, or they will receive answers in prophecy to assigned questions.

JESSE: Sometimes we are asked to stretch. For something that I have a lot of personal feelings about or opinions about, I'll sometimes write back and say, "I don't feel I have the faith for this, I'd rather not." Other times, I'll just do it. I'll pray and ask the Lord to help me receive the prophecy anyway. In a sense, I don't really personally care about the Lord's reputation. If I receive a prophecy, whether it's used or not doesn't really matter to me, because I just pass it on through the process. Mama listens to it. She's the Winetaster, and I feel that she can tell if it can be used, or what it needs to be used for in particular.

According to our WS sources, a distinction is made between "work" prophecies, which are assigned to WS for a particular purpose as discussed above, and "personal" prophecies, which any member may receive on any topic. These latter prophecies may wind up being incorporated into GNs, disseminated only within WS, or simply filed away.

VIVIAN: If anything is going on in anyone's life, they'll just send it "of interest" to Mama. She knows it's their personal life and not something for work. But oftentimes they can encourage other people who are going through the same problems. The Lord speaks to us, and it can be encouragement for someone else as well, or an instruction or lesson. So she not only gets the work prophecies, all of that volume, but the volume of all the adults here that regularly ask the Lord about things. These unsolicited prophecies can go in two directions, either to the whole Family, or we often put together compilations of people's prophecies for WS use only. When things happen that are affecting everyone—for example, a recent rash of driving accidents here at WS—we encourage everyone to pray about it, their driving or whatever it might be. Then we'll take prophecy excerpts, put them together in a compilation, and read it together at devotions in the morning before going to work. Then everyone can benefit from what the Lord tells us to do.

ALECIA: If you send a personal prophecy to Mama, it will be filed. Except she has one confidential directory [on the WS server] that you can send to, and that will not get filed. So if it's very personal, and you don't want it to go into the archives, then you just send the text file or the MP3 to Mama. Unsolicited prophecies from outside WS are cataloged and filed too. People from the field often send in their prophecies.

VIVIAN: You think, "Mama can't possibly read—or hear—all these files," but she can! It is phenomenal. She has this "reader" that she speeds up. It's a Text Aloud program that transforms text into MP3 files; she listens to them at the speed of 380 words per minute. And she remembers who got what prophecy, because she comments to people. It's amazing.

ALECIA: As far as the prophecies go, she listens to them all, as far as I know. Sometimes some might slip past, and she might accidentally miss a few.

VIVIAN: It's pretty supernatural, I think.

JESSE: And she really understands what's going on. Because she responds, and she'll comment on things I don't even remember receiving when I got the prophecy.

ALECIA: And she just loves the Lord's words, so she does it when she works, she does it when she wants to relax; that's what she likes to do.

JESSE: So that's what we do. I'll get a prophecy. I will put that prophecy into the Text Aloud program, where it is converted to the MP3 file. Then I take the MP3 file and copy it to Mama's directory on our central server and then send a copy of the text file to the secretary who files things.

Peter had told us earlier that his current contributions to GN prophecies are less than they used to be, now that there are enough other practiced channels available.

ALECIA: I know that Peter and Mama receive at least one prophecy every single day. They take their prayer time every morning to hear from the Lord, and sometimes those prophecies are used in publications.

VIVIAN: I don't know the actual process of how their prophecies are cataloged and filed.

THOMAS: They might be filed separately if they have to do with more confidential issues. Peter and Mama might pray about things that we're not aware of.

JESSE: As far as I know, it isn't like Peter is relied on to receive special prophecies for special big events; it's sort of like he is one of the channels, right?

ALECIA: Yes, Mama and Peter have just as much faith in everybody else's connection with the Lord. It's not like they think that what Peter gets is more the Lord's words then what somebody else gets.

THOMAS: At the time when Dad passed away, at the end of 1994, then the emphasis of prophecy became more pronounced, and Peter did do a lot of prophesying. Then Mama encouraged the staff, so over a period of time various people with gifts starting popping up. At that time, it was mainly Peter and Mama, but since then the burden has shifted.

What has been described so far (with much more to come) is an amazingly complex system. Our perception, reinforced at various times, is that nobody—even at WS—really quite understands how it all works.

VIVIAN: It's true. The Lord just does it somehow. He's in control. It's based on a very simple principle and that's "ask Me everything." Whatever you do, ask the Lord about it. And then, if you don't understand, ask Him again. If someone else thinks differently, ask Him again, ask Him together.

CHAPTER 5

Illustrating and Laying Out Prophecy for the *Good News*

This chapter continues the selected interview responses of GN Department staff begun in chapter 4. Our own comments and information summaries are set off from WS staff responses in italic paragraphs.

INTERVIEW WITH ART AND TEXT DEPARTMENT HEAD ROBERTA

As head of the Art and Text Department, Roberta oversees the production of all materials (with the exception of Family *GN*s, which are under Maria's exclusive direction) that are designed specifically for members of the Family. For the most part, these latter publications seldom circulate outside of Family Homes. Besides her supervisory responsibilities, Roberta also does "locals" for submitted works and edits various children's publications (including some for Aurora Productions—see chapter 6).

Roberta is a 25-year-old, second-generation member who joined World Services in 1999. Although she had a talent for writing, Roberta was brought into WS as an editor with no previous editing experience. Among other things, Roberta works with WS staff artists and writers (some of whom are identified and discussed in the context of our interview) to assign text and illustration projects for particular publications. She also chairs the Art Review Board (ARB) and sits on the Publications Final Approval Committee, which must approve all in-house publications (excepting Maria's *GN*s) before they go to press. The ARB looks over artists' initial sketches and evaluates them by employing prayer and prophecy. Commissioned illustrations for Family publications vary in the amount of detail specified by Roberta and her staff. Artists are given a certain amount of creative leeway in their work, but ARB members must be mindful of different cultural and national norms. For example, is the artwork under consideration too "sexy" for prevailing cultural norms in some parts of the world where Family publications will be distributed? And, over the years, there also has developed an increasing sensitivity for what is appropriate for readers at different age levels. Compared to the much more freewheeling days of the Children of God (whose literature illustrations were sometimes fairly graphic), these latter kinds of concerns have led, over time, to more conservative controls being imposed on the production of Family art.[1] Similarly, the Publications Final Approval Committee is concerned not only with editing grammar, spelling, and punctuation errors in Family texts, but also with text content. This reflects similar concerns about normative cultural differences and variations in age level appropriateness for different Family publications.

Thus, we see once again the way in which Family International leadership has matured by making accommodating reforms in their missionary methods while simultaneously attempting to stay true to their core beliefs and end-time commitment. An additional theme that reemerges in this interview concerns the growing emphasis in World Services on effective staff training and personnel management.

As was true for a number of people we interviewed at WS, Roberta was not sought after as an already established expert in her current position, but rather came by faith and what she believes was God's direction.

ROBERTA: I wasn't actually hoping to come to WS. I was in South Africa at the time, and a want ad came out in the *Grapevine* [the Family newsletter] asking for WS personnel. One of my friends said, "Oh, I found the perfect Home for you!" And I laughed and said, "Right, I'm in Africa. Africa is cool. I'm going to stay here." But I prayed about it, and she prayed about it, and the Lord said to apply. So I applied. I had mostly done missionary outreach and child care, so I wasn't really sure what I was going to do if I came to WS. But when I applied they took me in to be an editor, all by faith. Ha! I hadn't done any previous editing, but I enjoyed writing—creative writing, embellishing my letters to my family—African tales. Ha! I had sent in testimonies to World Services from what we did in our area or a youth camp that we held.[2] But when they called me for an editor position, I was like, "I think you've got the wrong person." And as for art, although my family is fairly artistic, I don't have any artistic talents. I just coordinate the work here at WS and oversee it.

Thus, as we learn above and in other interviews, people at WS are not infrequently placed into positions that require certain kinds of technical skills or experience that they may not currently have. These may particularly be supervisory positions that require managing others who, in some cases, do have experience and skills that the supervisor lacks. The system depends fundamentally on the reciprocal faith and high motivation of all parties.

ROBERTA: In some cases we have responsibility that we don't necessarily feel capable of. We want to make sure that it's correct, that things are done right, because in the end we're the ones who are going to have to answer if anything goes wrong, or if it doesn't quite hit the mark. You almost want to do it yourself, because then you know that, "I'm going to keep all of these things in mind." Whereas if you let someone else do it, perhaps someone who has only been in WS for six months, and you are working with them, it takes a lot more to say, "Part of your training is you're going to take this, and you're going to run with it, and I'll be praying for you, and if you have any questions you can ask." It takes a lot to take that step, because you know you are ultimately responsible, even though they are doing the job. In my case, I've only been doing the job I presently have for a little over a year. So it's not that I have 15 or 20 years of experience, which would probably feel a lot better to me. You have to take it by faith and trust the Lord that, if you hand the job over to someone else, they are going to be able to do it.

But in some things, like art for example, you don't really have to know how to draw yourself in order to be able to coordinate and plan the work. So before I became the department head of art, I worked with certain artists, and I already organized their work and worked with them and knew their abilities—what they could do and what they couldn't. So it was basically just expanding that a little. Each artist has a skill. Some artists can draw realistically. Some artists are very cartoony. Some are humorous. Some are very serious. So you have to know all the different talents and attributes of the artists. Some can flip-flop and do a variety of things. Generally, each text person has the ability—if they are working on a specific story or they're working on an article that needs an illustration—to have an idea they can present to the artist. But, overall, it's up to the artist as well to pray about it and hear from the Lord as to how He wants them to illustrate the textual story line, and what the artistic message should be. Or if there should be a story line within the art itself, that's often left up to the artist.

We have a number of artists, some who work in WS and some who contribute from different mission fields or service centers.[3] For example, let's say, Alvin in South Africa: he contributes to *Xn,* and he communicates with us. We give him all his assignments. He sends them in, and we take them through our procedure. We communicate back to him. Savannah, one of the WS staff artists, does that. He currently has a cover illustration. It's the vision in Ezekiel with the "inside/outside eyes."

We had learned from another source that Alvin's initial concept for the cover assignment resulted in a letter from WS that basically said, "This isn't quite what we're looking for, can you change it?"

ROBERTA: Ha! I didn't actually write the letter; I only did that in an advisory capacity. Savannah and I worked on it together. Of course, we went through our usual procedure. Most of our artists do a simple sample sketch of what they plan to do, and then we put it through a review board here in WS, which consists of usually four to eight people who look over the art and give their comments. Then we take all of their comments, compile them, and ask the Lord about it. If after hearing from the Lord further questions come up, we bring those to the Lord again, and then we sit down and write the person and pinpoint: "This needs to be fixed in the picture," or "would you mind doing this?" We have certain parameters for what we can do. Because our publications go to so many different countries, there are certain things we have to keep in mind. For example, you can't have skimpy articles of clothing, because some of the Family lives in conservative countries. So part of our job is to keep an eye out for those things. If an artist drew something a little too skimpy, we'll say, "Please make the shorts longer." Ha! If you compare our artwork to secular comics, you'll notice a big difference in conservatism.

In other conversations with artists, we were told that there's perhaps a little greater potential for tension in working with artists in the Family, because in many cases they have themselves prayed and gotten what they regard as guidance for the vision or the concept that they use in producing their art. They send forward what they've received. Then they get a note back, saying, "We don't like this," or "change that." These instructions might totally alter the vision the artists feel is generated through their own prayer and prophecy. This tension is resolved in various ways.

ROBERTA: Here in WS the artists very much understand this. It's sort of a, "in the multitude of counselors there is safety," concept. All the artists here are very fluid with that, and they've been doing it, some of them, for 15-odd years. But in the field, generally, when someone writes in and says, "I would like to contribute to a publication via art," we generally have a form letter where we explain many of these things. For example, we encourage them to hear from the Lord on any specifics He would like to give them regarding the illustrations. But then we also explain that, once it comes to us, we will counsel about it, and that we also hear from the Lord in case there are any things that may have been overlooked or not taken into account. On a very practical level, for example, if there is someone who lives in Brazil and they're accustomed to drawing girls topless, that is something that we can't allow to fly in our publications anymore, because it may not go over so well with a Home in the Middle East when someone picks up a publication like that. So we have a more overall view of it, and we'll explain to them, "We love the picture, but just put a top on the girl." (Laughter.) A bikini works. Ha! So that's an example, because sometimes we have a more in-depth background on why certain things pass, or why certain things don't. And our artists in the field are very gracious about it.

Sometimes they do have a battle. Alvin had a battle, because it was a much bigger project, and it was a form of art he wasn't accustomed to doing, as well. So it was branching out and stepping a little beyond the normal. It was an assignment, but not an in-depth assignment. It was taken from a Bible verse; our assignment to him was, "We would like your help on four covers. Would you want to pray and hear from the Lord about what the cover should be? Here are the general things to keep in mind for the cover. For example, covers for an *Xn* magazine go through several more steps than just inside art, because they're the face of the magazine. Also, all covers are in color, so that's one more additional step." We didn't actually give him the verse from Ezekiel for the assignment; that was something he prayed about and heard from the Lord. We were actually thinking he would draw his cool little egg men characters. But he had a vision of how he could portray what is described in that verse. He didn't like the way it had been illustrated before, so he wanted to do something that would speak to him personally, and that he would like. The end product was great, but it was a trying process. It's not always like that.

Overall, though, in our assignments to people in the field, we rarely spell out something like, "Please draw a girl handing this to a boy." That's uncommon because we like to give the artists leeway in interpreting whatever they're illustrating and getting the insight from the Lord. That's their job—they are the artists. In many cases, we are just the text person, or we are merely coordinating the work. On occasion, we do have very specific assignments. For example, "We want to do four covers, and when praying about it, the Lord gave these different concepts for you as an artist that would complement your skills, but . . ." There's always a "but" clause that says, "but please feel free to ask the Lord if you don't have a burden or personal inspiration for this, or if you get another idea." We're not set on, "You must draw X."

As indicated earlier, there is more oversight over Family art today; it appears that Family art has become more conservative, less "sexy" in response to concerns about varia-

tions in cultural norms or greater sensitivity about the reaction that might come from outsiders. In the old days, the Family didn't have such a wide range of different publications targeting different age groups. The question, "what's most appropriate" wasn't considered earlier, according to some of our informants. Before 1990, everybody got the same publications. Family Homes would get MO Letters *or* GNs, *and their children would see what everyone else saw. But that's changed, as Roberta tells us below.*

ROBERTA: *Xn* targets a 12-year-old range. Our children's publications target from 0 to 11. So you don't really need sexy stuff in that material, because you are actually trying to convey to them God's Word in an elementary way. If we were targeting a 16-on-up audience, we probably would make more allowances. There are other reasons for the changes. I remember from a very young age the latest *GN* or *MO Letter* would come out, and we would all sit down in the evening, and we'd read it and take notes, and that was just the way we did it. But, nowadays children don't have the same attention span. It's much harder to keep their attention. Therefore everything has to be highly illustrated, with condensed text, so that they can actually absorb it. Reading a *GN* with a child that's 24–25 pages is too much for them to absorb nowadays, so we take portions of it and condense it and put it into a 16-page illustrated publication where the child can visualize it. Children absorb things much better if they see it, rather than just hearing it. So that's what we target. I think perhaps it's a matter of us understanding the needs of children more nowadays than we did 20 years ago, when we were just developing our child-rearing structure.

By the way, we don't stigmatize the production of anyone's initiative. Maggie, for example—she's one of the child-care workers here at WS—is producing her own illustrated key promises for the children she teaches. That's great! Agnes, in Mexico, did the same thing. We put out the key promises for children, and she made beautiful color posters for them, which we then uploaded to our members-only Web site; Family members anywhere around the world can get them.[4] [For more about Family-only Web sites, see chapter 7.] Also with the development of the Area Boards, they all produce stuff as well, which is not necessarily from WS.[5] In fact, it usually isn't, unless we take it on and officially make it a WS production. But a local child-parenting board can create something for the Homes in their area; they coordinate that through their board, and it doesn't come through WS publications.

Because I coordinate publications as well, different International Board chairpersons [all of whom are situated at World Services] will also send things. You know, "Here's an initiative that's taking off in India. What do you think?" For example, here's a recent one from the JETT/Teen Board in India. [JETTs is the age designation used for 12- to 13-year-olds in Family Homes; "teens" are between the ages of 14 and 15.] Several years back they produced a little witnessing booklet that had all the basic verses about salvation and the Holy Spirit that young people could use in their outreach. There were also little explanations about how to present *Activated!* magazine to teen contacts, or how to explain your upbringing or your education. They produced that and gave it to all the teens in their area. I think it also went to other JETT/Teen Boards around the world. Then they sent it in to WS. We took it, as the team, and we filled it out a little more. For example, when they put it together, they only had the references. We included all the verses. We added some *MO Letter* excerpts of quotes [from David Berg] on witnessing. We included a bigger explanation about presenting the Family International to someone who doesn't know anything about us. We then produced that as a little booklet that teens around the world could use. And it was courtesy of the India JETT/Teen Board in conjunction with WS. That's an example of where we took something somebody else worked on and produced it.

Roberta does need to be personally adept at proofreading text because, as she explains below, the Publications Final Approval Committee, which she sits on, constitutes the last review before any in-house Family publication (excepting the GNs) goes to print, and people are needed at this point who can make sure that everything is correct.

ROBERTA: I guess when you do something for five and a half years, when text is just a part of your work, you know what to look for, what's important and what's not. You have a mental checklist that you work through, such as serial commas. Ha! Often people miss the comma before the "and," or they wrongly divide words. It depends. There is one stage where I see it, and it's already all laid out, and you see the text as it will be printed. But then there is also the text file that you see, and I go over that as well. So I see it all at several stages. If you miss something at one stage, you hope you can catch it in the next. I look for misspellings. I look for wrongly capitalized words, things like that. That's the technical side. As far as content goes, I don't know, I just pray really hard. Spotting content glitches is part of my job.

What would be an example of a content glitch? The text has gone through so many layers of review already—people praying, and obtaining follow-up prophecies, and making changes as a result—that at this stage one wouldn't expect to see many major glitches.

If, for example, we're working on a publication for children, and we've had to ask the Lord for a simplified version so that children can understand it, of a prophecy that was in a *GN*, or of a spirit helper explained in a *GN*.[6] Generally, what we'll do in the creation of something like that, is study everything that the Lord has already said about it and then ask Him for a child-friendly version, so that it's on a level that children can understand and that makes sense to them. But every once in awhile you might receive a prophecy that wasn't necessarily clear in the original *GN*, or needs further clarification, or one word was used in exchange for another, and it alters the meaning. So you might notice something like that and then go back to the original prophecies received in the *GN*, or in whatever publication that original spirit helper or message was given, and ask: "Does this actually work together?" That's a content example that would be spotted later on.

But the *GNs* themselves, in terms of final approval? No. That's Mama. Ha! We look at all other publications aside from the *GNs*. And the Aurora publications, we're not involved in them either, unless we are contributing a story or some sort of content for an Aurora publication. [See chapter 6 for a detailed discussion of Aurora Productions.]

INTERVIEW WITH WS STAFF ARTISTS SAVANNAH, SYLVIA, AND CORRINE

The in-house World Services Art Department consists of all women, but both men and women artists contribute regularly from "the field" (communal Homes outside of World Services). Savannah, who works closely with Art and Text Department Head Roberta, is art coordinator and assistant department head. She is a 27-year-old second-generation member with eight years' experience at World Services. Sylvia, also an SGA, is 24 years old and has worked at WS for two years. In contrast, Corrine is a first-generation convert, age 47, who has 21 years' experience at WS. Sylvia specializes in "comic" art (not cartoons) but helps out everywhere, including doing illustrations for General Public publications. Corrine specializes in pencil-and-ink drawings and is the primary illustrator for Family *GNs*. Both Savannah and Sylvia do computer as well as brush art.

As brought out in Roberta's interview in this chapter, art and illustration requests are submitted by text editors. Savannah prays about assignments and consults with Roberta and various text editors before assigning projects to different field artists. As with musicians and writers who contribute to a wide variety of General Public products, Family field artists are given monetary "gifts" for their work (which typically go to the artists' residential Homes for disbursement); they are not paid standard commissions or royalties for their artwork. Sylvia is responsible for sending artwork to be reviewed by WS art "locals," who are not always themselves artists. Family artists are expected to respect locals' "anointing" for spiritual assessments of their art. Feedback from locals helps relieve WS staff artists' editorial burden. Along with Roberta, Savannah communicates with Family field artists regarding editorial changes in their work, some of whom are more sensitive to criticism than others. With regard to Corrine's *GN* illustrations, however, final approval comes from Maria.

Some of the dialogue in this interview overlaps what we learned earlier from Roberta about Family art and text production. However, we retain the overlap because it expresses the extent to which shared faith and belief in constant guiding communion with the spirit world governs all WS operations. Family artists see their artwork as a form of revelation, and WS art production is modeled on the same interactive process that is followed to obtain prophecies for the publication of texts. In conformity with the Family member's ultrasupernatural beliefs concerning intimate intercourse with the spirit world, WS artists have discerned that their department has a specific "spirit helper," who has been identified as Minerva. In addition to Minerva, each artist also has cultivated a connection with her own personal spirit helper. One conclusion to which we are led is that the cooperative process of "teamwork prophecy" among members of the Art and Text Department has (as in all other WS operations) become integrated with effective negotiating skills and management practices.

Toward the end of this interview we found it helpful to differentiate our dialogue as being either Gary's or Gordon's.

Although many WS staff members have not had previous training in the areas they are assigned, a large part of the confidence they demonstrate in carrying out their jobs— even those based on possession of actual talents, such as artistic or writing skills— comes from their belief in the power of "anointing"—God's endowment of individuals with the abilities necessary to carry out specific duties they have been called to perform in God's service.

CORRINE: I was a field artist many, many years ago when they first put out a call for artists for the *TK Komix* [a Family comic book for children]. I was a mommy with a little baby at the time in India, and I'd drawn before I joined the Family. I thought, "Ok, I'll give it a try." I drew some comics and sent them in, and I became a field artist for a long while. Then I got called to come into WS to help with the Life with Grandpa series [illustrated magazine stories with moral lessons for children]. I was doing backgrounds. It was like a production line: someone would do the people, some would do the backgrounds, someone the lettering. So I stayed on after that. Then I didn't do art for many years in WS. But just five years ago I started doing art again. It's an anointing [empowerment by God], that's for sure! It's not me. I think they want a realistic style. I'm sure Maria and Peter prayed about my work, if it would lend itself to the *GN* style. I was asked to try it out and see how I did.

SAVANNAH: The Lord may give you a gift in one thing, and you're really challenged in another. I'm very challenged when it comes to talking and writing.

But even talented, or anointed artists, are subjected to the same prophetic judgments and revisionist inputs from staff "locals" as are all others who contribute to the WS publication enterprise. This was the case with Alvin, the artist who illustrated a recent Xn *cover that we discussed above with Roberta. Savannah works closely with Roberta and does the actual communication with artists like Alvin. Here we receive more details on how the interactive process between field artist and WS works.*

SAVANNAH: I'm not the one who makes the call on whether changes need to be made in the initial submitted artwork. It goes around to various locals. We are artists on staff, but then there is the text person who does the *Xn*, there is the layout person, and there are a few other people who usually notice things. So we could be getting critiques from others who are not themselves artists, but they have a concept of what the cover should be, overall. It may be different than the vision of the artist who produced the work, and that's where some of the difficulty comes in. It falls to me to communicate that to the artist. Artists, whether they are visual artists or musical artists or literary artists, are very sensitive about their creations. An artist feels inspired, has a vision, communicates that vision on paper, then sends it in, and then, when it comes back, it may not be what he or she had in mind. That is sometimes especially difficult with artists.

You must find a way to communicate your concern, but do it in a way that's acceptable at the artist's end. You have to really pray and ask the Lord about it. And you learn. People are different, and certain wordings for some people are a little harder to swallow than for others. Some people I write to are like, "Really, you don't need to give me all the pillow padding. I'm fine. Just tell me what you want me to change and I'll change it." Or "it's kind of irritating for me when you're super, super calm and soothing me with feathers." And then other people you have to really be careful with. So you sort of learn through trial and error, and you have to really pray.

We were told that sometimes, in response to a critique that has come from WS back to the artist, the artist may say something like, "Let me give you a fuller version of my vision, and why I think you're wrong and I'm right." This is sometimes persuasive; Savannah and Roberta may respond to the merits of the artist's argument, but, according to Savannah, they will first subject the question to further prayer and prophecy based on the new information they received.

SAVANNAH: We sent Alvin a picture to do, for example, and we thought the humor of it was very cute, but then on the flip side, it just didn't seem right, you know? So we sent it back to him and said, "Well, is there a way that you could change this particular picture?" It was super cute. This was a little comic strip with two brothers together, and one guy was kicking the Devil in the butt. On the flip side of the picture the other guy was helping the little guy who had kicked the Devil, so then he's standing in front of him squishing him behind a wall, kicking the Devil. You see the little guy's arms and legs in the back. So we said, "Is there any way you can just move him to the side a little bit?" And Alvin responded, "I thought about it, and it just didn't seem right." So he put a little caption from the guy who is being squished saying, "I'm feeling safe, bro." We just looked at it, and we prayed about it, and we decided it was fine. It fixed the issue we had.

We were told that there are a lot of aspiring artists in the Family and that many apply to come to WS, although working as a field artist is a more realistic prospect for most. Savannah explains below what constitutes a full-time field artist (who is in a regular Home and has other ministries in that Home), and how they are compensated for their work.

SAVANNAH: I had a folder that had about 25 different artists who were applying as field artists. Then what we did to hit all the birds with one stone was send a published memo to everybody in the *Grapevine* that had a list of what kind of art we can publish, what we're looking for, and gave a few pictures for them to draw. They're supposed to email me and say, "Well, I'd like to do this, and here are my pictures," as per what we asked them to draw and what personal information we want to receive from them. We have three artists right now who are starting to be full-time field artists who applied to the *Grapevine* ad that we put out. Some just aren't quite able to come here to WS. I'd love to have Alvin here, by the way; that would be so cool.

In some cases, we've had to say, "We really like your art and please keep practicing on these particular things and get back to us." In other cases, we weren't soliciting art for younger kids, whereas their talent is very much in kiddie artwork. So we said, "Well, we need more adult artwork or comic work, so we'd be interested in seeing that, because that is what we are looking for and needing at the moment." They can post all their stuff on the Web site. Sometimes we flag people and say, "Oh, that's a good one. Keep an eye on her!"

As for working field artists, some do a certain page amount per month, and some get an allotment, like Phil, for instance. He does 10 pages for us a month, so at the end of every month I send him 10 more pages. By comparison, Alvin does batches of 10 pages, whenever he can finish them. So people who are on a regular schedule either do a certain amount per month or they are given batches of a certain amount of pages.

Because they are giving up a certain amount of their time in their Homes to do this work, field artists get a gift or compensation for the artwork that they do. We send a check to their Home, and it's the Home's decision as to how much the artist is allowed to keep. I know that in some Homes, if it's something artists are doing in their personal time, in their free time, then they're allowed to keep it. I'm not sure what each Home does and how they do it, but if it's a substantial amount, the first time I write an artist it's like, "We'd like to start sending you a gift if we can count on you. We know that we're taking your time, so we'd like to send you a gift for the artwork that you do." We ask them to show a copy of our letter to their Home Teamwork [elected Home officers] to make sure that we're not pulling on someone the Home really needs, and we are trying to compensate for any time that we do take. And then, yes, in varying degrees, they do get a gift. Every so often we send them an appreciation gift saying, "We love you and thank you so much for helping us." Artists need lots of encouragement.

We had learned from a number of sources that, unlike all of the many other publications, every aspect of a GN, including its artwork, must receive final approval from Maria. Maria is herself a frequent subject represented in GN art—something that has contributed significantly to her iconic status in the Family.

CORRINE: There is a final approval. For instance, I have my own set of *GN* locals. But then, after they've gone over it, and they're happy with it, it goes to Mama and Peter. So Mama not only passes the text, but also the art. And if at that point she says, "I don't like this illustration." Weeeep! Usually there's hardly anything she doesn't like, or there might be a little thing.

SHEPHERD: Up until a few years ago, very few Family members had ever actually seen Maria, so their conception of her was based primarily on illustrations in *GN*s. Visually, she was like a cartoon.

SYLVIA: Yeah, black hair and a bun.

CORRINE: Somewhat consistent so people can recognize her. You get it down after awhile.

SHEPHERD: When are you going to start drawing Mama with gray hair? (Laughter.)

CORRINE: I think we could do that now. (More laughter.)

Many religious groups produce religious art to create a general spiritual atmosphere. The pope commissioned Michelangelo to do the Sistine Chapel, the Latter-day Saints Church commissions artists to do large murals in their temples or other church build-

*ings, and so on. We asked whether the Family produces any religious art that is not
simply illustration.*

SYLVIA: Not really. There are a lot of pictures of Jesus that people have done
   in the field throughout the years. At least in the Homes I've been in, people
   print out a picture they like of Jesus and usually have it on their wall. I don't
   know if you saw in Africa, but they sometimes have African Jesuses and stuff
   like that, adapted to their cultures. I was in Africa, and some of them have
   some pretty big ones. People just pick a Jesus they like from our Jesus site
   on the Web and print it out big and put it on the wall. All our pictures that
   we do in the Family publications, all the spirit helpers, all of Corrine's stuff,
   are there without any titles or anything, so anyone can print it out and put
   it up. Lots of people color them.

CORRINE: People have their own preferences of what kind of Jesus they like.

SYLVIA: It's called Scrawlathon [Family Web site that displays unsolicitied
   member artwork], and everybody in the Family who has drawn a Jesus usually has sent them in, so you've got tons of varieties of Jesus, lots of different
   nationalities, too.

SAVANNAH: There is some artwork that is dear to a particular person's heart.
   I really like Lawson's old work, like the "Rich Man, Poor Man" picture with
   the rich guy reaching into the poor guy's pocket. There is this little poor man
   standing there holding a little can, and the rich man is reaching into the poor
   man's pocket and saying, "I can't find any money to give you." Ha! But, no,
   we don't have any "history" art. We haven't put a focus on it, let's put it that
   way. We've mostly been concentrating on going forward with the work.

*As we learn next, family artists think of their work as a spiritual process, one in fact,
like every other activity engaged in at WS, that is guided through teamwork prophecy and channeled supernatural assistance. In this case, assistance includes the aid
of artistically specialized spirit helpers, who supplement the artists' personal gifts
and anointing as artists with specific directions for their art. All of the artists claim
Minerva, for instance, as the primary source of their inspiration, but have additional
personal helpers as well.*

CORRINE: From start to finish it's a very spiritual ministry. I think artists are
   spiritual receptors; they receive from outside themselves. It's an inspirational
   thing; any art. Minerva's our helper generally—for the artists and the layout
   people, the creative department. But then we all have our personal helpers.
   Minerva broadens our channels, our faith, and helps us to stretch. You can
   definitely feel a difference. We can only go so far in ourselves; we need the
   extra spiritual help.

SAVANNAH: Sometimes my test is just to keep going even when I don't feel it, and I feel stuck, like I'm banging against a brick wall. But the Lord wants me to keep trying and keep having faith to keep going with it, and then it comes, and the picture starts to pick up. That happens to me a lot.

SYLVIA: I usually get it in the beginning, when I don't think I can actually do it or that it might not turn out. But then it's just amazing how it comes out every time, and it's like, "I don't know how I did that." Our art is very much a form of channeling, especially when it's specific spiritual concepts that you illustrate in a spiritual sort of way. You have to have the right spirit in your subject, and you want that to be portrayed; it's not really something you're familiar with, and you know it's not you.

CORRINE: It's a very exciting ministry; it's a receiving sort of ministry. I just love it, to be able to illustrate the words like that; it's just fantastic.

SAVANNAH: Every new project is like a new present. You have to really pray, and depending on the picture that you're doing, you have to be careful. Like if you're doing a picture that is primarily evil. I was just doing one where it was a witchcraft star, the pentagram, with an evil-looking snake going through it, so the picture itself is very evil. And I had to really pray that I wouldn't make myself feel dark to portray dark. Does that sound weird? I didn't want to start getting that way. Another time I drew this thing, and it was a whole story about a girl who was very into witchcraft. Of course it had a good ending, though sobering. But I wasn't able to channel it right, and I started getting a little weird, where I was just getting too into it; I wasn't being prayerful enough. So the people who were checking the pictures at the time were like, "there's just something that doesn't seem right, could you re-pray about it and redraw some of them or fix them?" and things like that. Because I wasn't as used to drawing, and I didn't have the amount of knowledge or wisdom I needed. I hadn't been doing it long, and it took me awhile to realize the influence spirit can have on art. It's no laughing matter.

As Savannah implies above and Corrine and Sylvia confirm below, there is a spiritual reaction looked for or expected from locals who may not be artists. They can't really critique artistic technique, but it's the feeling they get from looking at the art that is important.

CORRINE: It's the spirit that locals feel.

SYLVIA: Or even understanding what you're trying to draw. Sometimes the concept of what you are drawing makes total sense in your head, but to them, they're like, "How does that relate? What's it trying to portray?" Because you have it in your head, and you totally know what you're doing, but they don't get it. You don't want something that nobody can understand; locals pick up on that.

CORRINE: Locals have an anointing of their own. That's something that I have had to come to grips with, because I was a very sensitive artist. But in order to keep progressing as an artist you have to get over sensitivity. You have to come to grips with it at a certain point if you are going to keep going and be prepared to improve and be able to take people's input on your art. I had to have some major breakthroughs in that regard. But the Lord has really helped me. I think that in a way the locals represent a segment of the Family out there in the field. I think that every person on my *GN* locals team sees things in a different way, and in a way they are probably proportionate to certain people in the Family who see art a certain way. Sometimes as an artist you are so close to the trees you have to stand back and see the forest, and that's what locals help you to do, because they are not so intensely involved like the artist is, intimately with the picture. So they are able to pick up anything a little off in the spirit or something that just doesn't quite hit in the right way, something that's not clear, something that can send a wrong signal through the picture.

According to the artists, generating publications that go out to the Family worldwide, and knowing the impact these publications have on members, engenders a genuine sense of responsibility in the production staff. Illustrations that accompany the text in some ways have an impact equal to the text, because people remember visually the image, and they associate the image with the text. As many people know from their own childhoods, it's the vivid illustrations that accompany stories that most stay with them. WS artists do think of this responsibility for conveying images to the Family around the world—to both adults, and especially to young people—that they will carry with them all their lives.

CORRINE: Yes. It scares me a lot. It really does. It sobers me. It gives me a fear of the Lord. It makes me want to do a really good job and get the spirit really right. That's why I'm thankful for locals, again. It's a team effort, it's not just me. I know it's not just me. It's working together to get it right, and it's a reassurance to have locals and other people going over my art.

SYLVIA: I think it helps me stretch as far as coming up with things that are interesting in art. Or something you know will appeal to the age range you're trying to reach. Because with art it's hard to actually do something that's a little more challenging for you, or to try to think of a concept that is out of the box that might help people see it in a new way. So I like trying to make it more interesting, trying to make it something that will hit the mark for them, that they will appreciate as art, or that will reach them, if they are young people; something that will appeal to them.

CORRINE: Dad [David Berg] loved pictures. That's the way to capture the message. You have so much more freedom through art, too. They say that people remember more what they see in a picture than what they read, so that is a real powerful way to convey a message.

SYLVIA: Also, the kids can color stuff. That's what kids need too. You can give them a book with words, and they won't be interested. But if you give them pictures, they're interested.

SAVANNAH: It's fun. It's cool.

Our interview with WS staff artists concluded with a lighthearted request.

SHEPHERD: Well, here's an assignment for you. Before we leave Monday morning, we're going to commission you to do a little piece of art for us.

SYLVIA: Of what?

SHEPHERD: We're going to leave that up to you. It's going to be an inspiration.

CORRINE: For you, personally?

GARY: Yes. We want you to collaborate on this. It's going to be an interactive project.

GORDON: He's just making this up.

GARY: Yes, but it would be nice as a remembrance of our time here with the artists and something that we could take with us. But don't spend a lot of time at it. Obviously you're busy, and there's not much time before we leave.

GORDON: Don't send it to the locals. (Laughter.)

SAVANNAH: Sylvia could do portraits.

SYLVIA: Do you guys have spirit helpers? I've drawn them for people at parties.

GARY: Here's an idea: Do a little comic strip, a sort of snowball thing where maybe Corrine would start off and do a frame, and then give it to you, Sylvia, and you have to do the next frame in sequence and come up with something, and then, Savannah, you do the final frame.

GORDON: The adventures of Gary and Gordon.

CORRINE: That would be a good comic strip. (Laughter.)

SAVANNAH: Okay. Would you guys mind us putting you into little outfits and stuff like superheroes?

GORDON: As long as we don't have to model in them. (Laughter.)

The artists collaborated on a color cartoon poster of both of us buffed up in physique and wearing Superman costumes, with Gary holding a digital recording device and Gordon holding a notebook and pencil. The caption reads, "Gary and Gordon Take on WS!"

INTERVIEW WITH LAYOUT DEPARTMENT HEAD BEKKA

Once the text and art for World Services literature have been obtained and edited, they must be formatted and laid out for publication. Head of the Layout Department is Bekka, age 32, who, as one of Peter's daughters, has grown up in World Services. It must be remembered that WS assumes the task of publishing numerous periodicals that, at any given moment in time, are at some point in the WS production pipeline. This pipeline is constantly monitored by the Layout Department, which has final responsibility for formatting all WS publications (excluding Aurora General Public publications for nonmembers) on deadline for distribution to Family Homes worldwide. *GN* issues have a priority status over all other Family publications in the pipeline.

Recent movement from print publishing to publishing that utilizes digital technology has greatly expedited the WS production process. Furthermore, WS programmers have developed a Web-based work management site that can be accessed by all WS editors and department heads, as well as by layout personnel. As digital publishing and computer programming skills have become increasingly vital to World Services operations, WS staff members have had to stay abreast of advancements in technology, much of which is self-taught or learned through trial and error. Their ability to do this is, as usual, attributed to their religious anointing and serves to reinforce their faith in supernatural empowerment as God's chosen end-time servants.

Because of their religious beliefs regarding the need for corporate prophecy in discerning God's will, the overall amount of collective input required for the production of Family literature probably surpasses anything done in secular publishing. Thus, for example, in addition to her layout responsibilities, Bekka sits on the Final Approval Committee for all Family member publications. Other committee members are Jessica (one of Maria's secretaries in the MPL ministry) and Roberta (department head of the Art and Text Department), as indicated in previous chapters. Once everything that goes into a publication has been laid out, the Final Approval Committee reviews all final drafts, along with the multiple, attached prayers and prophecies that writers, artists, and editors submit with every draft. Prior to forwarding formatted texts to the printer for publication, the committee prayerfully deliberates and sends a written record of committee members' own confirming prophecies regarding final copy to all WS department heads. Family language translators get their copies for translation once everything has been approved by the committee.

For this interview, we were again accompanied by WS shepherds Vivian and Thomas.

———————

BEKKA: I don't do much magic. Ha! I just make sure everybody else does it. I just oversee the layout aspect of publications. There are other aspects of publications that I'm not involved in. We have a really good team. There's a high turnover of work. A lot of people in WS have projects that take considerably longer, whereas our work cycles are done in two-week increments. We get it, we get it processed, we get it done, and then we start over again. Yesterday, we uploaded our mailing, and today we have to divide up the work for the next two weeks.

We used to send Family publications out via mail many years ago. We'd print it all out on our printer and cut up all the pages and check them all. At that time we had six printing centers, worldwide, that would print for different countries and areas. We'd print out the masters and check them all here, and then we would mail them off to the print centers, and they would print them and send them. Now we've centralized things, and with the advances of the internet, it has facilitated our being able to get things done faster and better. We send a mailing off twice a month, on the 15th and 30th of every month.

On average there are about eight to ten publications per mailing [to Family Homes worldwide]. So we have to communicate with the *GN* team and those who work on the text and content of the publications. We're always looking for ways to improve things and keep up with the times and do our work more efficiently and better. Recently, we have started developing a management workflow site, Web-based, that everyone can access and have input. We have different kinds of publications: the *FAR*s, the *GN*s, the *Grapevine, Grapevine* supplements, and the *Gen-Up*. They're in-house Family publications only—they don't go to the "activated" Family membership, with the exception of the *Link* magazine, which we're just starting [as discussed in chapter 6].

There are a host of details that need to be worked out with the *Link*. We're just going to be launching that magazine in mid-July or end of August—it's going to go to our full membership: Family Disciples, Missionary Members, Fellow Members, plus Active members. [See chapter 1 for a description of member categories.] And it's the first time we get to do one with the cover in color. It has always been black and white and gray. A lot of the publications are for children. The *Xn* is for teenagers. *Kidland* is for parents.

We created our own software. This is a real miracle, because it's one of those things we've needed to do for a long time, and we didn't have personnel to do it. So the Lord led us to just start working on it on our own. We got someone in to temporarily help our department, which frees up Sylvan to work on the software for this and create the site. Sylvan hasn't really had a lot of experience with programming, but the Lord is anointing him and miraculously this thing is coming together. Then we're developing the actual workflow, so that it takes the publication through all the various stages, more automated than we've previously been doing, which was just mailing things to people, including various reviews, checks, and proofreading.

The art department works mostly on the illustrations, and they have also been working with the text, especially in the children's publications that are highly illustrated. For the publications that are illustrated, we get the text and the art at the same time. Then we just lay it out. There is a lot of prophecy involved in the creation of the publications from the beginning. In the content phase, when the text is finalized and it's been approved, whoever is working on it will at the end ask the Lord, "Is this what You want to be in this publication? Is there anything else that should be in it? Is there any aspect that we're not covering?" So they will, in essence, get the final okay from the Lord on the text. Likewise with the artists. When they are compiling the last bit of the art, and praying about it, they'll do a final confirming prophecy over the art. Likewise, we do the same thing in the Layout Department. All of these confirming prophecies then go to the Final Approval committee, which reads over them. So people do use prophecy in their work to a huge degree, from the artists asking the Lord who they should be assigning the art to do for this particular part of the publication, to text people asking the Lord if the content is correct, and the layout people asking the Lord if He has any thoughts, or if they have captured the spirit and the portrayal of what they're doing.

By the time, then, that the Layout Department gets it, the text has already been proofed, and the art has already been fine-tuned; this is now the last step in the production process. Before going to print, however, Bekka explains that a final check-over must be done, and sometimes technical glitches are detected, either in the text or illustrations. The Final Approval Committee conducts a last P&P (prayer and prophecy) for the overall product.

BEKKA: When you are manipulating the text at the layout stage there is room for error, so we have a fairly lengthy process. The layout is checked, it gets a final proofread once it's laid out. We have a layout review board that okays it. The final approval is at the very end where a group of a few people look at it. Right now there are three people on the Final Approval Committee;

I'm one of them. The other two are Roberta, who is the department head of text and art, and Jessica, who is one of Mama's secretaries.

We're not approving the content of any publication, which has already been determined by those who work on it. We're approving the final layout. I do read over all of them, and sometimes I find mistakes. But not very often. Everybody prays about it and hears from the Lord about the various aspects of the work. Then at the very end of the process, one of us on the team will ask the Lord if there is anything that we're not catching, or if's there's anything else that He wants to show us about that particular publication before we send it off. Frequently, He'll bring something to mind that should be adjusted. At each step of the process, we have specific designated times where we check in with the Lord as far as, "Is all well, is it ready to go to the next step?" The answer might just be "fine," "good," or "go to press." Or sometimes the Lord will say something more detailed about the publication itself. We send this message to all the people who have been working on the publication.

We make our own deadlines. If significant issues come up with a publication, it may be postponed to a subsequent issue. We are servicing such a wide range of Family members in so many countries, there are a lot of things that you have to take into consideration—things like sensitivities in different cultures. We get a lot of feedback from people, especially if something went wrong [in a previous publication]. Ha! Or if something we didn't realize was sensitive for a certain area of the world or for a certain time period. So we have to be kind of global about how we approach things, and that's one of the reasons for different kinds of checks. Hopefully, with enough people looking at it and enough prayer involved, we'll catch these things.

Once the publications have been uploaded for printing in English, translators get them at the same time, and then they go to work. They are on a very different schedule, because their work is just beginning once our work is done. Their deadline may be a month later to get the final version of something, let's say, in Portuguese.

The translators have their own review process. And not everything gets translated. The most frequently translated publications are in Spanish. All of the GNs, as well as most of the children's publications, are translated in Spanish. In other languages, all the GNs are translated—that's what they prioritize, because there are some people that don't speak English, and the GNs are the only way for them to get the Word [officially approved revelations from Jesus in support of Family policies and teachings]. However, publications other than GNs are sometimes translated, sometimes not. It's really up to the translators' discretion, their financial capabilities, and also their personnel. We don't control that. It's very indigenous.

Family publications are originally written in English, as implied above. We were later informed that major translation centers operate in Latin America, Brazil, Thailand, and Taiwan to produce versions in native languages. Everything has to go through another set of prophetic checking procedures to produce these translated publications.

CHAPTER 6

Activating Religious
Interest of Nonmembers

In conjunction with their millennial expectations, WS leaders have proclaimed the 21st century an Era of Action, in which the Family International's attention will not merely be focused on witnessing to and saving souls, but also on greater follow-up efforts aimed at building a broader membership base through recruitment of "outside members" (as explained below). Among other things, it is hoped that outside members will become a source of financial support for the Family's end-time cause. Currently, outside members are being recruited primarily through subscriptions to a Family publication titled *Activated!*, a monthly magazine featuring short articles on theological topics and practical religious applications for daily life. The names and addresses of interested subscribers are funneled through "Activated Desks" and passed on to local Family Homes for follow-up visits.

Activated Desks is a term used for those communal Homes worldwide whose assignment is to oversee the distribution of *Activated!* magazine subscriptions to Family field missionaries, monitor follow-up efforts, and function as information centers for nonmembers' questions about the Family's teachings and outreach programs. Subsequently, through their dissemination of *Activated!* magazines, local field missionaries make contacts with people for follow-up visits, Bible lessons, fellowship, and additional instruction in Family teachings. A major goal of the Activated program is to cultivate outside members (alternatively referred to as "Activated members") to become part-time distributors of *Activated!* referral subscriptions and financial supporters of the Homes that recruit them. The Activated program is relatively new, and results have been uneven worldwide. Nonetheless, according to Family membership statistics, there were over 79,000 *Activated!* subscribers by the end of 2003.

Issues of the *Activated!* magazine must be prepared five to six months in advance of publication; 100,000 copies are printed monthly and are translated into 23 languages. At present, however, complete editions of *Activated!* are published only in English, Spanish, and Portuguese. Printing is done in Thailand under supervision of the World Services General Public (GP) Department. In addition to WS staff members, there are several regular contributors to *Activated!* who reside in Family Homes in the field. Unsolicited articles may also be submitted in response to ads run on Family Web sites. In addition, both the editors and contributors to *Activated!* can access material from a Web-based database called Infostore, which contains all Family publications.

The editor of *Activated!* is David, a 56-year-old first-generation convert who has been at World Services for 12 years. David is assisted in the *Activated!* ministry by his wife, Kendra, who has served even longer at World Services (25 years) as a staff writer and as one of Maria's secretaries. At the time of our visit, however, Kendra was suffering from poor health and was not present during our conversation with David. David is one of the few WS staffers who had been to college, having majored in fine arts at Ohio State University in the 1960s. David claims he was a mediocre student, however, and says he hated English classes. But his father had a journalism background and helped him in his coursework. Rather than citing his secular education, David credits his ability to edit *Activated!* primarily to his "anointing" for the work in World Services. At the same time, he disclaims any personal prophetic gifts and says he relies heavily on other Family members' prophetic confirmations concerning what he writes or chooses to put into the magazine. In attendance with us for this interview was Vivian, one of the WS Home shepherds, who made occasional comments in response to our questions about *Activated!* magazine and the Activated program of recruiting a stronger network of supporting members.

In an earlier publication we have observed that what is most interesting about the current Family emphasis on growth through recruitment of "Activated members" is the way that it has been conceptualized in official prophecies and leaders' publicized statements.[1] The shift in leadership's rhetoric concerning these topics signals an important transition in the Family International's institutional moral career. "Activated," or "outside members" (that is, living outside of Homes and not dedicated to being full-time missionaries), are now compared to the members of established churches in which paid clergy minister to their congregations' spiritual needs. The Activated program is envisioned as a potential vehicle for every Family Disciple (FD) Home to build a supporting congregation or "church" of outside members who would tithe to a local Home. This would create an opportunity for older first-generation disciples to begin assuming pastor roles to their congregations of outside members, as age and health concerns eventually limit their ability to actively engage in the Family's strenuous outreach and witnessing efforts. Adopting conventional

Christianity's model of a salaried ministry also is projected as a way to help alleviate concerns about the future well-being of disciple members who have forsaken secular occupational careers to devote their lives to a religious cause without accruing any retirement or health-care benefits.

Thus, while the end-time is pending, Family leaders optimistically hope to accelerate greatly their religious agenda of Christian evangelizing worldwide through the full-time dedication of its core, missionary disciples and the financial support of an expanding "Activated" member base. The eventual need for second- and third-generation leaders to adjust institutional priorities in ministering to a much larger body of individuals, who maintain conventional lives and obligations in the outside world, significantly increases the likelihood of a greater degree of Family integration with mainstream institutions. To the extent that their growth-oriented, Activated agenda is successful (Family leaders themselves acknowledge that there are no guarantees that it will be), the formation of Activated congregational units will introduce a new organizational dynamic in the Family's development that is likely to generate internal pressure for a greater degree of social and religious accommodation in the 21st century.

INTERVIEW WITH *ACTIVATED!* MAGAZINE EDITOR DAVID

Activated! *magazine (and its attendant teaching-learning program) has become the major missionary tool used in most Family Homes around the world. It represents a modern departure from the traditional "litnessing" and other street witnessing strategies originally introduced in the earliest years of the Children of God and widely employed until the mid-1990s.[2] Like all other WS personnel, David, the editor of* Activated!*, attributes his performance to being "anointed" for this particular job rather than to his own inherent talent. He then summarizes how* Activated! *was inaugurated, how it has evolved into a more complex program, and how it currently operates.*

DAVID: Within the Family, we have to work with what we've got. I was solidly in the bottom third of my high school class. I made it through high school, and I actually hung in for four years of college; didn't graduate, but I hung in there. That was at Ohio State; I'm from Ohio. So anyway, I still read at about an 8th-grade level, probably, and I'm not the sort of person who can take in tons and tons of information; actually, it's not my job to do that anyway. That's the difference between the Family and the secular world. I didn't major in journalism; I majored in Fine Arts. I guess it's just proof of the Lord, because even in the Family I'm one of the least likely people to do this kind of work. I hated my English class.

But my dad's love was journalism when he was in school. In the army, the Second World War, he was six feet tall and less than 120 pounds; they said: "The gun weighs more than you do. We can't send you into combat." So he'd had some training in journalism, and that's what he did during the war. Afterward, my mom had my brother, and then me, and he realized he couldn't really support a family as a reporter for a small-town newspaper, so he went into real estate. But he always would rather have been in journalism. It came in handy when I had to do papers in school. I'd always wait until the last night. Then, usually the morning before I had to turn them in, I'd put something together, and he'd get up and he'd type them for me and do a little editing and polishing. Basically, I think 95 percent of what I learned, I learned from reading my papers before I turned them in, so I'd know what I was turning in. I think that was my training.

But in the Family, it's basically the anointing. It's a gift. You've probably heard other Family people say something like they never picked up a guitar until the "inspirationalist" in the Home backslid, and they were the only one left in the Home to do it.[3] These are people that are now some of the best Family musicians, and that's how they learned. That's sort of how I got here. The people who were much more capable aren't with us anymore.

So I know it's the Lord, because I know that I don't have the natural gifts or the education or anything else to do the job. Then a few years ago [late 1990s], along came the increased use of prophecy in the Family. And here I was just kind of grooving on the anointing [God empowering him to do his work], so for me that's been a bit of a change. It's really helped me to appreciate the rest of the publication team, because most of them are stronger in hearing specifically from the Lord.[4] I can just kind of work away and see things that need to be changed or whatever. I just do it by "feel," and that's good to a point, but then to make sure that it's really what the Lord wants, we need confirmations and all of that. So that's one area where I really rely on some of the others, to keep reminding me to take it back to the Lord to, make sure it's not just the way I'd like it, but really the way the Lord wants it.

The way *Activated!* started was, about six or seven years ago, we had some meetings to discuss "How do we need to change the Family's outreach, and what sort of tools do we need?" And that's when the whole idea for *Activated!* came about. Cassandra, now at the Activated Desk in California, was one of the people that had the most ideas and the greatest burden for it. ["Burdens" are duties that members feel inspired to carry out.] So she started out gathering material and sending in rough drafts. I guess a team of us first hashed out getting a basic instructional course in place, and then a few more issues, and then eventually it was decided it would be a monthly magazine. When we started we didn't know if it was going to be a monthly magazine, or just a basic course and a few extra issues, or what.

Cassandra started putting together rough drafts, and then she got busy with other things and passed it on to another girl named Carol, who kept up with the rough drafts. Usually about half of the material she sent would go into the magazine. At WS we'd find other material that we thought would round out the magazine. Just recently, Carol had her second or third baby, so she's sort of bowing out now.

With the whole Board Vision, we've got people who are on the Church Growth and Outreach Board, and our General Public publications go hand in hand with their outreach.[5] So we've recruited some of the regional board members to help provide material for us. One thing we do, for the last few years anyway, is before starting on the next year's material, we put together a lineup of what topics we want to cover, because each issue has a central theme. So now we've just finalized the lineup for 2006—which topics we want to cover in which month. January, traditionally, has been New Year's, personal goals and a personal-growth-type issue. December is Christmas. Easter is Easter. And that leaves eight or nine other topics. We try to keep going back to some of the real basic topics like prayer and faith. But we also work in some topics that are priorities with people these days, like stress and combating depression. And we usually try to have one issue a year that is sort of family oriented. So, first of all, we solicit possible topics and then try to push it around until hopefully we get a well-rounded year.

We put plugs in the *Grapevine* [a regular Family newsletter]. The idea behind our advertising in the *Grapevine* is: "You people out there in the field, we are doing this for you, for your missionary outreach efforts. So if you have any ideas, if you have suggestions concerning existing material, or if you'd like to write something, or if you know someone who could write something, send it in."

We have a few regular contributors. I don't know if you'd recognize their names yet. We've got a fellow in England, for example, by the name of Jedediah. He's an old-timer and kind of an Endtime buff, so we recruited him to help with the Endtime articles. Also Elston here at WS, who also goes by Scott MacGregor, is a regular contributor and is also the author of *God on God*.[6] Between the two of them, they usually come up with the Endtime material we need. Once we have it edited and the magazine put together—you've heard about "locals" and that whole process—so, with the *Activated!* magazine, because it's going for outreach all over the world, we send it out for locals [editorial critiques that employ prophetic channeling]. We have in-house locals, and we have field locals. And some of the field locals, because they are now more involved, will get Active Members, who they know, to write stuff. The Family has many more good writers than we ever get material from. But we have a few that have kind of gotten into that groove. So we're starting to build up a little stable of regular contributors who we can call on for outsourcing.

First of all, though, we get input on the themes. Then this year, once we had the themes, we farmed them out to four or five new people to come up with material. They don't necessarily need to try to edit it or write new material. For example, one of the issues for 2006 would be pride versus humility. So they can go to the Infostore and pull material that they think is suitable for that. I'm not even really sure how it works computerwise. But Infostore is basically just a big database of all of our publications. It was done by a couple in the Ukraine, some SGAs [second-generation adults], who had the vision and burden and enough computer know-how to do it. From what I understand, they did it working together with our WS Web team. I don't know that much about it. We've got all of the Family publications here, so I don't really use Infostore, but it's been put on CD and sent to the Homes.

At any rate, when people are assigned a theme, it's like, "Go to Infostore and see what you can find on topic X." Also, the advantage of them being in the field and being involved in outreach is that, hopefully, they know Family members or Active members who can write new material to go with it. We also send out to these four or five field writers a skeleton outline of how the magazine works, because they follow a pretty standard format. There's a little message from me on page two; page three is usually easy reading relating to the theme that is like an anecdotal thing. Then we usually have two pretty meaty Word articles [articles that contain prophetic messages]—something from Dad [David Berg] or Mama [Maria]. Sometimes we use *Meditation Moments* [a small Family publication filled with spiritual quotations] or something that Peter has done for a *GN* that we can adapt to the general public. So those are the meatiest part of the magazine.

In short, in addition to new pieces that are sent in, we adapt articles for *Activated!* that are drawn from already-existing Family literature. We edit those and rewrite them, so that they are more appropriate for our audience—sort of like a *Reader's Digest* condensed version. Except I think *Reader's Digest* just has to cut it down; we've got to try to translate it from our lifestyle. In other words, we have to simplify articles written in a prophetic style and vocabulary the Family uses to language the general public understands.

We basically put the cookies on a lower shelf for the general public. We run into certain things, kind of routinely. For example, last January, we wanted to finally attack this big issue of vices—alcoholism, drug addiction and things like that. But you can't get into a topic like that without involving spiritual warfare. It may be a physical addiction, but it's also spiritual, and how these things tie in together [meaning that addictions are viewed as tools of Satan for destroying peoples' lives]. Because of the 100,000 copies that are printed every month, about half or more of the magazines get distributed on the street to new people, and most of those go to people that are getting them at stoplights or wherever. You can't assume that those people know anything; you have to always be providing enough explanation so that some of it is going to make sense to them. When I first was converted into the Family and started reading the Bible, none of it made sense to me, but I kept reading until it did. So we have to assume that that's how the Lord's going to work with people who get the *Activated!* magazine. At the same time, everything can't be simplified to the very simplest terms or it wouldn't be spiritually feeding the people who've been reading it for years. So we have to strike the right balance. And that's where we have to really pray and trust the Lord.

We just did the January edition of *Activated!* for next year. It's a fifth anniversary issue, so it's all just reprints of articles that have already been published. In the little Personally Speaking section we put in some statistics, and we've published over four million copies now, 60 issues. Not per month, but that's the total. I think we publish *Activated!* in 23 languages, but some of them are only a few issues that are translated in bits and pieces. The only three languages that we translate complete magazines in are English, Spanish, and Portuguese.

Each language area, depending on its size and the translators available, has figured out what they have the faith for. Some of them use the basic *Activated!* course, two issues a year or something, or they'll do a modified basic course.[7] But something that's nice for them is they can just pick and choose from whatever material we put out, and they can use stuff they think is most relatable in their area. Unfortunately, you have to start some place, but if you look at other magazines like *Time* and *Newsweek* they've got an Asian edition, a European edition, a South African edition, etc. But right now our material, for different reasons, is sort of top-heavy U.S. But in the local language editions they have the freedom to pick and choose and adapt it to whatever they think will be most effective in their area.

Activated! is actually printed in Thailand. That's why we have to work so far ahead. Right now, we've done the next Christmas issue, which is already with them in Thailand. It's kind of a funny thing, because for Christmas we print twice as many, so it gets printed separately. Normally, we print two months' [issues] at a time, and every other year we print a separate Christmas issue that basically throws things off, because instead of doing six printings a year we do six and a half. So right now November and January are in the works, because they've got to print it, it's got to get translated into Spanish and Portuguese—which they also print in Thailand—and then it's got to get shipped all over the world, and the Activated Desks have to ship it to Family Homes. I guess compared to other publishers it's actually a pretty small deal. I think the Jehovah's Witnesses do 20 million a month, and of course, *Time*, *Newsweek*, and all of those can afford to do things differently than we can.

Because other publishers produce so much, they can do it cheaper, and because they can do it cheaper, they can afford to spend more on shipping or distribution or whatever. It kind of limits us on how much we can mention items that are actually current in the news, because if something happens today, by the time it comes out in *Activated!* it's six or eight months later.

In this year's Christmas *Activated!* magazine we had a Family Home in Phuket, Thailand, that was doing Christmas outreach when the December 26, 2004, tsunami hit, so they could do an article about that for this next Christmas issue, but by now it's the first anniversary of the tsunami.

Last year, a year ago Easter, the film *The Passion* came out, and all the other magazines had it on their covers when it was in the theaters. We had "The Passion" tract, which we used in the next Easter issue, but we're a year behind. It's just the way it goes at the moment. My dream, actually, is some day when our circulation is up, to be sent to India, where I've never been, to do an Indian issue.

Vivian explains what the connection is between Activated! *magazine and the Activated program, which functions to recruit more financial and missionary support.*

VIVIAN: Rather than the exclusivity of our membership consisting only of Disciple members—only the inner circle—there are so many more people in different walks of life that are a part of us in spirit. I think our Activated membership [program] acknowledges that. So we hope to expand the Activated member category, to broaden the circle of our fellowship and membership.

DAVID: I think it's happening. I'm sure you've heard the analogy of the Family as a huge oil tanker, or the *Titanic* or something that takes a long time to steer a new course, and that's sort of what's been happening. The *Activated!* magazine's been out for five years, so the Activated program has also been in place for five years. Circulation is slowly climbing, and I think the other aspects of the Activated program, which includes personal follow-up on subscribers and involving them in the work of the Family, is also picking up steam, but slowly.

The various Activated Desks around the world take care of subscriptions in their regions. I've never visited any of our desks, so I don't know, but my guess is that some of the people that subscribe to the magazine are in close contact with local Homes, and some are pretty much on their own without any direct Family fellowship. They may have just gotten the magazine from a road team and written in for a subscription, and at that point it's pretty much up to that person's initiative to get in touch with the desk to get something going, other than just receiving a magazine each month.[8] Some people, that's all they do—they just receive the magazine, and we don't know whether they read it. We assume that if they sent in the subscription fee, they intended to read it, at least. I guess how far each person goes is up to them and how the Lord is working in their life.

As an example, Gary learned from his world travels that the Family Home in Bangalore, India, has over 1,000 "Activated members" in something like 36 different towns and villages that are within traveling distance of the Home. These towns are regularly visited by an "outreach team." The team has a computer program that indicates who's getting what issue of Activated! *magazine and how often. They know if someone only wants to be visited once a year, or every month, or every week. The team divides the towns up, and they go out and make those visits. It's a very organized follow-up, as David confirms.*

DAVID: Bangalore is one of the better programs in the world. If we could get all the Family Homes in the world doing that, then we'd be on our way. It takes time, and it takes numbers, too. That's a small Home in Bangalore. I think the goal of the Bangalore Home probably is to train a few people in each of those towns or villages that can help take care of the people in that town. That's the long-term goal. But it takes awhile to develop that kind of work, even to just give people the spiritual training that they need in order to start helping to pastor a little church in their town.

INTERVIEW WITH GENERAL PUBLIC DEPARTMENT AND AURORA PRODUCTIONS HEADS BARBARA AND FRANK

World Services' General Public (GP) Department and Aurora Productions involve closely connected Family enterprises. They are responsible for producing and distributing Family religious materials primarily for consumption by non-Family members, which is to say, the "general public."[9] Through Aurora, the GP Department operates as a business enterprise, functioning as a relatively small but active actor in the global marketplace of religious literature and related supplies. For various legal reasons Aurora Productions is organized and incorporated under Swiss law, although it doesn't have a physical office there. In order to perform their production and distribution tasks competently, GP Department and Aurora staffers have to understand and engage in secular business practices and comprehend related legal issues. They are, perforce, largely self-educated in these areas.

Revealed in the following interview are some of the ways in which the Family International's business operations have developed rational, market-oriented strategies for successfully competing in the sale of religious materials, especially literature and music products for children. Decisions regarding the creation, production, and distribution of Aurora products are made at by the International GP Board, which serves in close conjunction with the International Church Growth and Outreach Board. The GP Department within WS is responsible for and carries out the actual creation of products, which are then produced and sold by Aurora. Family products and materials (books, magazines, tapes, CDs, DVDs, posters, greeting cards, etc.) are marketed and sold to non-Family as well as Family members. These are important revenue sources that are reinvested in upgrading or producing new products, which Family members worldwide use as fund-raising tools to meet their Home expenses.

From the point of view of unconventional and highly committed religious organizations like the Family International, the outside world commonly is viewed to be spiritually and morally corrupt. Entanglement with worldly institutions and their ways is considered to be spiritually dangerous and potentially contaminating. What secular authorities see as the need for accommodation to secular norms and practices by legitimate organizations is typically resisted by heretical new religions as a corruption of their efforts to build and sustain a purified community separated from the world. In the face of accommodating pressures and perceived spiritual laxity, revivals, reformations, or retrenchment campaigns typically emerge in new religious movements. In many respects, Aurora Productions and the GP Department are those administrative units of the Family International that are in closest contact with the outside world. This predictably makes them and their operations potential pressure points in the direction of greater Family accommodation to the secular demands and legal requirements of contemporary life. At the same time, continued resistance to secular influences and renewed devotion to core beliefs have, in fact, become major motifs in recent Family retrenchment campaigns.[10] Renewal movements typically serve to sustain, rather than reduce, tension between sponsoring religious organizations and their detractors, including disenchanted former members who have not left the group on good terms. Thus, for example, in this interview (as well as in many of our other WS interviews) defensive comments are periodically made about former members who have attacked the Family for its alleged economic exploitation of individuals and abusive practices with regard to second-generation children.

While hoping to realize a profit from the sale of Family products, the GP Department defines its primary mission as providing missionary tools for the

Family International's field Homes to carry out their basic religious duty of witnessing and conversion. Thus, even though Aurora Productions and the General Public Department have adopted a rational, secular approach to the manufacture and sale of their religious products, they retain a fundamentally religious orientation to their work, the goals of which supersede the primary profit motive of secular business organizations. Family artists and authors for Aurora products receive a one-time only, monetary compensation for the time and work they have invested, but they are not paid conventional salaries or royalties. Furthermore, as Savannah observed in chapter 5, compensation is not given to individual contributors but to their local Homes. This practice is accepted by loyal Family disciples as an application of the basic principle of egalitarian sharing in communal living and of their commitment to what they believe is God's work on earth.[11]

We obtained information about General Public publications and Aurora operations through a joint interview with Frank and Barbara. At age 36, Frank is a second-generation Family member who has been assigned to World Services for the past 11 years. He is the international board chair for Church Growth and Outreach (CGO), while simultaneously overseeing Aurora Productions. Barbara is a 29-year-old SGA who has been in WS for nine years. She is the department head of GP publications and also sits on the CGO Board. Frank is involved primarily with the legal and business management side of Aurora Productions, while Barbara focuses on publication content concerns and editing. Both Frank and Barbara also are considered to be "exercised" (reliable) channels for *GN* prophecies.

For this interview we again were accompanied by WS shepherds Thomas and Vivian, who occasionally joined the conversation. In our conversation we were reminded that before new staff members are brought into World Services they must first be screened by WS shepherds who, among other things, form an in-house personnel committee. In addition to whatever specialized talents or technical skills they might possess, WS applicants also are evaluated for their spirituality and ability to work cooperatively with other people.

Prior to meeting with Frank and Barbara, we had heard mention made of a new Family publication called *Link*. So that is the question with which we began the interview.

FRANK: *Link* is a magazine that we created specifically targeting our "Active Members" [recruits who subscribe to *Activated!* magazine and meet periodically with Family missionaries for fellowship and religious instruction]. It's the first time that we've created a magazine especially for them. We've had the *Activated!* magazine, but that's something more for the general public at large. *Link* magazine is for Active Members who have gone through the Twelve Foundation Stones course.[12] With Active Members you know they've reached a certain level of knowledge about basic Christian and spiritual principles. When you're developing content for their magazine you know that they know at least this much, and they are being visited, they're in personal contact with a local Family Home, so you can put content in the magazine that reflects that.

But with *Link*, we purposely are using only new material, so that when the Family Homes get it, it's new for them too at the same time that it's new for the Active Members. It makes the Active Members feel more a part of the Family, because they're getting something at the same time that Disciple Homes [Homes in compliance with all disciple standards] are getting it. And it will make Disciple Homes read it as well; it's important for them to know what their Active Members are getting in the mail.

Frank and Barbara go on to discuss the complex operation of Aurora Productions and its relationship to a multitude of GP publications and products.

FRANK: Aurora is a company that holds the rights to all of the material that we put out for the general public. It's something we started doing in 1999. Aurora was established in 1998, which is when we first started printing a couple of General Public publications with our small beginnings. The *Mottos for Success* calendar was one of the first things we did in 1999 or 2000, and now we've done two versions and we have it in close to 30 languages. The Aurora Company was set up for the purpose of holding the copyright, so that the copyrights of all of our products that go out to the general public, whether they be audio, video, or print, are securely held by a company. Thus, they are not in some individual's name who today is in the Family and tomorrow is no longer in the Family, and then you're sort of stuck, in that Family missionaries might not be able to continue distributing material that we have created.

We were in a situation like that in the mid-'90s. In Japan, the Kiddie Viddie company was set up, and that company on paper owned the rights to the *Kiddie Viddies*. [*Kiddie Viddies* are music videos for young children.] The company was set up by two people—it was just a small, little company—and over time the person who had the majority share left the Family. He was an old-timer. Not that he turned against the Family or anything like that, but he just left. So we realized, "Wait a minute. Now we're not in a good situation with this." So we wanted to set up a legal structure that was going to be solid, that was going to stand the test of time, and that wasn't going to be in the name of a particular person who might decide not to be in the Family, and then you've always got to scramble.

We did recover the rights to *Kiddie Viddies*. What we did was set up the Aurora Company in Switzerland, and the Aurora Company bought all the assets, all the intellectual property of *Kiddie Viddies, Treasure Attic* [another video series for children], and Aurora, which was another company in Japan that held the rights for the first audio tapes that were done.[13] So the intellectual properties of those companies were transferred to Aurora in Switzerland, and the other companies just dissolved.

Aurora is an actual legal company in Switzerland, but ultimately it's overseen from here. I'm ultimately overseeing it, but I'm not employed by Aurora or legally involved. We have people who actually are employed by Aurora and do the Aurora work. There are different onsite departments in Switzerland. We have a department that takes care of the legal work, and the bookkeeping, and the financial, and making sure that we have the rights to all of our products, and that all the legal paper work is done properly. Then we have a production department that is located in Southeast Asia, in Thailand, where we print all the stuff.

By "productions department," I mean we have a small team. For example, when we create something we send the files to Thailand. They get the proofs made, they get the plates made, and they work with the printers. They work with warehousing and shipping it out to our distribution centers worldwide. So that is quite a job. We have a huge warehouse there with tons of all of our products. We've created about 100 to 150 products in the last five years. So that is a lot of stock; we have to keep our distribution centers supplied. We have to have inventory, and then the distribution centers order from Aurora, and in turn Family Homes order from the distribution centers. Some products are produced locally by the distribution centers in cases where it's either cheaper for them to do so or because of import restrictions they're not able to bring it in from Thailand. For example, India can't import CDs because of government regulations. So they produce their CDs locally. But books they can import, so those they get from Thailand where we're able to print in larger quantity for a cheaper price. So that is all part of Aurora too.

And then we have a commercial marketing department; they have been going to the international book fairs and representing Aurora there. The Aurora marketing team has been going to the biggest international book fairs now for the last four or five years. Two thousand might have been the first year we went. We have a booth in Frankfurt, which is the largest book fair in the world, and we go there every year. I've been there twice.

BARBARA: I went once, but mainly it's Frank's dad.

FRANK: Yes, actually, it's my dad heading up the marketing team. His name is Joshua. They live in Ireland now [as the marketing team], he and a couple of other people, and they go to the book fairs. There's a circuit that we've been doing: Frankfurt, which is the largest international book fair by far; Bologna, which is the largest children's international book fair; and London, which is the largest English-speaking book fair. We went a few times to Chicago to Book Expo America, and Guadalajara, Mexico, which is the largest Spanish-speaking book fair every year. And last year we went to São Paulo and Rio. We go to New Delhi, and we've been to South Africa. We haven't really gotten into the video and audio CD marketing. We have done some deals for the videos and audios with book distribution, but a lot of them don't carry video or audio products. So that's not the main thing that they're looking for. And to be honest, we haven't really gotten into that because our resources are limited, so we're mostly focusing on the books.

It's been an investment. The first couple of years you're just getting exposure; nobody knows you or your products, so you're mostly spending, and you're not making anything. Then the last couple of years have been looking quite good. They've been more than worth the time and effort and expense. It's also taught us a lot. Going to these fairs has caused us to increase the quality of our products tremendously, and we've learned a lot through the process, because we didn't know anything about this sort of thing at all. We had to learn it pretty much completely from scratch! Thank the Lord we can hear from the Lord, and we have good people to work with.

As Frank and Barbara relate below, they both grew up in the Family, both are second-generation adults, and both got most of their schooling in Family Homes. Since the General Public Department, and especially Aurora Productions, more than any of the other WS units, have connections to the outside world, Frank and Barbara have to understand and function as actors in relationship to the outside world, in terms of established business practices and law. They're responsible for an enterprise that functions in the world market place. They have become primarily self-educated in how all this works.

FRANK: I went to System school, what we call System school—that means school outside of the Family—for four years when I was a kid in France, in French; sixth through ninth grade.

BARBARA: And I went to a System school for one year in Santiago, Chile, when I was five—first grade. Where did I get the basic language and writing skills that I have to have in my position? I guess from my parents' homeschooling. I always loved to read. Since I can remember, I was constantly reading. I don't remember learning how to spell. I just always seemed to know how to spell everything right, and I liked to write. I've written a diary since I was seven years old. In school, anything having to do with language or with writing or spelling was always my area of expertise as a child. I just sort of did it and learned it. I never took courses for it. The editors and writers who work in this department are much better than I am, like David [*Activated!* editor, see above], for example. But I have a handle on it.

FRANK: Basically, my formal schooling ended when I was 13.

FRANK AND BARBARA TOGETHER: We don't have MBAs; Oh, no! (Laughter.)

FRANK: I never even took the GED [exam].

BARBARA: I took it just to get it. I thought, "Oh, it'd be good to have at least a high school diploma." So I went and took the test and got the diploma.

FRANK: I'm already doing the job of an MBA, so I don't need the degree to tell me I can do the job, ha!

BARBARA: Frank does more of the business aspects than I do. I mostly focus on the content of the product, the editing, and managing the people in WS and in the field who contribute.

FRANK: I used to do both of these jobs, but thankfully now Barbara does the creation side so I can focus on the business side.

FRANK: With regard to my job before, and now Barbara's job in managing the team: we don't have to possess all the skills ourselves. We just have to manage everyone who has the skills. Like Jerinda, who does the graphic design for all of these books; she is very, very talented, very skilled.

BARBARA: And, again, entirely self-taught.

FRANK: Yes. Those are skills that Barbara and I don't have. I taught her the technical side of it; how to use the programs, but as far as the creative talent, that is something that the Lord gave her.

Frank and Barbara discuss the difficulties and ironies of selling Family-linked products to Christian publishers, such as Zondervan, as well as the difficulties Aurora faces in a competitive publishing environment generally, and the business model they believe is most appropriate for the Family's end-time mission.

FRANK: Our products that get the most interest are the kids' stuff, and the From Jesus with Love books. These are just the latest in the series. We have five or six of them. A Christian publishing house is distributing these in the U.S. And they do get placed in Christian bookstores.

BARBARA: Southern Baptists. By the way, didn't Zondervan publish Deborah Davis's book [*The Children of God: The Inside Story*]?[14]

FRANK: Yes, that was the first anti-Family book that I know of, and it was published by Zondervan in 1981, or something like that.

BARBARA: Now they are only publishing our stuff in Spanish, for the Latin market and Puerto Rico.

FRANK: We've been talking with Thomas Nelson, and they've also been interested in our books. We used to have a distributor in the U.S. for our products. They were called Faithworks, and they were a division of National Book Network, which is one of the largest book distributors in the U.S.—their Christian division. And it didn't go so well. It was an experience that we're not going to repeat. Working through a distributor in the U.S. is difficult. Not that they didn't like our products; they did, but the sales didn't go well. What we do now is deal directly with the publisher. Instead of dealing with the distributor, you ship them the books, they try to get them into the stores, and if they can't do it, they ship it back to you. Well, we had that experience and now we're like, "No, thank you." Now we work with publishers who have their own distribution network. They agree to buy X number of books and that's it. And it's their problem if they sell them or don't or however they distribute them; it's up to them. Of course, it's in the contract what markets they can sell them to, and that's basically the only thing that we're going to do now. There's an interesting story about Faithworks in relation to the issue of knowing who we are.

On our business card it doesn't say "Aurora, a Division of the Family International," or something like that. It just says "Aurora Productions." But if people ask, we tell them, "Yes, these products are made by the Family International" or "distributed by the Family." And the people who attend the book fairs and represent Aurora, they are Family members. Legally, Aurora is not a "Family" company, because the Family is not an internationally registered entity that owns companies. So, legally, Aurora is just its own independent company, that happens to have Family members running it and that produces products created by the Family, which it sells to Family distributors, as well as to other commercial publishers and distributors.

But in one case, once our books started getting in the stores, Sam Ajemian, who is one of these guys who really fights against the Family, figured out who it was that was distributing our books in the States and started sending emails to them. He emailed the CEO, and we got wind of it, because he posted about it on one of those ex-members Web sites.[15] So we were thinking, "Okay, good to know." My dad was just heading to New York for a book fair, where he was going to meet with a representative of this company. We got a copy of the letter that Ajemian had sent them, and everything was in there, the usual accusations: flirty fishing [see chapter 1], Loving Jesus, child abuse, all the things they accuse us of, all in one letter.[16] So we prayed and we asked the Lord, "What do we do?" And the Lord said just be open and honest and don't try to squirm in your seat, just be up front. So we sent that message to my dad. When he met with the company president, who was sitting there with the email, this man said, "You know I received this very disturbing email. Are you from the Family?" And my dad said, "Yes." And he told him his testimony and witnessed to him and said, "Well, those are just accusations that people who are embittered about the Family and are fighting us bring up. But you've worked with us now for some time. You know our products. You know the message that is in them. So I think that the products speak for themselves." And this man said, "Okay. Let's talk business."

That was it—it never came up again. Eventually we ended up discontinuing working with them, simply for financial reasons. But that was an interesting experience for us. And he was a Southern Baptist. Ha! I think he was probably unusual among other Baptists in that respect. There's another company in Italy that was interested in the Feed My Lambs series, which was another one of our products, and they also asked us who we were. We said "the Family," and they looked it all up. But again, it's the products themselves; they see the message we're trying to get out, and that is our biggest witness, which I think can overshadow whatever kind of muck people try to throw at us.

One thing also that we're learning with our commercial marketing—we recently had meetings to discuss this problem—is that there are two different business models and we've been pursuing both of them, yet they inherently are in conflict with each other. One is a distribution model whereby we make a deal with a large distributor who then sells throughout a whole country or territory, such as, for example, we did with the From Jesus with Love books in Spanish. A company like that will want exclusive rights to the market or territory that they are going to distribute in, because that's just the way companies operate. They don't want you then going and selling to their competitors. Unless of course you are in such a position where you can dictate the terms, and then they just have to accept your terms or you're going to go to the next guy. We're not in that position because we're not Disney or Microsoft.

We're not DreamWorks, we're not Pixar. We're just a little guy, small fry. So that's one model. The second model is where you have your own distribution network, where you sell to you local distribution centers; well, we have local distribution centers and they sell to our distributors—our Family Homes—and they sell to individuals or to small stores and businesses and places like that. That's more of the Avon or Mary Kay type of business model as opposed to your standard Disney business model. So we've been pursuing both, but in countries where they overlap, we run into conflicts. So we're in the process of trying to sort out those conflicts, and we've been praying, hearing from the Lord and asking the Lord as to which of these business models we should pursue; should we continue to try to do both, should we just throw all of our weight behind one or the other, and if so, which one? Or should we do one in some countries and one in others? So we just had some meetings about that recently with Family representatives from around the world. You've got to cover your overhead and cover enough to be able to reinvest in new products. Otherwise you're eating the eggs, but then the goose is slowly dying and you don't have enough money to raise a new goose.

We are competing in a highly competitive industry, one with very small margins. But one advantage we have is that our writers, contributors, artists, and so forth are not getting paid in the usual way. So our overhead in this regard is much smaller. This allows us to produce our products cheaply enough to give our Family Homes a substantial margin when they sell the products. In comparison with a normal distributor, a non-Family distributor who would be in the same position as the Home, their profit margin might be 20 or 30 percent. Whereas a Home's profit margin on the products they sell is usually 100 to 200 percent, which is really unheard of in the industry, and is only possible because, number one, we're not interested, as the publishing company is, in making most of the profit for ourselves. And secondly is our overhead. I mean, we operate on a shoestring budget. From a purely business point of view, if we were running this as a business, if we were just focused on one particular territory and a couple of markets within that territory, we'd be very successful.

BARBARA: Or even one line of products, like videos only.

FRANK: But one of the reasons why we're not very successful, perhaps, in dollar terms, is because we're trying to accommodate a lot of needs all over the world. Whereas from the business point of view, you shut down your unprofitable lines, the ones that aren't bringing in a lot of revenue, and you focus on the ones that are. Then once those are stable enough, you can expand, whereas we expand everywhere at once; we subsidize. And we try to accommodate our members' needs in different languages—materials to reach different target audiences and different cultures. And that, of course, spreads us very thin. So it may not be good business sense, but it's good missionary sense, because, of course, our main goal is to be missionaries and not to be businessmen.

We, of course, sell a lot through the Family, through our own distribution network. Our own distribution network is not big in terms of visibility; it's not in Wal-Mart or Target or Barnes and Noble. The actual amounts that we sell worldwide of our products are quite good in industry terms. For example, *The Mottos for Success*—which we have sold a half million—that's a best seller. In fact, a best seller in the industry is 15,000 copies, and most of our books hit that and surpass it. So we actually do quite well in terms of numbers, even if it's not necessarily through the commercials venues. We have done some bigger deals; for example, we sold 40,000 copies of our Discovering Truth books. One is called *Bible Basics* and one is called *Keys to Happier Living*. They are all Bible verses arranged categorically on different topics—two really good books, and they are popular in Africa. Forty thousand of our books have been distributed to African churches. We have a lot of testimonies of pastors in Africa who use those books as the basis of their teaching, and they're not all affiliated with the Family. And *God on God?* It has mostly just been distributed in India, believe it or not. We really tried to find a U.S. publisher who would take it. So far we haven't found one. Random House almost took it. We went back and forth a number of times, and in the end they decided not to.

God on God is somewhat unusual, we have learned from other sources, because there is a sole author who is identified as such, which is not typical for either Family or Aurora publications. Below, Frank and Barbara explain how Aurora handles copyright and royalty issues (for authors, artists, and other creative producers), as well as other legal requirements.

FRANK: We assign all the rights to Aurora, for all the original authors, artists, etc. We have contracts whereby all the rights are signed to Aurora in exchange for a one-time payment rather than author royalties. And that's something we have debated and asked the Lord about a number of times when we started this whole Aurora Company: whether we should have a royalty-based system. Not only for books like *God on God,* but we have songs that are recorded by musicians, all kinds of things—art that's drawn for a children's book, etc. There were some good arguments for why we should allow it, such as it would help those missionaries with some residual income that would perhaps encourage them to contribute more. That was a very good pro. But the main reason why we didn't do it is because, in the end, it fundamentally goes against our general economic system in the Family, which is based on the Bible verses in Acts 2:44 and 45 about sharing all things in common.

You have a musician in a particular Family Home, or the studio producer, who spends two weeks recording a composition. But while he's doing that, someone else in the Home is taking care of Family business so he can do his job. So let's say some member gets the royalty on a song. Well, what about the person who was taking care of his kids? They should in turn have a little contract with him whereby they get a percentage of whatever he gets. And if we start going that route, that is a breakdown of the Family economy. It's a breakdown of living communally. So we figured that we couldn't allow it. What we do instead is compensate people on a one-time basis. If a producer spends two weeks recording a song, we give him a one-time gift for his time that goes to his Home. It compensates the whole Home for his time to produce something that then is going to be used by the whole Family. But then he has no authorship rights after that. Or if you are in World Services, like Elston; well, he's getting his free room and board, and that's in exchange for whatever he does. Actually, that's not uncommon in the world, either. The artists that work for Disney, they don't own anything that they draw for Disney. Disney owns it all.

Over the years, we occasionally have had artists—either musicians or painters or writers—who have created something that has been successful, and then the artist or the creator has subsequently left the Family and wants to have control of their creation. These cases are resolved in different ways. One example is a brother named Jethro Salm. He's one of the old-time Family members, one of the original members. He wrote a lot of songs that were used in the Family, and still are. God bless him! He actually went to be with the Lord about ten years ago. Before he died he had left the Family, and a number of his songs were featured on the Kiddie Viddies. So he wrote us and said, "My songs are featured on the Kiddie Viddies, and I want all this money to be compensated for that. Otherwise, I don't want the Family using them." So we took his songs off the Kiddie Viddies. We just basically rearranged them. Instead of six Kiddie Viddies videos, we rearranged them to five, and we dropped off all of his songs. In this case we didn't have any contract with him for the use of his songs. We had another case with someone else who left the Family, Slim Becker, who is also a famous singer.

BARBARA: He was FM [Fellow Member] until recently.[17]

FRANK: In his case, from what I understand, he has a couple of his kids who are quite anti-Family. It seems like they were telling him, "Hey, Dad, you're getting ripped off by Aurora making money off of your songs," which actually wasn't true at all. He had recorded a CD that WS had funded originally, and he was compensated for it. Then we released it to the Family for distribution to the public. We didn't sell that much of it, but some sold, and he wrote and said, "I want royalties for all those CDs," and you could tell he had talked to a lawyer because of the language he used in his letter. We wrote back and said, "This is how many we've sold, and it's not really that big of a deal, but since you're so uptight about it, we'll just stop distributing your CD."

VIVIAN: We wrote it nicer than that. (Laughter.)

FRANK: Yes, we did. We wrote it very nice, actually. It was sad, because they're great songs that could be a real blessing to the Family, to our sheep [contacts and people who are interested in learning more about the Family's teachings]. We never heard back from him further on that, but we just stopped producing his CD. Now, of course, we have contracts on all of our products.

BARBARA: In comparison, the Capstone brothers [former Family performing artists] turned their rights over before they left. We keep using them, and they haven't made a stink about it at all.

FRANK: There are lots of people who left the Family whose songs we still use, and it's not a problem. The contract we do for songs actually allows them to continue to use the songs in whatever way they want, in addition to Aurora being able to use them however we want, without paying them any royalties other than a one-time compensation.

BARBARA: So if they get discovered by someone out there, they can do whatever they want.

FRANK: They can still record their songs. And we told Slim Becker that, too. In fact, we even offered to give him 1,000 of his own CDs for free that he could use and sell in order to make money off of them. Actually, we offered him a very good deal, but he wasn't interested, for what reasons I don't know. But for the most part, even though we have the contracts in place, we're not likely to go to court with people over these things unless it's really of such fundamental value that the whole Family is depending on it, and then we have to go to court in order to show that we actually own the rights and we have the right to do this. Because going to court is messy and expensive.

BARBARA: We have a Swiss lawyer, because Aurora is a Swiss company based in Switzerland.

FRANK: All the contracts we do are all under the jurisdiction of Swiss law, not American law, which greatly simplifies them, because American law is extremely subject to litigation. Other countries don't subscribe to the same sort of philosophy as the American legal system. In Switzerland, it's very difficult to sue someone unless you have a real legitimate case to do so. In the States you can sue someone for whatever reason. It doesn't matter if you win the case or not, you can just run someone down financially through a court case, which is why we didn't set up Aurora in America.

We have templates for a number of different contracts that we designed over the years. We actually wrote them ourselves for the most part, but then we had our attorney go over them, to make sure they're right. Fortunately, under Swiss law, things can be a lot simpler than U.S. law. In the U.S., the equivalent of our two-page Swiss contract would be fourteen pages. Because in the U.S. when you say, "can you use this," it's "how do you define 'use.'" Whereas in Switzerland, "you can use it" means "you can use it." It's much more straightforward.

There is a functioning Home in Switzerland that has various ministries, but there are a couple of people in the Home who are employed by Aurora to take care of Aurora business—all the legal business part of it. We do have a team in Thailand. And I'm here at WS; Celia helps me—she's a secretary. And then we have our team in Ireland that goes to the book fairs. So it's spread out. But, yes, in Switzerland, we just have a couple of people. We have an actual little office there. So it's not a vapor-paper company. It's a real—what the Swiss call an AG [joint stock] type of company, which is the equivalent of a corporation in the U.S. And we get audited every year and jump through all the legal hoops, the Swiss hoops, of which there are many. Mostly, it's just the auditor going over all of our files. We also hire a company to do our official bookkeeping. Because the Swiss way of doing it is complicated, and we don't really have anybody who has that kind of training. So the guys there just make sure that the bookkeeping company gets a copy of all of our invoices, all of our contracts, all of our paper files so that they have everything.

In some ways, in our judgment, Aurora is the face of the Family around the world. Because Aurora has so many facets that represent Family interests in such a major way to nonmembers, Frank and Barbara solicit suggestions and critiques from people outside of the GP Board in World Services, although they do assume final responsibility for making routine product and policy decisions.

FRANK: We get input in two ways. When it comes to the creation of products, there are people within WS who review content and do "locals" on it. But in addition—and this is something that is only done with our products for the General Public that are created here—we have an online collaboration Web site that all of our local distribution centers, as well as our Church Growth and Outreach [CGO] board members, can access. We have six International Family boards, one of which is CGO, which I chair. Barbara and I both sit on this Board, and it dovetails with our production for the General Public. Those members all have access to this forum. We put things that we produce up for comment and critique before they are produced. So that is one way of getting input at the creation stage. We also get a lot of input and ideas and suggestions from other Family members or from the board members themselves.

BARBARA: Unfortunately, we can't act on even a fraction of them, but we try to go over all of that input: "Well, there are 40 Homes asking for this. Maybe we should pray about this thing as a new type of content to 'create,'" whereas if only two guys wrote in asking for something else, maybe that can wait awhile.

FRANK: Or when we have our International CGO Board meetings, we'll discuss what we feel as a board are the priorities for us to focus on as far as the creation of content for the Family distribution, which we did at our meeting last year. Then of course there are many little decisions that affect exactly how it's all done, or little requests that come up that we have to handle as they come up. But there is quite a bit of input that comes from the grass-roots, because the Homes are very concerned about what products they get in order to meet their witnessing and teaching needs. As Barbara brought out, we don't have the resources to be able to meet everybody's needs, and that is something we struggle with.

BARBARA: We do have a lot. There's material for children, for adults, and for newer Christians or more developed Christians.

FRANK: Something that we are going to need to focus more on now is materials to feed [spiritually strengthen] our expanding membership, our new levels of membership. That is something that we don't have enough of. We do have in the pipeline a series of classes for new members, the Twelve Bridges classes [follow-up indoctrination classes to the Twelve Foundation Stones lessons as a crucial part of the Activated Program].

BARBARA: And we're starting the *Link* magazine, and we hope to be able to do some products for the children of Active members [subscribers to *Activated!* magazine] and the kids of those people, who also need feeding at their level.

FRANK: With regard to our authority in making these and other, more basic decisions: We don't report to anybody about routine matters. But we do have a GP Productions Board, which exists on the international level only. That's the two of us and five other people who represent different continents. We had our annual meeting just two weeks ago, and together we make the major decisions that affect the course that we're going to take with the creation, production, and distribution of our products. Those decisions are made by the Board together.

If a decision falls within the mandate that the Board has already set, and it's just a matter of how we are implementing that, then I'll go ahead and make that decision. Or we'll counsel about it together, or maybe I'll counsel with some other people who may be involved. If it's something new that goes outside of whatever decisions we made as a board—the direction we are go-ing to go—then of course we counsel with the whole board and make the decision together. If there were a deadline, rather than having a face-to-face to meeting, we would do it by email.

CHAPTER 7

Defending the Faith in the Cyber Age

This chapter covers in selected interview excerpts how the Family uses the internet to communicate with outsiders to share its particular message of faith and to engage its public relations arm to combat negative information about the Family. Authors' summary and informational comments are distinguished from staff responses as in previous chapters.

INTERVIEW WITH WEB DEPARTMENT HEADS CYNTHIA AND DENSEL

The considerable level of human capital and resources invested by World Services in producing and disseminating "the Word" through its assorted publications notwithstanding, proportionately more people today are learning about the Family International and its teachings by way of the internet. The Family currently maintains four major Web sites and hosts or sponsors numerous smaller, more specialized sites. In addition, individual Family Homes may set up (and many have) their own home Web sites. Many Family members (including WS staff) routinely post music and internet pictures online. At the time of our visit in 2005, there were approximately 28,000 pictures and photos available for viewing on Family Web sites. That number, of course, has subsequently been greatly increased. After two years on display, photos are archived.

Co–department heads of the World Services Web Department are Cynthia and Densel. Both are second-generation adults. Cynthia is 27 years old and is partnered with Peter's son, Jethro, who also works at World Services as a computer tech. Cynthia has been at WS for eight years. Her primary responsibility is to supervise the content of Family Web sites. Densel is 23 years old and grew up in WS, where he received training in computer programming from his father, who pioneered the development of internet technology at World Services. His wife is Savannah, who is a staff artist and art coordinator for the Art Department. Densel's primary responsibility is Web design.

The promotion of Cynthia and Densel to department heads again illustrates the Family's current emphasis on cultivating second-generation youth leaders and placing them in administrative positions of trust and responsibility. Both Cynthia and Densel say they want and need to update current Web sites and create new ones. Densel is particularly concerned about being as transparent as possible in providing internet users up-to-date and candid information about the Family's controversial history and beliefs. At the same time, the great majority of Web content is not new or original material; most of it is compiled, condensed, and edited from other Family sources.

Like all other WS departments, the Web Department's development of Web sites and their contents is ultimately subject to the "locals" review process that requires prayer and confirming prophecies from individuals outside the department, especially if sensitive rather than routine topics are involved. The primary locals for the Web Department are performed by the WS international board chairs, particularly the Church Growth and Outreach and General Public board chairs. The latter's public relations orientation represents a conservative, moderating influence with regard to the presentation and content of materials posted on the Family's open sites for public access. The more conservative orientation of these board chairs appears to create a small amount of tension with Densel and Cynthia's desire to gain support for greater openness and innovation on the Family's Web sites. At a higher level of authority, it is usually Peter with whom Cynthia and Densel communicate about Web Department plans and concerns. This reflects the apparent leadership division of labor between Peter—who focuses primarily on organizational and administrative issues—and Maria, who focuses primarily on "spiritual concerns" and publication of the GNs.

In addition to its public Web sites, the Web Department also maintains a member only (MO) site. This, for example, is used by Family Homes who submit their monthly home reports to World Services via email. Every Family Home has a password, which Cynthia oversees. Homes must change their password every time a Home member leaves or transfers to another Home. There also are different access levels to the MO site depending on one's level of authority and reporting responsibility. Like other complex organizations, the Family International in general and World Services in particular must anticipate and protect against unauthorized access to its internal, computer-dependent operations, where untold mischief could be done by unscrupulous hackers or organizational antagonists.

Among other topics of conversation in our interview with Cynthia and Densel (and also WS shepherd Thomas, who accompanied us) there emerged discussion of the Family's movement away from the specificity of David Berg's earlier end-time preaching to a more abstract characterization of conditions and events that betoken the final epic of human history. Like countless other millenarians before them, Family first-generation converts have been forced to adjust to the fact that the eagerly anticipated end did not transpire in their youth, as many thought it would, and subsequently they have had to rear a new generation with still fervent yet muted millennial expectations.[1] As the end-time calendar is pushed further back, first-generation parents now have faith-promoting stories to pass on to their children of their early sacrifices and struggles and God's miracles that sustained their commitment. Along with the second generation an oral history has begun to emerge that offers potential material for the Web Department's ambitious hopes of expansion and development of Family Web sites.

In this interview we also broached the topic of finding ways to ease the path of second-generation youth who lose their faith and attempt to make the transition into more conventional, secular lives, a recurrent theme in other WS interviews as well. And, in a somewhat related vein, we discussed the Family's growing need to provide technical training for its loyal young people, who represent the future both at World Services and in its international network of missionary Homes. Regarding recruitment of new blood into World Services, Thomas emphasizes that WS shepherds must authorize *all* World Services' department hires, including personnel for the Web Department. According to him, financial resources and budget limitations are not a significant problem in hiring new staff. Rather, the main hiring concerns are twofold: assuring that applicants have proper spiritual qualifications for the work, and keeping up with security issues associated with circulating an increasing number of individuals in and out of World Service positions.

Densel and Cynthia spoke with us at length about their backgrounds and job-related experience.

DENSEL: My parents, Timothy and Veronica, were working here at WS when I was born. Veronica was the very first WS staff person. When Dad [David Berg] and Mama [Maria] needed help in London, way back in 1970, they asked for my mom. She's a secretary—the very first WS staff person—and has helped Mama on the *GN*s for many years. She's Canadian; my dad's American. I don't know what she was doing in London at that time. My dad pioneered the Family Web sites. He got the first one up in 1995. It was pretty early for the Web, actually. He's extremely gifted as far as computer programming. He pioneered the whole computer system for World Services.

He has some interesting stories, like in 1981 or '82, about going to some of the first Apple expos and saying, "I've heard about these things called home computers, maybe we should get into that." And Dad and Peter were like, "I don't know what we need those for." But he kept looking into it and eventually computers came in. We couldn't operate without computers now.

My dad still keeps up with the latest advances. He always has an idea about something; he's a big innovator; he's always reading and studying up on it. He doesn't work here anymore at WS. He went into other things when Cynthia took over here in the Web Department, but he's very much up on all that stuff, much more so than me. I'm not actually as big a geek as he is—into all the actual technology and stuff. He still works with servers and access and all sorts of different stuff with people. He does the Family Board stuff [the Family's Area and International Boards, as discussed in previous chapters].

So, my parents were here since the very beginning, and I've grown up here. I started actually working on WS Web sites in about 1995. My dad said, "Well, I think you could help," and started training me. First it was every Friday and Saturday, then a little more, and then a little more, and then, when I finished my Family homeschooling, I just went into it all the way. We provide emails to different people that are on Boards, all over the Family. There are like 300 people that need email and email services, and my dad helps with that. And he ran some sort of a newsgroup type thing for communication at all the Board levels, not just here.

CYNTHIA: I guess I've been department head here ever since there were department heads, which was 2001 or 2002. That's when "the department head revolution" happened.[2] I took over from Tim. I came to WS in 1998 to be Tim's secretary. Two years later I became the team head, and then when we came here in 2001, we got into the whole department heads and work reports and work excellence emphasis.[3] When I first arrived at WS, I came to be a secretary and to work on content for the Web sites. So I did that, and then I just sort of got more involved over time. I'm not a real computer geek, but I know what I need to know to do what I need to do.

Before I came here I was a Regional Shepherd field secretary.[4] So I knew how to do secretarial work. I knew how to use a computer. I knew how to type. I knew how to do all that kind of stuff. But I'd never done Web work before. But Tim was involved in all of the technical stuff, so then I also got involved. He just actually gave me a lot to do. He'd say, "Here, I want you to do this." I was super happy to do it, because I like the Web, and I like learning new things.

Densel and Cynthia explain below their division of labor, which includes oversight of a number of Family Web sites and hosting of several others.

DENSEL: I set things up; I do the Web design.

CYNTHIA: I do the content and the administration, because we have 1,500 users for our members-only site. It's password protected and all of that. Each Home has a unique password and login. If you are a Home member, then you have the right to have access to the password and the user name to the site. If someone leaves the Home, then the Home teamwork has to send in a new password to us; they have to change their password. That then ties in with the TeleTRF, which are the Family's monthly reports.[5] A Home reports in their monthly reports when someone leaves. Only current Home members are supposed to know the password for that Home's login.

We give "service" people their own individual logins, because you can subscribe to get the *GNs* via the site, or the *MO Letters,* or any of the Family's publications. So a lot of people who are service-type people need to get it to their own email.[6] If they have access to the site, then they have access to whatever level of access they have. If they're Fellow Members, then they have access to all FM publications. But if they're Family Disciple members, and there's a *GN* that is for FD only, then they would have that access. We're hopefully going in the direction of giving each person their own login, but it needs to tie in with the TeleTRF, and that's not ready yet.

So I work on that kind of stuff, and Web content, and then just coordinating the department and the people. We have a programmer, a maintenance and server guy, and we have another guy who helps with maintenance. We have all sorts of small sites, but we have four main sites including, thefamily .org, activated.org, and Family Members, which is the Family members–only site.[7] And then we have smaller sites like Ricky's site, Angela's site, etc.[8]

Myconclusion.com is run by three young people in the field who have no connection with WS.[9] We designed the Aurora Productions site. And countdown.org is becoming ours.[10] We're hoping that each Home will have its own site. That's the goal. There are a lot of Homes out there that have sites. Also, the Activated ministries have sites. And we host local language sites. We have activated.org, but then there is Conéctate [conectate.org], which is Spanish, and we host for different Activated programs; but often the Activated desks do their own version of the site.[11]

DENSEL: There are probably over 100 sites in all.

CYNTHIA: But we really are only in full control of the WS sites. The content [for these sites] includes the text and the art and layout. We also have photos and audio and lots of text and testimonies and pictures, whatever it is that we put on it. Video clips, stuff like that.

With most of our sites, people contribute from the field, like testimonies, for example. But they need to be gone over and polished or in some cases rewritten, so I do that. On the Family members site we try to put up different things, like news articles that are interesting, or stories that we find that are good for children or for families—just extra little things, like Word compilations for people to use in their devotions.[12] Then on the GP [General Public] site, we put up news that the Family sends in, and stuff like that.

If it's testimonies and stuff like that, I P&P [engage in prayer and prophecy] to confirm it, then I make the decision to use it or not. If it's something *sensitive,* for example, like the Ricky site—we had to address suicide and that kind of thing—I pull content from a lot of things from prophecies the Lord has given, or General Public material that has been created, and pull it together and try to shape it into whatever it is that we need. Then depending on what it is, I'll send it around to say the Church Growth and Outreach Board or the Public Relations Board, or whatever board is affected. Then the International Board Chairs will go over it and give suggestions of what they think. They serve as my locals [editorial readers who employ "prayer and prophecy" in their reviews].

DENSEL: Creating *original* content [for the Web] isn't something that we've done in a long time, or not very often.

CYNTHIA: Not so much. We pull from other things, like taking something the GP did and something else we have and combining it to be exactly what we want; editing it, and then sometimes, of course, the Folks [Maria and Peter] will go over it depending on what exactly it is.

DENSEL: We run the site for thefamily.org. It's a little bit on autopilot right now. It needs a lot of help and attention.

CYNTHIA: We're hoping to redo it. We want to put a lot more into it, get it a lot better. It's an old site, and it's not really hitting the mark.

DENSEL: It represents the Family from 1995 to 2000, but not so much now. [Since this interview in 2005, the official Family Web site has been updated and undergoes periodic modification.]

CYNTHIA: We don't really feel it's what we want.

DENSEL: I'm chipping away at it little by little, trying to come up with a reimagined presentation for it all. There are two big stages. One I call the structure, and the other is the design. Structure will take me a long time. Both will actually take me a long time. Structuring it is actually just looking at all the content that we have, or even in some cases coming up with what we hope to have, and then giving it to Cynthia and saying, "We're going to make a new About-the-Family section. I think that's what we need. We're going to need this and this and this, and we want to present it like so." And she'll have to pull that all together. For instance, "I don't know that this section we currently have on the Endtime is really any good, so let's drop it and try to make something else in this other place." Sort of organizing it like that. And then the actual visual design, that takes time as well. It's a two-stage thing, and we're only in the early structure part right now, sort of looking at it, seeing what's needed, what isn't.

I'll draft it, and once it's at all coherent, I'll send it to all sorts of people. When I first started, I wrote a message to people here, even to my dad, saying, "If you have ideas when you look at that site or hear about things that it isn't doing or ways it may be missing the mark or things it could do a lot better, let me know." I sent that to the Church Growth and Outreach people and said, "Just give me ideas at this point." Eventually, once we have a little bit more of it together about how we're going to represent the Family with this site, we'll definitely send it in. I want there to be a lot higher level of input on a new site than there is now. The last one was created virtually alone. I came up with a lot of it, and Cynthia came up with a lot of it, and we just sort of did it ourselves.

CYNTHIA: Usually, for example, with thefamily.org, we look at it, and people in the Family also write us and say, "We think this about the site," or "We don't think it's doing this, or we think it should do this." So then I collect comments and we think about them and pray about them. With thefamily.org we look at it and ask, "Okay, what do we want to keep? What is it not doing? What do we want it to do?" Then we'll discuss it and get a general vision of where we're going and how we want it to be in the future. Then Densel will take it and break it down and structure it, and then we'll discuss it. We go back and forth and hash stuff out. Then I start working on getting exactly what we want it to say. Then he works on the design. The thing that holds this up the most is the programming, because that's really complicated and takes a long time, and we don't have the programmers that we need.

The main reason right now why we're not doing thefamily.org is because we've been redoing the Members Only site, and we're held up on the programming. Now we're just part-time doing thefamily.org, just as something to keep us busy while the programmer is still chipping away. We put up a big want ad on our site of exactly what we need and why it is so important.

We regard thefamily.org Web site as particularly important, because for the rest of the world it is the formal presentation of who and what the Family International is. It's the site that is linked to Family literature and everything else about the Family that goes out to the general public; people from all over the world visit this site.

CYNTHIA: We get tons of hits on it; generally, about 30,000 or 40,000 a month—not just hits, but distinct visits. We update it very week or so with more stuff, but we don't feel it is hitting the mark as far as giving as much information as we'd like about the Family, and also the "meat of the Word," which are the more specific Family doctrines. We respond to all messages from Family members, but not the "Activated" inquiries from nonmembers. The Activated Desk in California answers all of those. If it's for another area, like Europe, then the Europe Activated Desk answers that, or the Japan Activated Desk, and so on. We get copies of all the messages, just to make sure that everyone is getting them, but we don't have to answer them.

Thefamily.org gets by far the most email messages of all our Web sites. Every month is different, and of course if there is some story about the Family in the media, it's lots more. When I was at thefamily.org we'd get about 30 to 40 emails a day, and that was eight years ago. I think they get more now; definitely during the Ricky-Angela thing they were getting probably around 100 a day for a while. It just sort of depends, and it fluctuates. Thefamily .org site has a "daily praise" and words from Jesus that we send out daily, and people subscribe to the daily or the weekly or the monthly feature. While I was there, there were probably eight people who wrote two or three times every week, asking questions or asking for prayer. Actually, a lot of ex-members found the Family again via thefamily.org site.

DENSEL: That seemed to be one of its big roles.

CYNTHIA: Then they asked to get more contact. "How can we get more Word, because we used to be in the Family," and that's how the *Winepress* [a publication for former Family members] was born.

DENSEL: For me, I feel people need to know our history and doctrines, because if they're not hearing it from us, with the way the internet is now, they can go to the sites that our ex-members have and find more information and extreme details. Myconclusion.com deals with some of this sort of stuff, and down the road there may be development of a new "press room" site that will focus somewhat on controversial issues

CYNTHIA: Yes, there is a lot of exaggeration and stuff out there that could blow anybody away.

DENSEL: Extreme information, all the information you could want, all the dirty laundry and then some. So there's less harm now in tackling these things head on.

CYNTHIA: We feel like we want to get more of that out there, but there is the other side where members put the Web address on their tracts and give it to someone who knows the Family and loves the Family, but doesn't know everything in our history. Then they go on the site and read something that they're shocked or blown away by. So it is something that we've had to communicate a lot with the Church Growth Outreach and the Public Relations Boards about, and pray about, and come to an agreement about, with everyone on the same page, concerning what we want to do. We also talk with Peter regularly and tell him, "Look, this is our general idea." Of course, with any major site we are doing, we cc all the messages about it to him and have him look over it and, of course, Mama too if it's not too hard on her eyes. Like with thefamily.org, Peter said, "I really want you guys to get more out there. I would like it to be like a church, where every week we have a body of people that maybe can't go to a church, but they come to the site, and they get a weekly feeding, and they know that they can count on that." We have so much of God's Word, and the Web is a way of reaching millions of people with very little cost. It's very cost-effective as far as getting out the message. The reason we haven't made more progress really is because we don't have the programming help and personnel that we need. If we had two full-time programmers then we'd be able to do a lot more.

We have only one programmer, and he's been learning. When he came he didn't know that much, and he's really grown and learned. But the Family member site is very complicated, because you have the individual users and the different levels of access, and then you have the adding and editing, and the back end is really complicated. So it's taken him a long time to make progress on that, and we've had some serious setbacks. Then, of course, something like the Ricky and Angela murder-suicide thing happened; then we had to put everything aside and get two other sites up quickly, so that we could get our message out there, because the ex-members were just saying all this stuff and we weren't [responding]. Most people that had a memory of Ricky or Angela or whatever pretty much sent it in right away. But we still get feedback every once in awhile. However, most of it with the Ricky site is generally sort of negative.

We had learned elsewhere from Family public relations representatives that efforts are now under way to develop a special site for transitioning SGAs (second-generation young people who make a decision to leave the Family).

CYNTHIA: Yes, they are doing that. It will be called Changing Lanes. It was something that a number of people wanted, and we had put on the Members Only site quite a while ago, including different information on how to write a résumé, how to get a job, information about education, how to try to get a scholarship, how to do your income tax—all of these different things that people who leave the Family need to know. Then somebody wrote in and said, "Oh, it'd be really nice to have this out there for people." It will be open to everyone, so it'll probably help people besides those who are leaving the Family. It will demonstrate the Family's concern as an organization to assist those people within the Family who feel that being a missionary is not for them, and it will help to defuse the charge that the Family does not provide any assistance for people who leave it. And it also will save time, because not every parent will be trying to do that on their own. They'll have a lot of resource material that they can use.

Densel elaborates on his own hopes and future plans for Family Web sites, especially a new presentation of the Family's understanding of the end-time.

DENSEL: We're also involved in the countdown.org [posting items concerning the end-time]. We need a comprehensive Web site for our Endtime beliefs. It's sort of there, but it's not very well done, and it's not very well presented. It never has been. That's where a lot of original content is going to come into play—all the material that's been written, Dad's writings, and some of the new things the Church Growth and Outreach Board is putting together. Aurora is producing an Endtime series of books. I'll look at all that and try to make a Web site out of it, because that's been a neglected area for sure. If you look up other group's apocalyptic Endtime stuff online, it's all very poorly done, kind of stupid, UFO junk—little dancing aliens. It's not really anything very good. We can make a lot better presentation and get a lot of our basic stuff out there. Even the normal Christian eschatology stuff is not well presented, because it is a hard thing to present. Just doing these new sites is what I would want to do.

One of the main reasons for updating is, in fact, the Family's evolving theology of the Endtime. I posted on activated.org the other day; they have a section on the future. *Activated!* magazine has periodic Endtime articles, and there's something called the 14 major points of the Endtime. Reading that one article made me get a lot more excited about this project, because a lot of our understanding has been refined away from certain dates and specifics. I think what we aim to present would be the overall things that, from the Bible, we know have to happen; but not like "this has to happen by this particular time and this person today is that particular person prophesied in the Bible." We can look at the overall picture and say, "okay, at some point there does have to be a Rapture, there does have to be the Man of Sin, and one thing tends to follow the other," presenting it more like that.

My personal goal would be to try to steer it away as much as possible from specific dates and predictions. I even thought it would be kind of funny— maybe reinforcing the negative—but on the home page of countdown.org, have a little image counting down that says, "Click here to see when Jesus comes back," and you click there and then it's, "Ha, ha, of course we're not going to tell you when Jesus comes back!" No one knows when Jesus is going to come back. That's not what this is about. This is about what Jesus said would happen in the last days; look at our times we're living in; is there a connection? Keep it a little bit more general, which I think all Family theology is at this point. I don't think there's been a "date" given for a long time, so I think we're in a good place to present a lot of this. It'll probably raise interest.

End-time topics are of great interest to a lot of Christians. The Family's own sense of mission is organized around that sense of urgency; its mission is predicated on this idea of the end-time.

CYNTHIA: Yes, that's why we feel it's so important, because we haven't done anything like that in awhile, and also, one thing that sort of jump-started this project was we recently got a note from NBC, and they said, "We went to your Countdown site, and it's awesome, and we featured it as the top link to our revelation series."

DENSEL: It doesn't have bad information or faulty dates or anything; it's just very general and doesn't say a whole lot.

CYNTHIA: So we want to address everything: 666, the Antichrist, the Tribulation, the Rapture, and give our scripturally based take on what all those things are. Mama and Peter would have to go over it and approve it; and then there's Chuck. He works on the *END* [*Endtime News Digest*], so I would consult with him. And Scott MacGregor [*God on God* author], he works on the General Public Board. He also worked on the Endtime book; and then Frank and Barbara, because they're Church Growth and Outreach; and Joseph and Allan, because they do Public Relations. Those are the main people. I would work on the content and send it to them for their input, and "locals," and all of that.

Our conclusion, reinforced below, is that World Services operates like many other complex organizations in which departments have development needs but must formally justify expenditures and acquisition of new personnel and other material resources.

CYNTHIA: The plan is also for us to get a secretary, because if we had a secretary then she could be answering a lot of the mail or whatever, and that would free me up to focus more on content and also on coordinating things. All the International Board Chairs here want their personal sections on the MO site, and they all need it because it is so important; and we're like, "Okay we want to do all of this, but we can't do it unless we get more people."

So, we have to make that justification in a formal way to get approval in order to send out an advertisement. Approval requests go to the Shepherds; it's like almost every department needs personnel, and so the Shepherds say, "Write up exactly what you need and why you need it." Then they get the final approval from Mama and Peter.

THOMAS [ONE OF THE WS SHEPHERDS]: Well, I'd like to make a comment on new personnel. We put out want ads to Family Homes worldwide. We've had a lot of applications. One problem we've had is visas. We have people in the Ukraine or different places who would be perfect for WS, but visas are a problem. Another person wrote in and had all the qualifications to help her designated department, but she concluded with, "by the way, I'm married and have 12 children." So that's a little difficult. Finances are not a problem. We'll just keep going, right up the block to expand WS facilities if we have to. The Lord always supplies. Finances are not a problem. The *spiritual standard* is important. It's a unique personality that can live behind the scenes doing WS work. Presently in the Web Department they have someone who may be moving on. As much as they need valuable personnel, they have someone who can't work with the department, and we've got to have people that can work with the department. To get a person like that we've got to ask the former Shepherds he worked with, "How is this person?" There is another 18-year-old boy in South America, a programmer, who has all the qualifications, but he can't work with people. We could get him, but we've had some people come in to WS, work in a department, and then they leave the Family with valuable information [which the Family perceives as a potential security risk].

CYNTHIA: It's also hard to find programmers, because we don't have that many in the Family and it's a difficult job to do.

THOMAS: Yes, it's like an artist or an editor or a writer. They are creative, gifted, but they're temperamental.

DENSEL: Almost always young, single men.

CYNTHIA: Or sometimes they get into high-tech programming, and they conclude, "Oh, I could be making a lot of money in the outside world."

THOMAS: We've had a couple of people who came in to WS and then moved on and got very good System [secular] jobs out there. Some were favorable toward the Family and not enemies, but they're out there making lots of money. There also is a tremendous need for programmers and laborers out in the field, as well as here at WS. Tim, Densel's dad, who is an idea guy in computer programming, would love to go out and teach people, to organize seminars. Every year he goes to the computer fair in Las Vegas, and he looks at all the new inventions and tries to figure out what the Family could use and comes back with all kinds of ideas. So it's true, we need some kind of educational program that will motivate our young people and challenge them and teach them.

DENSEL: We don't want too many people though. Nobody else seems to ever worry about that, but I always worry about it. I worry that someday all of the Family is going be WS, and there's not going to be anymore Family—we're just all going to be doing office stuff. Ha! I guess for every person who's willing to do this sort of office work, there are many more people who would rather be regular missionaries. At least I hope so. We need so many people; soon it's going to be 1,000 of us in WS per 9,000 others in the field.

THOMAS: As the work becomes more technical and specialized, it does require more training. In the old days people could come in and go out and a new person coming in could quickly acquire the particular capabilities required for their job. That's no longer true. Now that there are people like yourselves, you're a scarce resource and WS doesn't want to lose you.

CYNTHIA: Also, the kind of programming that we need is pretty high level programming. Web sites used to be like HTML, which is very simple and user friendly, but now we're using major databases and scripting and all of this difficult code; people can't [just] come in for a few months and go through a Web course and know how to do it. It's more like years of working and studying. It makes it a little more difficult to find those kinds of people.

But with the Web you can do so much. I'd like to do a Family history site, where we outline our history with photos and multimedia, and a site about Dad [David Berg], and a site about Mama [Maria], and really get a lot of our information out there; our take on what our history is as opposed to what our enemies say our history is.

INTERVIEW WITH PUBLIC RELATIONS AND COACHING/ SHEPHERDING BOARD CHAIRS JEFF AND MELODY

In the Family International's organizational structure, all international board chairs (IBCs) are part of World Services. Collectively, World Services IBCs form the steering council for all regional boards and meet periodically with them to review the work being done in the Family's major "pillar" areas, namely: church growth and outreach, children and parenting, preteens and teens, Family education, coaching and shepherding, and public relations. A principal task for the international chairs is to coordinate the related agendas and activities of the Family's regional and national boards, which in turn are comprised of members from missionary field Homes in different parts of the world. International board chairs also sit on the Family Policy Council (FPC), which is the Family International's highest governing body. Every 12 to 18 months the FPC convenes Family "summits" in different locations around the world. In effect, summits are the Family's "Congress," consisting of various WS Leaders, international board chairs and regional shepherds, who, utilizing the same prayer and prophecy procedures described elsewhere in this book, debate Family issues and formulate official Family policies. Summit meetings demonstrate the contemporary democratization of Family governance at the international level, just as the decision-making procedures instituted at World Services do at the headquarters organization and Home steering councils do at the grassroots level of Family field Homes.

In the following interview we talk with two of the international board chairs, Jeff and Melody (we were joined in this conversation by WS shepherds Thomas and Vivian). Jeff and Melody are husband and wife; both are first-generation converts with considerable WS experience. At age 59, Jeff currently is the IBC for the Public Relations (PR) Board. With 14 years at World Services, he also continues to be involved in WS business and finance and is a member of the WS Administration Committee. Melody is 52 years old and, with 16 years in World Services, she is considered to be one of Maria's most reliable channelers and contributors to prophecies published in the *GN*. (Melody was one of the staff members present when we met with Maria and the GN Team, as summarized in chapter 2.) Melody currently is the IBC for the newly formed Coaching and Shepherding (CS) Board.

At the outset of our discussion with Jeff and Melody we concentrated on the public relations consequences of the "Ricky-Angela" murder-suicide that occurred in January 2005 (also referenced in chapters 1 and 9). Family leadership interprets the negative media coverage that this incident swiftly spawned to be part of the persecution to which God's servants must always be subject. Like other heretical religions historically that have been denigrated and attacked by outsiders and (especially) disillusioned former members or "apostates," the Family considers persecution to be a fundamental test of faith and commitment. Furthermore, in accord with other Christian fundamentalists, persecution is believed to be an essential ingredient in the anticipated "Tribulation of the Endtime" and, therefore, is also considered to be part of God's ultimate plan of redemption.[13] Loyal Family disciples believe they must be severely tried, that they must struggle and fight against Satan's surrogates' in order to be strong and worthy of God's commission.[14]

As is well known, conflict with other groups is, in fact, a major source of in-group solidarity and boundary maintenance.[15] In particular, it is the perceived unifying impact of the negative publicity that followed from the Ricky-Angela murder-suicide on second-generation Family youth—who were mobilized to defend against charges of misconduct and abuse leveled against their parents and Family leaders—that our respondents address in the beginning of this interview. At the same time, WS leaders have become increasingly sensitized to the problems of second-generation youth who lose their faith or no longer desire to be full-time Family missionaries. Concurrently, they have given increased attention to developing ways of easing the transition for young people who choose to leave the Family and enter mainstream society. In the final analysis, however, our WS informants maintain that their primary obligation is to continue to "serve the Lord" and to concentrate their primary efforts on encouraging their second- and third-generation young people who want to do the same.

_____

Jeff and Melody supplied us with further background information.

JEFF: I'm the International Board Chair of the Public Relations [PR] Board, along with Anson. We're supposed to stay on top of news about the Family worldwide, things that are happening, all the various activities. Usually, the bad news, ha! We work closely with Michael and Clarissa. They're the regional PR Board Chairs for North America. There are 12 world regions, and each one has a regional PR Board chair that we work with.

I was a little bit involved in making arrangements for your trip around the world to Family Homes. But Michael and Clarissa did most of it. The Family is very open to that [legitimate investigation]. We're very adjustable, very adaptable. I guess we have to credit most of that the Family's flexibility to Dad [David Berg]. He kept us very adaptable. He was always changing everything, ha! He had a saying, "If you don't like the way things are, wait two weeks and it'll change."

You met Melody's son, Mathias, in Mexico. I'm not his father, but I'll tell you a funny story about that. Melody and I first met in Japan, before we got together; then she went to WS, but Mathias fell in love with my eldest daughter. So then Melody and I got married, and our two kids got married too. Ha!

MELODY: We have three grandchildren. Jeff's daughter, that Mathias married, is not in the Family any longer. They have since separated, and he married Eunice, whom you met in Mexico.

JEFF: My oldest daughter lives in Atlanta. She's got three kids between her and Mathias. Then I have five others in various places—London, California, Africa, and Ireland. My youngest daughter is still in the Family, and she's in Dublin, Ireland. The rest are all out.[16]

As indicated here, the Ricky-Angela tragedy consumed a lot of time and worry for the Public Relations Board, but it has probably created more internal concerns than actual consequences with outsiders. Our respondents also perceive it as a faith strengthening test.

JEFF: We had an International Board meeting last summer in the Baja, down in Mexico. The murder-suicide with Ricky and Angela happened, and we all got quite involved in that, of course. It's been a major PR problem for the past six months, since January. A lot of this was Michael and Clarissa's [public relations directors for North America] backyard, so they handled most of it. We just counseled and communicated with them, prayed and would get Prayer and Prophecy for them, things like that. The funny thing is that it didn't impact our Homes much worldwide. The way I see it is that any tabloid stuff goes in one ear and out the other for the general public. It's just entertainment for them.

Often it works to our advantage, because people in contact with us—Family supporters and relatives—love us; they've known us for years, and they see that what we've been saying is true, that there will be religious persecution.

SHEPHERD: Well, what you say is true for those who have weathered the occasional media storms over the years. But there are new supporters, and there are relatives who have never been fully reconciled with the Family, who are just on the margins. Then something like this comes along, and it throws them for a loop.

JEFF: Yes, that's true.

SHEPHERD: In Michigan we had recent visits from Rochelle and Jordan from Hungary and from Nadene from Uganda. Both have parents who live in Michigan, and in both cases they have very tenuous relationships.

JEFF: Home visiting and trying to build fences.

SHEPHERD: Yes, to reconcile. It's been a very tedious, difficult process over the years. And then out comes this story—most recently a very negative *Rolling Stone* article [by Peter Wilkinson]—and it just revives all the old tensions again.

VIVIAN: But you know when we prayed about it and asked the Lord about it, the Lord said "That's part of My plan." Just like in the Bible, "there was a division among the people because of Him" (John 7:43). People have to make choices. It brings people forward. They have to make their choices in life. Some choose for the Lord. Some choose against Him. Some are confused, it's true. But it is a test and it was for a purpose. It brought people either closer to us or drew them further away, one or the other. It's part of the Lord's will in people's lives to make those choices. So even with the persecution, it does that. And it's really hard personally for people, because when your relationship with your parents is damaged because of some lies or slander, you have to trust that God is going to help people and bring each person individually to their choice about it. It can be discouraging when it happens, but it's all part of His plan.

THOMAS: Another thing: you refer to it as PR problem, and it was definitely a PR problem. But last year the Lord said that this was going to be our Year of Strengthening. We saw the effect that the Ricky-Angela murder-suicide had on our young people as far as their convictions were concerned, leading to the development of the My Conclusion site, and it had a very positive effect. I am sorry for the negative PR image with relatives and outsiders and the *Rolling Stone* article, but as far as our young peoples' personal convictions, it was the best thing that ever happened. They rallied together and are fighting for the Family. Sometimes we try to move the young people to grow and to take responsibility. In this case they felt that "they're attacking me and my lifestyle, and I'm going to stand up for it!" So what we saw with our young people was that it had a very positive effect.

MELODY: Yes. I think during the media blitz, when that happened with Ricky and Angela, the fight from our point of view was much more for the minds and hearts of the young people in the Family. Michael and Clarissa were doing the media interviews and writing the news releases and all that, and we were really scrambling to get the information to the Family, to answer when news articles would come out, helping Peter to do the notices that were posted on the MO [members only] site. These things were really critical to the success of coming out of that incident without too much damage to our own young people. The problem is, it brings up again questions that our young people are already shaky on, things that are under the surface, that they have a hard time with; and the apostates use anything they can to keep bringing up this old stuff from the past that has already been answered as well as it can be answered. It's over, water under the bridge, but not for them. So they just keep bringing it up and harping and using anything to try to stir up the pot again. And young people in the Family get destabilized, "Oh, did you read that?"' They're not forbidden to go on the ex-member sites, the apostate sites, obviously—they do, and even if they don't, they still get the apostates' barrage. They just send their junk to every email they have, and it's a real war of words.

JEFF: The Lord says that persecution makes us strong. It's what keeps us on the cutting edge and fighting for the truth, for what we believe.

VIVIAN: You don't have the victory without the battle. It's a test.

MELODY: And for us, on this end, it's really a lot of work, but it doesn't bring good fruit and make us stronger if it just runs its course without really fighting. You have to fight desperately in prayer, and fight to get the information out, and fight the Enemy's lies, and fight to get the Word. So many *GNs* have had to be prepared, and Peter's notices, and all kinds of things. It was unfortunate timing, because Peter and Mama were very, very tired, so it was a real hard few months. Peter had just come out of an enormously huge year, and they were actually trying to get some rest when it happened. It was really difficult to try to make it through those months—a lot of counseling; a lot of writing; a lot of praying and hearing from the Lord; lots of time on the phone with Michael and Clarissa. It was a very strenuous time. The fruit of it is wonderful, but had it not been such an attack, I don't think it would have turned out as it did. It doesn't work that way in the spirit. You have to really fight. Because those guys [detractors, enemies] are fighting. They were thinking that they had gotten a great victory. They were really going to do it this time. It was a pretty powerful attack. Their words were very strong, anointed by the Enemy [Satan], very powerful. So it took a lot to push it back, overcome it, and neutralize it. At least it did for us. And for you guys [now speaking to WS shepherds Thomas and Vivian], I'm sure, with all the shepherding and strengthening of the young people here at WS, it was probably very time-consuming for you.

THOMAS: I think it was a little easier for us. Melody's talking about the world-wide Family. The people here at WS know Mama and Peter, so their faith is a little stronger; their convictions are a little stronger. It did bring up issues that we needed to address, things that the youth didn't know about. But a lot of the attacks were against Mama and Peter, against WS—and our youth here live with them and know them.

SHEPHERD: One remaining issue coming out of the Ricky-Angela situation is with the youngest kids, the little ones. We know that you haven't said anything to them here, and that's generally true in most cases in the Family Homes that we visited; in most cases the children don't know about this. Of course, several young people here at WS grew up with "Grandpa and Davidito" [David Berg and Ricky, who as a child was called Davidito]; so that is a continuing issue that you need to address somehow. Do you have any plans for how to address that?

JEFF: I don't think we've crossed that bridge yet.

MELODY: That would be for the Child Care and Parenting Board to consider.

VIVIAN: I thought I already read something about that. Something like, "How do you read your Davidito stories [the Life with Grandpa series for children depicting David Berg as a wise and kindly father-figure] now with the kids?"

MELODY: Yes, there was something, but I don't recall where it was.

THOMAS: I don't really remember, so I wouldn't want to be quoted on it, but I believe that a GN did come out explaining that we're still going to teach the morals of the Life with Grandpa stories; they're still valid.

VIVIAN: It talked about Cain and Abel and Absalom and all those other Bible examples; that just because someone makes wrong choices later on, as Ricky did, it doesn't make their whole life wrong.

THOMAS: Yes. And I think that it's going to have to be explained to the kids at some point in their life what happened with Ricky and Angela.

JEFF: When they reach a certain age.

VIVIAN: The older ones already know. It's been explained to them.

SHEPHERD: We would guess that down the road there's going to have to be some alteration in the way history is presented to kids in terms of Davidito [see chapter 1].

JEFF: Yes, I would think so.

SHEPHERD: Although, as you say, you haven't crossed that bridge yet.

JEFF: Well, I wouldn't be surprised if the Child Care Board has crossed the bridge a bit, at least in their discussions and prayers.

SHEPHERD: But to the extent that this is incorporated into reading material for little kids, would there be new or different versions of the Davidito stories?

THOMAS: See, I don't know, it's not my portfolio, but many years ago we just had the Davidito stories. We still have them, but there are so many other children's publications now that it's just one of many. It's not like their whole faith is built on that one publication, or on one person.

JEFF: And it's not the *Davidito Book* [a quasi-documentary description of Davidito's early childhood, published by the Family in the early 1980s], because the third-generation children today don't even have it. We still have the Life with Grandpa that children now read, but the *Davidito Book* was a very big part of what our SGAs [second-generation adults] grew up with. Now it's not really used, although there are still very good things in it. Most of it is still excellent counsel.

We learned that the departure of SGAs from Family Homes has emerged as a signifi-cant issue. Various WS departments and international boards devote considerable thought and effort to moderate the attendant difficulties that arise when young people reject their commitment to the Family's communal missionary lifestyle.

JEFF: With regard to the proposed new Family Web site for SGAs who want to leave and need help in transitioning more effectively to living outside of the Family: Yes, it's still in the prayer tank. We have International Board meetings every year to year and a half, so at our next one that's going to be one of the main things we tackle—how to go about setting up more help for young people if they leave, so that they can get in touch easily with their PR boards around the world to find out how they can get help. The Child Care and Parenting Board is involved, and the Family Education Depart-ment Board is also involved. We're counseling about it and praying about it, getting different options on how we can do it.

SHEPHERD: Would there be a way of developing some statistics on people who have left the Family and have successfully made the transition, without be-coming antagonistic? The great majority have done that. It's a small minority who appear to have difficulty and who have become antagonistic. But that's impressionistic, and it seems to us that it would be helpful to know specifically how many have made a successful transition, what they're doing, and in what ways their experience growing up in the Family might have facilitated or hindered this transition. In many cases their Family experience has given them coping skills, interaction skills, people skills, performance skills, and technical skills that have allowed them to be successful in the world. This is in contrast to the claims of those who say, "We've been handicapped" by growing up in the Family.

JEFF: That's really good. It's just that we don't have the stats on what people have done after they left, other than those we are in touch with. But as you know, there are many thousands who have passed through the Family. I think we are putting out a new Home report form, and in there we're asking when people leave, what they do when they leave. We're now gathering that information. But as far as the past, I'm not sure how we'll track people down.

MELODY: You could probably track down a lot of the second generation through their parents, or just through putting a poll on the Family's MO site: "We're trying to find everybody we can from the past, have their email addresses— and if you're still in the Family, let us know about your kids, or brothers and sisters." If there is any one person who is still in the Family, we could probably get a lot of information. It takes a lot of work. You really have to follow up on every lead.

THOMAS: A lot of those people who have moved on have literally moved on with their lives, and they have busy lives now. They have jobs and kids and everything else, and although they are not vocal against us, they don't have the time to be vocal for us. They might write something, and there were a few messages posted on the My Conclusion site; it would be helpful to have that statistic. My older brother left, and he's still favorable toward the Family. He's taken in 25 young people who wanted to leave the Family over a period of eight years. He has three young people who are living with him right now. He regards this as a personal ministry. He loves Family kids, and he says that the core is a good foundation. If they don't fit in the Family, they're still good kids.

JEFF: He's helped them to integrate into the System [non-Family society], and a lot of them are in college now, graduating.

THOMAS: He has two rules. You get a job, and you do not speak against the Family. Those are the two rules. If you speak against the Family you're out. And he's done that even with his own kids that spoke against the Family.

When I heard about so many young people leaving the Family, I personally had the burden to help with the transition, because I felt it was a worthy cause and they needed that, like my brother does. I even asked Mama and Peter if I could do it, and they said, "If you feel the Lord wants you to do that, go ahead." I actually talked to a few of the Continental Officers about people who had done ministries like that, and what they explained was they would do it for two or three years, taking care of kids who left the Family. And they discovered that these kids wanted to experiment with drugs, or they just wanted to lie around, or they didn't want to serve the Lord. After two or three years, those who were caring for these young people came to a personal conclusion: "This is not what I want to do with my life. I gave my life to the Lord, to serve the Lord." It just wasn't fruitful. Our goal is to love the Lord and serve the Lord and to win souls. So when you're taking in a bunch of people who are going in the opposite direction, you come to the conclusion that: "That's not what I committed my life to." So many of those engaged in transition ministries ended up going back to full service in the Family.

JEFF: To take care of the young people who *do* want to serve the Lord.

THOMAS: Yes, invest in people who are going in the right direction.

VIVIAN: Not to demean anybody trying to do something for someone, but there are so few people who are willing to go full-time for the Lord and actually do missionary work, that I think they have to come to the conclusion that maybe in society there are other people who can help on transition, like Thomas's brother for example. He just loves kids, so that's sort of his calling. Whereas the other people that we were talking about, their calling was something else. Their calling was full-time service to the Lord.

THOMAS: My brother helps kids to adjust, but he wrote me and said, "You either serve God or Mammon—that's what the Bible says. I'm serving Mammon right now." That's an extreme statement. He's just honest about it. Ha. That's what's important to him. His emphasis is not missionary work at this time in his life.

JEFF: I think maybe one of the major problems in the Family, and for people who have left the Family, like our children, for instance, is that they feel, "Why can't you be with us?" My children say, "Why can't you not be in the Family and come out and take care of us?" Of course they are all grown up, but they still feel the same way. But it's like Jesus said, if He calls you to a certain thing, He says you have to forsake—whether it's children, families, brothers, or sisters—you've got to forsake it to follow God. "You've got to do what I've asked you to do." So that's the battle that all of us have in the Family with our children that leave. We love them and we try to spend as much time as we can with them, but we're called to serve the Lord as missionaries. I don't know if there is any way to resolve that other than we do our best to try and love them and show them concern, but we can't do more than that. They say: "Why can't you be here with us so that we can have grandparents to take care of our kids when we want to go out?" If I was *there*, I'd be happy to do that, but that's just not what I'm doing. I'd love to take care of my grandkids. They are wonderful. But I'm a full-time missionary for the Lord.

VIVIAN: It's a difficult thing because your heart goes out to people you love, wherever they are. You want to be everywhere. But I'm always encouraged by the Bible testimonies of the great men of faith and the old missionaries who had to leave their family, sometimes their wife, their kids, or they died on the journey. How did they do it? They had to have dedication, a calling.

CHAPTER 8

Managing the World Services Home

This chapter contains selected excerpts from interviews on aspects of communal living that both contribute to and complicate the work of World Services staff. As before, author comments and informational summaries are distinguished from the discussion.

INTERVIEW WITH HOME MAINTENANCE DEPARTMENT HEAD DON

Dedicated to supporting and guiding the Family International's evangelizing and missionary outreach activities, World Services functions as a complex and technologically sophisticated work organization. While it does this, WS also attempts to model the required standards of Family communal life for Family disciple Homes worldwide. Like Family disciples in the field, WS staff members participate in communal home activities in which their domestic arrangements are ordered by the Family's basic home management template, and their spiritual lives and personal problems are monitored and guided by designated Home shepherds (we interview WS shepherds in chapter 9). In this chapter we report our conversation with one of the World Services "handymen." We had hoped to speak at greater length with representatives of both the WS Home Care and Maintenance Department and the Child Care Departments in order to gain a more well-rounded appreciation for staff members' daily domestic lives. Unfortunately, within the scheduling limits of our four-day visit to the World Services facility we did not have enough time to see everyone who was penciled in for us to interview.

At 30 years of age, Don is a second-generation adult with four years of experience at World Services. In addition to performing the handyman work that occupies most of his time, Don is department head of Home Care and Maintenance, which includes supervising the child-care staff and teachers. Don says he has had to learn listening and mediating skills to do his job effectively. His wife is Roberta, head of the Art and Text Department (see interview in chapter 5), who was also present during this interview. In addition to Don, we also interviewed Esau, another WS handyman who has been doing handyman work at World Services since 1984. Unfortunately, our conversation with Esau was not recorded.[1]

According to Don, even in communal organizations like the Family, which so strongly emphasize cooperative goals and collective action, there is a temptation for managers to micromanage projects when they are held responsible for their departments' performance and end results. Department heads and managers at WS must learn to trust people under their supervision to do their work and make their own contributions. In Don's opinion, this currently is a struggle for younger second-generation adults, who recently have been appointed to managerial positions in World Services. According to him, new SGA leaders often "feel desperate" and seek advice and counsel from more experienced first-generation veterans. As remarked upon previously, this willingness to promote second-generation young people into leadership positions has become a distinctive and important hallmark of the Family's international organization. Don emphasizes the importance of learning what he calls "life skills," which are developed through organizational opportunities and the Family's many cooperative enterprises. In spite of the sacrificial demands of the Family International's communal religious culture, he eagerly anticipates the emergence of a talented third generation of missionary leaders.

DON: I was in Argentina for three and a half years, from 1989 to 1993. I worked there with some SGAs and FGAs who were good handymen, and they taught me a lot. Then the Regional Shepherds came to South America telling people to leave Argentina and go to other fields, because the Lord had told the Family that we needed to go elsewhere. So they came and we had a big meeting. Six other people and myself were like, "Okay, fine. We'll go to the States, and we'll leave Argentina." So we left Argentina, and then two months later the persecution hit. The Home where my mom and my sisters and brothers were staying got raided.[2] I actually went to live with my dad for awhile, because he had separated from my mom. They had been separated for five years, and I hadn't really grown up with my dad, so I wanted to go and see what it was like. He's currently living just outside of Bombay in a city called Puna. My mom and my dad got back together again; they have my two younger sisters, and they have a Home there.

When I was asked to come to WS, they said they didn't want to take me until they could find a replacement for me where I was. WS was thinking of moving from where they were at that time. So they said, "You can come anytime you want after you get a replacement, but don't rush it." By the time I ended up coming here to WS, it was June 2001. This house was already here, and they had just put the well in. We had a meeting, and they were talking about the Celestial Manor. I was like, "What's Celestial Manor?" [one of the residences for WS staff]. And they said, "That's why we brought you here." Ha! I was like, "Whoa!" Because I don't consider myself a real "handyman" handyman. I'm not super good at a lot of the details, but I can do a little bit of everything.

So I worked with other people, and it was a learning experience. We've had a lot of local contractors up here—electricians and plumbers and anyone who builds anything; we've learned a lot from them. I've learned that some things are important to do, like making sure that the infrastructure is set up right, and that your electric cables are a foot below water, so you don't go digging through water and hit your cables.

As he indicates, Don's prior qualifications for Child Care Department head are somewhat lean, but his responsibilities, although significant, are more managerial than hands-on. Like many other WS personnel, he grows in his job through self-education, on the job experience, and teamwork support from others.

DON: I'm also the department head for child care. I help on the schedule, but I'm not with them full-time. I just kind of manage the people who do the child care. I am a biological father, but I'm not a parent per se. The parents of my child are a couple in Africa; in Guinea. How is it that I'm head of the WS Child Care Department when I'm technically not a parent? I think there was just a need, or there was soon going to be a need here, so they asked me if I could do it. I'm a Home Manager, too, technically, with Gwen and Mari.[3]

Here in Celestial Manor, we don't have any FGA parents. They're all SGA up here. I did child care in the past—I taught for a year. I had a child-rearing class in Argentina, and I also took care of toddlers. But that's the extent of my child-care training. As far as my job here goes, it's more making sure that the teachers are okay, that they're taken care of, that they're getting their Word time [daily scripture, and personal prayer and prophecy time], that they're not stressing out, that they're getting time off. Also, that they're giving input to the kids and training and teaching them properly. I don't tell the teachers what they need to teach the kids or how to take care of them. Alice is the point person, so basically I go to her and say, "How are things going in child care? Is everything working okay?" And she'll say, "Can we have a parent-teacher meeting or child-care meeting to talk about discipline?" Or health problems, stuff like that.

So I just oversee it. I don't actually get super involved. Maggie is an FGA. She's been in child care for 15, 20 years, and she's very good, she has a lot of ideas. Alice is an SGA, and she has a lot of good ideas too. They're both very good child-care workers. They both take their kids and do the best for them. I don't have any comments like, "Why don't you try this?" They have it under control. They both are very motivated teachers. I have to realize, "Okay, Maggie knows a lot more about child care than I do as far as the technical teaching of one- and two-year-olds." If sometimes there are miscommunications between them, then I step in. I counsel with Alexandria [the Celestial Manor shepherd], because I'm not technically a Shepherd teamworker. I don't talk to Maggie or Alice about issues they're having in their personal lives. I mainly focus on the work. If there is a conflict of interest within the Child Care Department, I get involved in that and pray with them or listen to them and try to work things out.

Then, as far as the parents go, if there is an issue between the teachers and the parents—like the teachers feel we're feeding the children too much sugar, and the parents feel, well, this is a surprise or reward for them. And the teachers say they had cake today, they had ice cream yesterday, that kind of stuff, and "the kids are going to get sick." So that has been something we have had to talk about and pray about.

Don reflected on his administrative principles and inspiring others in cooperative work situations.

DON: One way to think of administrators is that there are two types. One type likes to micromanage what people are doing. They're often the ones who have more problems getting along with people in their unit. Then you've got administrators who see their job as providing resources for the people who work for them, and who focus on helping them to do their jobs rather than criticizing them, or trying to do their jobs for them.

I think in child care I'm more in the latter category of administrator as facilitator. In handyman I would have to admit I have a tendency to micromanage just a tad bit more, and I've had to pull back from that. I've read a lot of articles about how to inspire people to do work without stifling their initiative. Because in handyman, after being here for so long, in my mind, there's a certain way to do things. Whereas the people I work with, maybe they see it from a different perspective. Sometimes their ideas are even more practical and more applicable than my ideas. In the book, *The Ten Top Mistakes Leaders Make* [by Han Finzel], one of the points is if you give someone a job, let them do the job the way they want to do it, if it doesn't negatively impact the actual product. For instance, "We need to rebuild this pump house." I'm not going to go in and say, "Okay, I want it 5 feet by 4 feet." I'll say, "Can you just pray about a way to build this pump house the best way, and then let's talk about it a little and see if there are any needed tweaks," then I'll just let them run with it. Because what I've seen is if people are inspired about doing a job, and they get to have some say in what they do, they'll do the job twice as fast, and they'll do it with a lot more inspiration, and they'll feel fulfilled about it.

The times when I have micromanaged a little bit, maybe it came out the right way or the way I wanted it to come out, but it didn't always result in people feeling so good about it. So it has been a learning process for me. Ha! Because I am a detail person, and believe if you're going to do a job, you might as well do it well and do it right. We did a lot of work on this house here. We wanted to resurface the roof—it was caving in. Doing the job along with the people under me made a big difference: instead of just telling them to do it, and then ordering them around, I did a lot of the work with the guys, got up on the roof and endured the sun and tar. Or I went underneath the house with the insulation and mice.

Dad [David Berg] always said, "It's a do-it-yourself-religion. You can do anything you have the faith for." I guess there's a balance, at least in my mind. It takes a person with initiative to do something, it takes someone to pioneer. But if you want help, then you have to get other people inspired to do it, too. For example, if you want to change the yard, you can get out there with the lawn mower and do it in three days. Whereas if you tell people, "Look this lawn is really long, let's cut the grass together. Can everyone help?" Like we did with the property a month or two ago, "Let's clean up the property." You get everyone inspired, "There'll be a surprise at the end," a drink or something like that, and the property was done in two days, and it's very cool. If you don't motivate people, you don't inspire them. You do the job, but you don't grow as far as life skills are concerned

There is so much to do, if you try to do it all by yourself, and you just stomp on everyone else, you'll never get the job done. In that way, it's imperative that you work with others. Not that that's the reason why you work with them— just to get the job done. Part of our life is the *living* of life rather than just the end goal, which for us is to win the world, to witness. At least that's what I have to keep reminding myself. I can be very goal oriented. Like, "Let's win the world for Jesus, no matter what it takes. Let's just do whatever it takes to do it!" But then it's like the story about the old grandfather who took his grandson on a boat ride to this special cove, and the kid was freaking out the whole time, "When are we going to get there? It's taking so long." Then at the end the grandfather says, "Well, the one thing you learn in life is that the journey is part of the destination." It's like enjoying the journey and getting there with others and having a good time doing it is actually part of the goal.

Well, those are the things I have to keep reminding myself of, because I've very idealistic; I try to change the world. I'm a perfectionist about certain things, like my work. I try to do the best I can, because I grew up reading the MO Letters, and Dad [David Berg] knew the difference between quality and quantity. He said that we want it done right, and we want it done now, but we shouldn't lose perspective of the bigger picture. So I'm a perfectionist by nature, but try to balance it out with, "Let's just get it done and do it the way the Lord wants us to do it." And that is what it really comes down to for me, hearing from the Lord.

We were told that Family first-generation adults repeatedly claim that the second generation of young adults is more talented and skilled than they, and that the biggest issue is to simply be able to turn over the reins and let SGAs take the lead. Don, as an SGA, sees the need for balance between the first two generations and then anticipates the emergence of an even more talented third generation.

DON: My parents have certain qualities that we as second-generation don't have, like more patience and long-term vision. We grew up thinking Jesus was coming back in 1993, so for us everything was "we have to do it now." Now, now, now! For me, I am continually faced with "today," with "let's do it!" Whereas our parents and FGAs are like the brakes a little bit, and we're like the accelerator. It takes all kinds to drive the car.

I for sure still look to older FGAs who have experience; you try to seek out their suggestions, especially when it comes to working with other people, interpersonal communications, and personnel issues. With energy you can do anything when it comes to technical problems, if you just try hard enough. But when it comes to working with people, it takes patience; it takes a lot of love just to listen, which I wasn't used to. Having been given the responsibility of administration jobs or managerial positions that we don't feel we have the talents or the capabilities to do, makes us very desperate to counsel with other people to get input and training. I had never headed up a department, and when I first started, it was eight people. I was like, "How do I manage eight people?" I have my own work ethics, but when it comes to helping others, it's really different. What it really comes down to is a lot of prophecy, a lot of hearing from the Lord, a lot of counseling with others and learning through both trials and successes.

I look at Shane and Servilla [two teens living with their parents at World

Services], and I see in them a lot more talent and capability then I personally have or ever will have. They're junior teens. I took them out for a hike yesterday, and these guys are just like fountains of knowledge and wisdom—maybe more knowledge than wisdom. Ha! But I look at them, and I say, "Wow, these are the guys who are going to be in the place that I'm in now. They're like 16, 17 years younger than me. It's a different generation. I'm inspired about them, their generation. I look at them, and I say, "I'd like to inspire them with the vision the Word has given me." They are so talented, and they have so much drive. I'm 30 years old. I'm not pushing old age, but in 10 years I'll be 40. In 10 years they'll be in their 20s. As far as continuing the revolution, Dad always said, God has no grandchildren. Every generation has to make the decision for themselves to keep things moving.

INTERVIEWS WITH THE SHEPHERDING TEAMWORK OF THOMAS, VIVIAN, LEM, AND ALEXANDRIA

The primary task of those assigned to be Family shepherds is to monitor the unity and spiritual standards of the Homes in which they live or serve. It is the shepherds' specific charge to maintain disciple standards at World Services, as well as in Family Homes worldwide. According to our informants, much of what WS shepherds do is personal counseling. We were told that the most common shepherding problems at WS turn out to be "relationship problems." These consist of both work connected relations and "personal" relationships, especially for second-generation young people concerning "mating" issues, jealousy concerns, and the Family's communal doctrine of sexual sharing. The shepherds conceded to us that marital instability is a major problem within the Family, one that can cause especially divisive conflicts when issues of child custody are involved and one mate wants to leave the Family while the other wants to stay.

In conformity with the positive value placed on human sexuality embodied in the Family's core Law of Love doctrine, WS leaders and first-generation parents expect (and want) their children to become sexually active. The Law of Love and corollary practice of sexual sharing are not tantamount, however, to sexual licentiousness. The Family charter explicitly details what level of sexuality is lawful for what adolescent or young-adult age groups and imposes strict rules against adult-minor sexual contact.[4] We learned that WS shepherds counsel youth against rushing into things and against getting too serious in romantic relationships at an early age; they urge young people to make responsible decisions about getting pregnant and assuming the obligations of parenthood. That parents and youth struggle with dating, sex, marriage, and parenting issues at the World Services headquarters organization—in much the same way that parents and their children normally do everywhere—serves to remind us that Family members cannot adequately be comprehended as "brainwashed" zealots who robotically obey the commands of unscrupulous leaders. Rather, official acknowledgment of these kinds of normal human problems and contentions—and their leaders' pragmatic efforts to grapple with them—helps to cast a humanizing light on the communal foundations of the Family's religious way of life.

The shepherds from World Services units meet together every Tuesday for assessment discussions during which they typically engage in prayer and prophecy regarding various WS organizational issues and concerns. The procedures followed at these weekly staff meetings illustrate the democratic communitarian ethos that has come to pervade the Family International's mode of operating at all levels of the organization. (By "democratic communitarian ethos" we mean the organized attempt to balance the needs and rights of individuals with the commonweal interests and concerns of the community as a whole.)[5]

The shepherds also consult periodically with WS department heads regarding the functioning of their units and discuss personnel issues and work related problems. They attempt to facilitate communal principles of sharing and cooperation among and between departments. The shepherds' job is not just to monitor and give counsel but also to discipline when necessary. WS shepherds are authorized to impose penalties on any wayward WS staff members who fail to meet disciple standards, either on the job or in their personal lives. (According to our informants, this is more likely to be necessary in Family field Homes than at World Services, were most staff members tend to be highly dedicated and conscientious about their roles in the Family's leadership organization.) In addition to their organizational monitoring and counseling duties, WS shepherds also are responsible for evaluating and vetting all WS job applicants, as indicated in previous interviews.

Three of the WS shepherds (Lem, Thomas, and Vivian) work together at the principal WS residential home. Alexandria teams with Wesley (who was not present for our interview) at Celestial Manor, another residential home. Noteworthy is the fact that all current WS shepherds are FGAs with many years of Family experience. In the field, however, young adults born into the Family (SGAs) are now being cultivated as "coaches" in a new Family oversight program to be discussed more fully in chapter 9. Lem, age 52, has served seven years at World Services. Thomas, 51 years of age, is married to Vivian and has been a member of the WS staff for 24 years. At age 48, Vivian has had 25 years of WS service experience. And Alexandria, age 53, who was Peter's young wife when they joined the Children of God in 1971 (they subsequently separated on apparently equable terms after having three children together) was asked to be a WS shepherd in 2002. Since we interviewed Alexandria separately from the other shepherds, we will detail her interview after first reporting the other interviews.

THOMAS: We [WS shepherds] meet once a month to touch base with WS department heads to see how it's going with their work. Our emphasis is the spiritual, so we try to arrange spiritual activities in their schedules. Their mandate and responsibility is the practical, in getting publications out to the Family. So there's got to be coordination, us working with them. Within the departments sometimes one will say, "We have a lot of deadlines, we have a lot of pressure," and another department will say, "Well, can we help you?" and so the communication helps to sort that out.

LEM: We try to reinforce the idea that, "Hey, we're here to make your job easier. We're here to keep your people happy and help you." And a lot of the department head meetings are about what are their problems, what are their pressures, how can we relieve them and how we can work together.

THOMAS: Any coordinated army needs a general or a boss, someone to keep things organized. The Folks, specifically Peter, started out coming to these department head meetings and explaining to the Shepherds that departments have their mandates, and they need to get their work done; and also explaining to the department heads that our communal living and community service is important too, and there's got to be a balance in that. So he sent a clear sound of the trumpet as to what the standard was. We have what we call four pillars in World Services: spiritual life, work life, personal life—which involves free time activities—and community life/community service. These are the four pillars that we try to balance out to make sure everything is getting the proper attention.

LEM: Someone might be extremely high on the work pillar, for example; they might work 70 hours [a week], but they might not be able to get along with the people they live with or have any social interaction or loving Christian fellowship. And that's important in order for their work to be carrying the right spirit, so we try to keep everything balanced.

It appears that a high proportion of Family marriages wind up in separation or divorce. The shepherds recognize this as a problem that needs to be improved.

LEM: Yes, I think it is a problem and has been a problem.

THOMAS: Of course we have quite a colorful history, as you know, along the lines of sex, and there were a lot of mistakes made. Our SGAs, our younger people growing up in the Family, said "we're not going to make the same mistakes that our parents made." But a lot of them have told us that they've done the same things or made the same mistakes. Now we, as Shepherds, can almost see when a relationship is not going to work. And we have counseled people that "you're not fit for each other; I would really pray and make sure it's the Lord's Will." And they were determined out of love for each other to go in the direction they felt they wanted to go, and it didn't work. So it's a balance between us making a decision for them and them making their own personal decisions.

VIVIAN: Like a recent couple, it just wasn't working. When we counseled both of them, we saw there were core issues, but they were thinking, "Do we have kids, do we get married?" They'd been together for three years and they had core issues. So with them, we had them pray, "Are these deal breakers? Look at these things that for three years you've been talking to us about." And they did, and they prayed and asked the Lord about it. We talked with them both individually and together, and they separated amicably. Now one of them is very happy with another person, and the other one has three girlfriends. Ha! That was a separation that we knew was coming from the beginning, but they wouldn't have done it without help. Because of what they were telling us, we had to honestly tell them, "You know, you guys have core issues. You need to pray about it. You need to talk about these issues."

LEM: There are so many cases. For instance, I come from a broken home. I was really affected by my parents' divorce. And then, like the SGAs in the Family today, I swore and was determined not to make the same mistakes. My goal in life was to have the perfect family, perfect wife, perfect kids, everything was going to work, and I was just convinced of it. But God has seen fit to work very differently than what I set out to do. And I can't say, looking back now, that it was a mistake or we failed. I've been in five relationships. I've been legally married three times. Each one of them was a success, because each one of them was used at a particular time in my life to accomplish what the Lord wanted to do, and not only in my ministry. I think in each case I got together with a woman because it fit a need, and it worked for a time. And then that need changed, and suddenly the relationship changed. And God just did it. It just happened.

We have observed over the years in our studies of the Family that some of the disaffected SGAs are bitter about the separation of their parents, claiming that parents were so involved in their ministries, traveling, and maybe mated with someone else, so that, as children growing up, this was, for them, a source of trauma. Although, from an adult perspective, this may have been part of a sequence of things that contributed to one's ministry, from the perspective of the children, it's a problem.

VIVIAN: In some ways, yes, and we've addressed this. We have what we call an R3 group [in which relationship problems are discussed]. It's during the young people's free time, and it's a voluntary thing. It's grown to include almost all of them now. But it started out with just a few that wanted to spend their Wednesday night really digging into the meat of personal issues in their lives. Right now it's just in WS; we started it in WS, but we're presently working on a publication to get it out to the whole Family.

VIVIAN: One of the questions we have addressed in R3 meetings is our Law of Love [Family doctrine that includes sexual sharing] issues. It was really interesting, because one of the girls said, "I was so bitter towards my mom for her relationships—from the perspective of a child. But now that I have my own children, I understand totally. Once I made the same mistakes a couple of times myself, my resentment is gone, my bitterness is gone, and my perspective is changed." It's so difficult for us, when we're younger, to have the right perspective on adult issues, and I think that's what we're seeing with some of our young people, that those who have matured, have totally changed their perspective. It was a sensitive issue. We had no idea what feedback we were going to get. We were like, "Whoa! We really need to come back and talk about this in smaller groups." Because we talked about it with about 40 of our young people, and there were all sorts of explosive things being said. People were looking at the other person and saying, "What are you talking about? You're not living the Law of Love! How can you be saying that?"

Then we got it down to smaller groups. Because we knew it was a sensitive and explosive issue we did scenarios. "So-and-so are living together in a Home, and a new guy comes, and this happens." And then we could talk about it as "not me," but they were definitely fitting scenarios. Then people got to talk about what was right, what was wrong, and how they would do it, and what they would do. They know what the Lord would say to do. There's the textbook answer, but how would you actually live it and how would you feel? So we addressed a lot of those things on that type of level, and it was very helpful and fruitful. It was interesting to me to see that, yes, as children we judge our parents in all sorts of ways. I had so many judgments of my parents when I was young. I'm sure they were trying to understand me, but to me they were clueless. But, as you get older, all of a sudden, all those perspectives change, because you go through the same things that your parents were going through.

LEM: Like, I said, I was greatly affected by my own parents' separation, and, of course, I couldn't blame it on "the System," or the world, or the Family, or anyone. I just blamed it on them. Then when at 50 years old, I finally talked to my dad and said, "Yeah, because you guys did this, and you guys did that." And he was like, "No, we didn't." I said, "Yes, you did. I remember." And he was like, "Well, you were just 10 years old!" That's the way I remembered it, but it wasn't like that. I saw the hurt in my own son when my wife and I were separated. He could have come out extremely bitter if he had chosen to.

But he chose not to. He made the right choices. And I'm sure his mother helped him to make those right choices. That's what parents have to do. We were together about seven years.

VIVIAN: I would say that we definitely counsel them [unmarried SGAs at WS] mainly to pray, mainly to ask the Lord and hear from the Lord on what they're doing, maybe to be a little safeguarded; sometimes with emotions things move very fast. We counsel them about being very prayerful about what they do sexually so that they don't end up with a pregnancy they hadn't anticipated. We're pretty open with them as far as getting them to pray about what they're doing. Maybe there's just not the enforcement to encourage people to pray. Even we don't do it as much as we could; probably because it's an invasive type of thing. It can be, if you don't do it properly. Otherwise, people will say, "This is my personal life. This is my relationship."

LEM: For instance, one of our current detractors was in WS when she was a young girl—pretty, smart—supposedly smart. We thought she was smart. But she was immediately attracted to one of the young men, and we said, "Go slow. Go slow."

VIVIAN: I mean we counseled her more than anyone.

THOMAS: We sat down and specifically said, "Do not have full sex. Do not have full sex," to both of them.

VIVIAN: And I told her, "I know your personality, if you are hot one day with him and then cold tomorrow, you're going to be so sorry. Don't do it. Don't go there." And she came awhile later and said, "I know you told me so, but I'm pregnant and I don't want anything to do with him." And I'm like, "Oh no!" But people make choices, and we work through that with mediation. I talked to him. I talked to her, and we agreed on a parenting arrangement. We agreed on all of that, and she refused any of his help. He would have married her; he would have been an excellent father. He loves his kid. Now she is an active ex-member, very active. And her whole thing is, "My daughter needs her father to visit every year." And I say, "Do you remember what you did to the father? Do you remember how much hurt you caused him, how you took away his daughter, how you refused to let him help?"

LEM: She's saying, "But my daughter is going to grow up so hurt that her dad's not there for him."

VIVIAN: So it's a very difficult decision for him now, because not only does she actively fight against the Family, she goes on television programs, she's actively attacking his lifestyle, and then saying, "But you need to come and be with the child." Even afterward she wrote us, "I'm so thankful you guys understand. It was really difficult for my dad, but I know you guys understand, you helped me. I know you did everything you could to help me." I still have those letters. But the tune just changes as time goes on, and they kind of forget what history was.

THOMAS: The father of this girl said, "You know, when she left our relationship was very favorable. She just wanted to flap her wings, to try something else." And then over time, it got more and more negative.[6]

VIVIAN: It's very sad. But now the fellow who is the father of her child is in a huge predicament. Of course he wants to see his child; that's not a problem—he's totally willing to go visit the child, but what he doesn't want is the mother there who is antagonistic. How are you going to cultivate a loving relationship with your child when you're being attacked by the mother? Her take is, "I won't attack you when you're here visiting my child." But what she doesn't realize is that she's trying to undermine him. What she does could easily cause persecution, could easily cause him to be attacked by others, his whole lifestyle. And she doesn't put those two things together; that's not reality to her. She thinks, "Well, I'm nice to you, but of course I'm going to fight the Family." And he has to say, "I'm in the Family, remember that?"

THOMAS: I think when it comes to marriage and relationships, it is a problem in the Family, but it's also a problem when people's values change. After a period of time, they don't want to live by faith, they don't want to be in the Family, and they've already had kids. Some singles have come to us and said, "I'm just concerned about getting married, because what if my husband settles down and wants to get a secular job? I don't want to do that. I want to be in the Family." This is a case where the young person decided to leave the Family. We've had other people in WS where the husband didn't want to live by faith anymore, so the wife went with the husband, but it was very difficult for her. And there have been situations where people wanted to stay in the Family, so the wife or the husband left. And there's a child involved there.

VIVIAN: I don't know what is happening in the rest of the Family, but here in WS, young people are waiting longer. We have 30-year-olds that aren't married. I think they're being more mature. I think we're having fewer single parents in the Family because people are praying more. They're taking more time to make those decisions. We're almost encouraging them to do the opposite now—not marry so young.[7] Ha!

LEM: I think they have an advantage too. I mean, Dad, always said from the very beginning, "If you don't learn anything else, you've got to learn to hear from God." That's what he taught from the beginning, but we didn't put it into practice until recently [i.e., Maria's renewed emphasis on corporate prophecy for every decision]. And if you want to hear from God about anything, it's relationships, because that's going to affect your whole life. So if there's one thing you want to ask the Lord about and follow His counsel on, it's that. And that's what our young people are benefiting from I think, at least the ones here at WS. Even when they make mistakes, they learn from it quicker because they go and pray about it, and the Lord says, "Well, you should have done it this way," or "you should have talked to him that way," etc. So maybe they don't go as far making the same mistakes we did.

Other Family members had previously told us that in the Family's earlier days people were sometimes "mated." It wasn't necessarily a consideration of compatibility or even mutual affection; it was more like, "We need a pioneer team, and you guys are it," as one informant put it. The WS shepherds explain what current attitudes are.

LEM: Actually, come to think of it, I did the same sort of thing. I got together with people who I thought, "We'll make a good team together." And we didn't necessarily make a good team. Ha.

VIVIAN: But I don't think that's still happening. People have free choice, free will. About that couple we counseled concerning separation, I want to clarify that that's probably just one in the last 10 years. And that particular couple, I used to read every week with them from the "Marriage Book," and we were trying to make it work. We really tried to get the communication going. And once the communication actually happened, they realized, "We don't want to go there." Once they could actually talk about it and get their issues on the table properly. But it's pretty rare that we'll counsel anyone to separate.

THOMAS: We really promote marriages working and keeping the families and the kids together as much as possible.

LEM: And thank the Lord, in that case, there were no kids.

VIVIAN: And that's what got us concerned. Their friends were saying, "When are you guys going to have kids?" They wanted to have kids, but they didn't want to have kids with each other, so that's a core issue. Ha! Both of them were dying to have kids, but if in their relationship they'd been together that long, and they didn't want to have kids together, someone needed to be helped out. I just wanted to clarify that. I think our main thrust is keeping people together and working through their problems and not bailing out; making sure that the people, who are together, get together for the right reasons in the first place.

INTERVIEW WITH HOME SHEPHERD
OF THE CELESTIAL MANOR HOME, ALEXANDRIA

Prior to coming to World Services at Peter and Maria's request, Alexandria was serving as a "Continental Officer" in the central United States (continental officers have subsequently been replaced by regional shepherds in the Family International's organizational structure). Alexandria had worked previously in

World Services from 1984 until 1987, when David Berg was still alive. Although now divorced from Peter, she appears to be on friendly terms with both Peter and Maria. Alexandria confirmed to us that "Law of Love battles" revolving around romantic and sexual attachments have been a problem for many SGAs. According to Alexandria, personal-relationship problems and their subsequent connection with management issues are of considerable concern to Peter, who sees it as a problem to be resolved through more effective leadership training. Peter is intent on developing SGA leadership skills through seminars and a new "coaching" program.

To be effective in their work, shepherds must have good people-handling skills and, like effective counselors everywhere, they must be sympathetic listeners and able to cultivate the trust of those they counsel. WS staff members often send their "personal prophecies" to their designated Home shepherds. These personal prophecies can provide shepherds with useful feedback regarding personnel functioning and potential morale problems. Staff members apparently understand that, in counseling with a shepherd in whom they place their personal trust, their occasional complaints, expressions of doubt, or personal troubles will be shared with the entire shepherd "teamwork," and that, in the event of confessed violations of disciple standards, they may be subject to disciplinary punishment.

In the shepherd's role as both confidant and rule enforcer we see a clear working example of Rosabeth Kanter's theoretical analysis of the structure of social control in cohesive community organizations.[8] In Kanter's analysis, institutionally channeled confession and discipline are forms of "self-mortification," which in turn function as a commitment mechanism binding members to group requirements. According to Kanter, however, in order for self-mortification to be effective in maintaining social control (which is to say, conformity to group norms), it must be balanced by shared transcendent beliefs (such as the Family's belief that they are God's chosen end-time disciples) that justify for believers the mortification of their personal egos in the service of a higher cause. Thus, Alexandria believes that her own trials and struggles living in the Family have served God's purpose of testing and refining his chosen servants, enabling her to empathically fulfill a shepherd's role in ministering to other Family members and their problems.

At the same time, we infer that the Family's ultrasupernatural belief in prophecies channeled from the spirit world functions, in part, as another commitment mechanism for reinforcing compliance with organizational rules and community values. Thus, for example, in performing their counseling roles, Family shepherds urge staff members to "to hear from the Lord," producing counseling messages attributed to Jesus, which subsequently are shared with the shepherds. In effect, when channeling personal guidance prophecies, Family members are asking "What would Jesus say or do about problem X," in the context of counseling with a shepherd, who is believed to be "anointed" or spiritually authorized in providing inspired guidance. The answers, as they comes to petitioners, typically reflect the voice of the religious community, embodied in the core values and doctrines with which Family members already are quite familiar and which, in turn, are most likely to receive approbation by the shepherds. These kinds of personal prophecies are what Rodney Stark calls "normal revelations"; they are revelations that reinforce foundational beliefs rather than expressing radically new directions or contradictory values.[9]

Joining us at the end of this conversation was Clarissa, a member of the Family's public relations board.

ALEXANDRIA: Before I came here, I was a Continental Officer in the central area of the U.S., so I did a lot of traveling in the States, and I got to see a lot of our Homes then. I've been here at WS for almost three years.

I was asked to come. I was very surprised. At that time Thomas was making a trip to Africa, and they said they really needed help, and they were wondering if I would pray about coming. It was very much of an answer for me, because I like working with people, and my job at the time was more administrative; more on paper. So when I prayed about it, the Lord indicated that it was His gift of love to me, and I've been here ever since.

The organization of shepherding has gone through much change, especially in recent years. But Alexandria indicates that she follows the same basic interpersonal process that she has always used, seeing shepherding skills more as a gift and as a result of personal experience than as the result of training.

ALEXANDRIA: In my shepherding over the years, a lot of it is just being there for someone, and encouraging them to ask the Lord and find out what He wants them to do; that's always stayed the same. I know there's been more training, especially for our SGAs. But I think sometimes people just want to talk about a problem and have somebody there to listen. I think almost everyone knows you need to go to the Lord, but sometimes it's difficult when you're right in the midst of a trial or a hardship.

I know over my life in the Family I've gone through quite a lot of tests and trials myself. Ha! And I know that the Lord has engineered that for a reason, because [with] almost everyone that I talk to, I can understand almost everything that they're going through and what they're feeling. Many times, when I've gone through bigger things in my life, I've thought, "I don't want to be in shepherding anymore," because it requires going through all of these personal trials, so that you can be understanding and know where people are coming from. I know that the Lord has used a lot of things in my own life where I've had to go through things; I've seen that that's the only answer. You have to stop and not look at it through your own eyes and your own perspective, but really try to get His perspective on it, which is not so easy to do when you're in the midst of some difficulty.

In our teamwork, I find that when I'm working with the managers, who are all SGAs, they tend to want to come to me—probably because I've been shepherding longer than some of the SGAs—people their own age. I know they do talk a lot with their friends, but most of the time I think friends encourage them to go to the Shepherds, because they feel that they're going to get better counsel in that way.

As we already knew, many parents have had to deal with the departure of their children from the Family, which becomes especially problematic if the children then become negative or even openly hostile.

ALEXANDRIA: I've talked to a lot of parents who have been in this situation, hearing the difficulties and the hardships and the heartbreak. I think a lot of that is putting myself in their shoes, to the best of my ability, trying to understand what it would be like, and helping them in that way. I guess any kind of heartbreak that you go through can help you in some ways understand another kind of heartbreak, too. I did wonder for awhile, even with Jason [one of Alexandria's sons], if he was going to stay in the Family.[10]

In addition to one-on-one counseling, the shepherds, as a teamwork, are also responsible for monitoring the overall level of group morale and organizational functioning and insuring that disciple standards are being met. Alexandria explains how these responsibilities are carried out.

ALEXANDRIA: Here at WS, a lot of it is just walking around talking with people. I hear a lot from one person about things that others are going through. I'll pray about it and then go talk to the other person. People are encouraged to hand in their prophecies; I hear a lot of what is happening through the prophecies that are sent in to me. Then, when we talk together, I understand where they're taking it because of what the Lord has given them in prophecy. People want me to be aware of what they're going through, and what counsel they're getting from the Lord, so I can help them to implement that counsel.

Because people do get a lot of beautiful counsel from the Lord. But it's sometimes difficult for them to put it into effect, so they just want the help. I can remind them of what they received and say, "Did you do that?" Or to come at it with more detachment so that they're able to see the whole thing:

"It seems to me that your prophecy is saying that three things are interconnected here." They may be seeing only one thing; they're not seeing the entire picture. So you can help them, in effect, to understand or interpret what they themselves have come up with.

I think you pretty much have to prove yourself to gain people's trust. I know when I first came here it took quite a while—maybe a year or so before people were comfortable with me. I did a lot of the staff work alongside people. For example, I would do dishes with them, or we would clean up an area together. I would be right there with them, and they felt more comfortable when I was a part of what they were doing. Then, if they mentioned something difficult they were going through, that's a time where it's easy to say, "Well, I understand, I've gone through something like that." Then you explain a little bit of your own situation that links you to them.

Alexandria goes on to explains how the shepherding teamwork at WS assesses what the problems are and how to deal with them. Counseling with other shepherds about individuals' problems does breach confidentiality, she acknowledges, but is generally accepted as a necessary outcome of the teamwork prophecy principle.

ALEXANDRIA: Our Shepherd teamwork—which is me, Wesley, Vivian, and Lem—meets every Tuesday for three hours, and we also send email notes back and forth whenever anything comes up that we need to counsel about. Then at our Tuesday meeting we always send in the agenda points ahead of time, and one of us chairs the meeting. We rotate alphabetically, and somebody gathers the points together; we pray about what order to present them in; and then we talk about them. Of course, most of the time we all end up praying and asking the Lord what the solutions are at the end of the meeting. We usually go home with a lot of assignments of things to pray more about.

Occasionally staff people will say to me, "I need to tell you something, but you can't tell anyone." And I'll say, "I can't promise you that I won't tell my teamwork." Everyone is pretty clear that I will keep their problems confidential except in our teamwork, because we have to counsel about it. Although some have struggled with this issue, staff members know that ultimately all of us are responsible for what happens in WS and for the WS standards, so everyone is pretty good about it.

The role of shepherds, in addition to counseling, as we were already aware, is to maintain the Family's standards, not just receive and forgive confessions of wrongdoing, as do Catholic priests. Alexandria reports that WS members understand this. If someone's personal issues involve a violation of standards, it is likely to result in discipline, in consultation with Maria and Peter.

ALEXANDRIA: I don't usually meet Maria and Peter here at Celestial Manor, because of the distance, but I know that Thomas and Vivian and Lem meet with them more. I chat with Mama every once in awhile. They do encourage us to report, and we do get feedback from Mama in particular. She's very interested. A lot of times, if she hears something, if somebody sends a personal letter or a prophecy to her, she'll chat and ask me about how it's going and what is happening with that person; she's very concerned about people.

When standards are violated, I've never made my own decision about reporting it or not. I don't feel comfortable in just relying on myself and the way I may look at things. I've always depended on somebody to counsel with; I've always worked in teamwork with somebody. I know, of course, that when you're sitting right there with a person you have a different rapport with them, but I always know that I need outside help to really see the overall picture.

People here at WS really want to be here, and they want to be a blessing to Mama and Peter. To be honest, there isn't a whole lot of discipline that we have to give, because most people do try their hardest to maintain the standard that is expected of them. They know what they need to do for the work. Most of the trials and battles that people go through here are relationship oriented and health oriented; or Home rules, very small things. I might say, for example, "As a Home, we decided that we're coming to devotions on Mondays and Tuesdays, and I've noticed that you haven't been coming, you've been sleeping in. I think I might need to monitor your weekends and what you're doing, so that on Monday morning you can be fresh." But I've never really had to discipline anybody.

It's definitely a different realm of shepherding being in WS than it was when I was in the field. In the field there were a lot of incidences, disciplinary infractions that you had to contend with. In the field, there were some excommunicable offenses for which there's no wiggle room at all. But with a lot of less serious offenses, consideration would be given to what the person was going through, the Home that they were in, the shepherding they'd been given, how much warning they'd received, and so on. But I know that recently it has tightened up a lot, because awhile back there was too much discretion.[11]

If something more serious did happen with someone here at WS, I would pray about it, I would take it to the greater teamwork, I would suggest an action, and then a couple of us would pray more about it before we did anything. But I imagine if something needed to happen, it would. We are authorized, under circumstances that we deem appropriate, to impose a penalty. Otherwise, I think the things which we would take to Mama and Peter are more the trials that people are going through which could affect their work, that we would want Mama and Peter to be aware of so that they are praying for the situation too, whatever it is—maybe a relationship problem—which happens a lot, because everyone is together so much.

The department heads usually take care of the work problems, so we, as Shepherds, don't get so involved with that. And if we do, it's more their interaction with each other—arguments, or maybe they don't say things nicely, or there are misunderstandings—that we might have to deal with. But with personal relationships, it's not like the field where, if something doesn't work out, you can just move to another Home. Here at WS there is the complication that when couples are together, and it doesn't work out, and one of the partners pairs with someone else, the other partner will know this is happening but may not know how to deal with it.

Relationship problems vary. Some of it is work related, where people don't see eye to eye on something. But a good portion of it is, in fact, love relationships between a boy and a girl. Because we live communally, with a lot of us living together in the same Homes, there's going to be more of this, I think, than if it's just people living separately in their apartments and only seeing each other at work. The younger people here, who have had less experience with actual application of the Law of Love in their lives, compared to the FGAs, do seem to have more difficulties.

Clarissa had arrived to escort us to our next interview, and closed this interview by discussing the promotion of less-experienced SGAs into positions of leadership, despite of their relational problems.

CLARISSA: We need to count on FGAs to have a certain maturity, kind of like what you were discussing concerning Law of Love battles. Our theology teaches us that we ought to look at it as a challenge to grow. That's part of stretching and the Year of Strengthening, to where you can humbly accept that, "This young person's hearing from the Lord, and even if they don't have the skills acquired over years, they have a channel of prophecy to be able to get the Lord's direction."[12] It's exciting! We'll see how it plays out.

CHAPTER 9

Managing the International Flock

This chapter contains selected excerpts from interviews on issues related to guiding and regulating the global Family organization. Authors' comments and informational summaries are inserted where appropriate.

INTERVIEW WITH MPL SECRETARIES MARILYNN AND JESSICA

MPL stands for Mama's Personal Letters or Maria and Peter Letters. Two of the GN Department secretaries—Marilynn and Jessica—are assigned more or less full-time to manage the MPL Ministry, which consists of handling Maria's voluminous correspondence (and occasionally Peter's too) with Family members worldwide. Both Marilynn and Jessica, ages 53 and 52 respectively, are first-generation converts to the Family, and both have been associated with World Services for over 20 years. Both regularly communicate with Maria through Voice Chat on computer headphones. Marilynn works directly with Maria, reading her daily emails and prayer requests. Jessica, on the other hand, monitors all email posted through the WS server, not just those that are specifically identified as a personal letter to Maria or Peter. These include WS staff communications as well as Home reports from the field.[1]

Every day Marilynn transfers a summary of MPL correspondence for Maria to review into Text Allow, a reading program that allows Maria to listen to the summary (Maria has a medical condition that makes her eyes sensitive to light and excessive reading). Maria has trained her ear to follow the Text Allow program at relatively high speeds. She is particularly interested in hearing any prophecies from her MPL files. Maria listens to letter summaries once a week and meets with Marilynn to discuss them. Occasionally Maria (or even Peter) will respond personally to their letters, but this is Marilynn's and Jessica's principal task. They typically employ a form letter with standard beginnings and endings. The middle portion of the response letter is tailored to the person who wrote the letter and is supposed to be obtained through prophecy. Forms are changed every month. Marilynn drafts the response and Jessica edits it. Marilynn and Jessica never send the same form letters to the same field Home. As explained in the interview, response letters typically are signed "Ashley."

The majority of communications to Maria elicit simple acknowledgment letters (100–150 per month). Approximately 30 response letters each month include WS prophecies. Marilynn tries to anticipate most of the prophecies that Maria wants included in her responses before meeting with her (these are usually "encouragement" prophecies that recognize the correspondents' diligent efforts in the field and encourage them to maintain their faith, especially during times of doubt or discouragement). A majority of these prophecy requests are farmed out to other WS channels. Marilynn and Jessica also extract particular letter questions and concerns from the MPL files and forward them to the GN Department. These items represent potential source material for future *GN* issues. Maria wants confirmation prophecies on all prophecies obtained from field letters that she thinks might have value for the Family as a whole. Confirmation prophecies are the result of asking God's further input on particular aspects of somebody else's channeled prophecy. Sometimes Marilynn or Jessica channel confirmations, and sometimes they ask others to do so. Usually it is the confirmation prophecies (which elaborate and expand the original field prophecies) that are actually published in *GN* issues. In Family terminology, people who are asked to obtain confirmations prophecies are referred to as "locals," as previously discussed.

Marilynn files MPL communications digitally by year, month, and sender's name and can search the content for retrieval purposes. Judi, another secretary who was away during our visit, organizes, codes, and classifies prophecies that are then sent to Maria. At the time of our visit there were over 65,000 prophecies on file. One other important source of information that Marilynn and Jessica monitor is the TRF reports (Tithing Report Forms) submitted monthly to WS by Family field Homes worldwide. TRF reports include Family Home tithes (10 percent of each Home's monthly income from donations or the sale of Family literature, educational and religious tapes, music recordings, and other materials that are distributed through WS to Family Homes), and evangelizing statistics. They also include Home members' personal comments, which Marilynn and Jessica read. In these monthly reports, Maria's secretaries can often discern emerging themes or collective Family concerns and problems to bring to Maria and Peter's attention. From a community management perspective, member access to the group's principal leaders through their personal correspondence helps to build morale and sustain a sense of collective identity. At the same time, systematic monitoring of field reports is an important way for World Services to maintain and enforce group standards, while also being responsive to periodic institutional problems arising in the Family International's global communal system.

In our interviews with Marilynn and Jessica, there is a certain amount of repetition of information gleaned from previous interviews. From a methodological standpoint we encouraged a certain amount of repetition in our questioning as a way to validate what we were being told about World Services operations. At the same time, each separate set of interviews—including this one—inevitably added significant details to our comprehension of these operations. One important theme, for example, that is both reinforced and particularized in our overlapping interviews is the way that WS has become increasingly integrated and complex as an administrative work organization. This development is consistent with various models of organizational change that we discuss in chapter 10.

MARILYNN: We use an MP3 recording procedure for Mama's email that uses an audio encoding format to record and store audio files, which can then be transferred between computers or other recording devices. The mail summary we produce for Mama runs about 20 or 30 minutes. Mama only gets a summary once a week, and then she listens to it, and she'll get back to me and go over the summary with me and make her comments. In the meantime, though, because I've been working with her for so long, I already pretty much know which ones she will probably say, "Oh, please get them some encouragement. Please have someone get a prophecy for them." So I'm already thinking ahead. The majority of prophecy requests to Mama are for encouragement prophecies.

The two of us both get prophecies for this purpose, and we also request others here at WS to get prophecies. Then we go over every prophecy, pray about it, and make sure all the person's questions are answered, that it's a complete prophecy. If it needs more, then we will ask the Lord for more encouragement, or instruction, or whatever is needed. Or if there is a questionable part in it, we'll ask the Lord about it. We'll take it back to the original channel and ask, "Can you get any more clarification on this?" We wouldn't be able to do it if we didn't have other people to help. We probably farm out the majority of these prophecy requests.

JESSICA: Sometimes we need something right away. For instance, when someone passes on and we want to notify their family members immediately; then we'll get the prophecy ourselves.

MARILYNN: Sometimes we may get a message from the departed person. We just ask the Lord for encouragement; sometimes the departed person wants to give a message to their loved ones, and sometimes they don't.

JESSICA: Sometimes people write in specific questions. A lot of times people write when they're going through a rough time or want prayer.

MARILYNN: We pray about each of these problems, what needs to be done about them. Besides getting them prophecies, Mama sometimes also wants to understand what's behind the problem, why they are having the problem. And those sorts of answers aren't given in prophecy to the particular people who make requests. They're for Mama's information, so that she can help the Family in general. We usually send out at least 30 letters that have prophecies in them per month. Then we also write [to] maybe 50 to 100 people, acknowledging their letters and thanking them. There are lots of people who write in just to tell Mama how much they love her, and there are lots of people who just want to send in a testimony. Or if they have specific questions, like doctrinal questions, then we say, "Thank you, we'll pray about it, and hopefully this will get published for the whole Family." If the prophecy we have received is exceptionally "feeding" [containing reliable instruction attributed to God], that would answer a question for everyone, then we bring it to Mama's attention: "Do you want to use this prophecy in a *GN*?" If she says yes, then we'll give it to the GN Department, and then we'll get another prophecy for the letter sender.

JESSICA: Sometimes we may get a prophecy from someone's letter instead of generating it ourselves. Then it's up to Mama to decide whether that prophecy has general significance, and we have published some of those people's prophecies.

MARILYNN: But also, Mama wants a confirmation on everything that gets sent in, so that's another thing that we generate. We farm out confirmation prophecies for other staff members to obtain, and we do some ourselves, too. Actually, we don't publish that much directly from the field [submissions by Family members outside of WS]. Usually we publish just the *confirmation* we've received about what they sent. Someone sends a prophecy, we ask the Lord more about it, and we get more details. For example, I don't know if you're familiar with the Elerian Horses—they're new spirit helpers that we've received. Someone from the field wrote in about this experience they had with seeing these white horses, and what they got in prophecy about it. Mama was very interested. We had people pray about it, getting confirmation prophecies, and now we have these new spirit helpers—the Elerian Horses.[2]

Since much of what WS does is produce publications, content has to be generated every month for a number of different periodicals. We asked how the staff copes with the constant need for material and where it all comes from, especially prophetic material.

MARILYNN: We already have a lot of prophecies on file; it's just processing it that takes time; polishing it. Plus, we all get personal prophecies every single day. And then, of course, another source would be Mama herself. She might say, "I have a question," and she makes a direct assignment for someone to get a prophecy about her question. Or she wakes up in the morning and says, "You know, I just had a thought . . ." She has so many ideas and so many questions, and she assigns them on prayer morning [scheduled bimonthly for all WS staff to attend], and we all pray about them. Sometimes we have "united" questions, and a lot of that material is used for the *GNs*, or sometimes a few people will pray about one of Mama's questions, and others will pray about different questions. It's actually "prophecy morning" more than prayer morning, because we have prayer "vigil" every day for half an hour, where we individually pray for Family members who are on the prayer list.[3] Everybody does that. On our prayer morning, we all gather together for an hour prayer vigil, following which we spend another three hours praying to get prophecies. We all have assignments from Mama. That's also a good opportunity for us [Marilynn and Jessica] to pass out MPL prophecies too. Also, department heads can bring problems to pray about and get prophecies for guidance. Usually people get more than one assignment to pray about, depending on how strong their channel is and how—I don't want to say quick, because it's not quick—but some people can get more in during that time than other people. That doesn't necessarily mean that they're better or anything, it just means that that's what the Lord has done with them as channels. At any rate, these prophecies are all submitted to Mama. That means they've got to be formatted so she can listen to them. Every person in WS puts their prophecies on an MPEG [compressed audio] file. These get sent to Judi [another of Maria's secretaries], and Judi systematically goes through them all. Judi's job is to coordinate the files, to keep the files. She doesn't actually listen to them.

JESSICA: It's more of a mechanical type of job. Judi also stores them and keeps up with the storage. For example, if Mama maybe heard a prophecy a week or two ago and wants to pass that prophecy on to someone else for whatever reason, she'll ask Judi to pull the prophecy, find it, and do whatever it is that she wants done with it. She's got a program—dtSearch—which we use to search on words.

SHEPHERD: How many prophecies are on file? How are they categorized and accessed?

JESSICA: [We have] 64,000 prophecies. That's what Judi told me when she left on vacation. I think she started doing this since Dad died, since 1995. Judi has a way that she files them under categories; like "discouragement" files or "young people battles."

MARILYNN: But I also digitally file all the MPL files, and I just have them by month, with the person's name inside their folder, and I have their letter and their answers. I recently have wanted to go through all the files and enter them by person, with everything under that, but it would be a monumental task. Plus to even try to figure out who was who, because we change our names so often, and we change locations.[4]

SHEPHERD: Because you have so much material here, you never just dump some of the stuff that comes in? It's all kept on file?

MARILYNN: Well, so far it's all been kept on file. Each letter has its own little file and the reply.

JESSICA: Somebody will write in, and we'll want to look at past letters that they've written to see the history of something.

MARILYNN: The confidentiality factor is very high. We don't discuss these letters with anybody other than Mama. Even the channels don't get the whole thing. But they don't get anonymity. Ha! If they've broken a Charter rule we pass it on to their Regional Shepherds [who are charged with monitoring Family members' compliance with basic Family rules].

SHEPHERD: Do individuals who submit personal letters understand that confessed rule violations will be reported, that that's part of the rules?

MARILYNN: Yes. We tell them that.

SHEPHERD: Does anyone ever write to Peter?

MARILYNN: Yes. It's Mama and Peter—the MPL or Mama [and] Peter letters. Peter gets the summaries too, like Mama, because he likes to listen to them, but he doesn't listen to them quite as extensively as she does. But if there's a letter specifically for him, and if it's answered in his name, he listens to it and approves it.

SHEPHERD: This last January, the Ricky-Angela tragedy occurred. All around the world Family Homes were, of course, shocked and upset. We're guessing that there was a huge flood of letters addressing that particular issue.

JESSICA: Yes, sympathy and condolences.

MARILYNN: And encouragement prophecies also, for Mama, Peter, and the whole Family.

It became apparent to us that Marilynn and Jessica are receptors and disseminators of a great deal of information about the personal problems and concerns of ordinary Family members from all around the world. Their role serves an important monitoring function that helps Maria and Peter keep track of both individuals and larger trends and allows them to address morale issues more effectively.

JESSICA: Another thing we do is that people send us a monthly report, the TRF [Tithing Report Form]. It includes the statistics of people the Home has witnessed to and souls won, but there is room on those reports for comments. These get sent to us, and we'll reply if somebody has a question. We'll go through all of those that come in during the month and write an acknowledgement or a thank you, or sometimes it will generate a prophecy because somebody has a problem, or they're going through something, and they need encouragement.

MARILYNN: If we see a trend like, "Oh, wow, we've gotten all these letters about such-and-such a concern" from different parts of the world, and they all have the same theme, then we'll bring that to Mama's attention.

JESSICA: I remember one. We've gone from people being "Visiting Shepherds" to being "Coaches," and when people were getting invited to attend these coaching seminars, there were some who had formerly been Visiting Shepherds—mainly people our age [first-generation adults] who had been in the Family for quite awhile—who were passed up for younger people, because we want to train the young people and give them more input. So we had some FGAs write in feeling left out, feeling hurt, feeling washed up.[5]

MARILYNN: They just didn't quite catch the point that it's not because they're not good, it's just that we want to train the younger ones.

JESSICA: But they were taking it personally. Like, "I've been in the Family for so many years," and some of them felt like, "What do I have to show for it?" Or "I was a failure as a leader, I was a failure as a Visiting Shepherd, and now I'm being passed up." The Enemy [Satan] just hits people in different ways.

MARILYNN: So anyway, now we have an Encouragement *GN* coming out to address that. But in the meantime, people who wrote in discouraged all got personal encouragement prophecies and an explanation. Because it's also our job to rally the troops, and to keep them fighting, and to keep them with the vision, and to explain what the vision is. "Don't despair! You're not washed up. Maybe you didn't quite catch what's happening, and this is what's happening." We very much try to keep people pointed toward the Lord and the Word, to follow the new moves of the Spirit, in our answering of their letters.[6]

JESSICA: We're the cheerleaders on the sidelines.

MARILYNN: The rescue squad too. Mainly we just try to encourage people. Keep going, Keep fighting. Keep persevering!

We asked what would be an example of a trend among SGA (second-generation adult) letters, particularly those who might be feeling pulled down by the fact that a lot of their peers have left the Family.

MARILYNN: We sometimes get letters from young people about their parents, who have left the Family and are trying to get them out, or their siblings trying to get them out, but they want to stay.

JESSICA: We also get youth who are discouraged, kind of like, "Everybody around me has left, and I'm the only one still here" type of thing, which is an exaggeration, or type of discouragement. Maybe there are young people, who are in a Home with their parents, and there's nobody around their age, they're living in a far-flung field, there are no Family Homes close by, and they go through battles about that because there's no one their age to fellowship with. Or we get young people who are having a hard time living with their parents. Or there's nobody they can talk to. We get a lot of young people saying, "You're the only one I can talk to. I can't talk to my parents. I can't talk to my Home Shepherds."

MARILYNN: And Mama wants that avenue to be open so that they *can* talk to somebody. We don't get mail from oppositional ex-members writing in, but there are a few people that, when they're leaving the Family, they'll write. We get nasty letters sometimes.

We asked what the general policy is when people decide to leave the Family and whether there are ongoing communications with them.

MARILYNN: Unfortunately, we don't, as a rule, get letters from people when they leave the Family. And we feel very bad about that. We have no way of knowing what percentages are leaving on good or bad terms, and Jessica and I don't even know everyone who leaves. This is something we've been praying about, and we'd really, really like to write everyone that leaves a letter of encouragement and thanks for their being in the Family, for their contributions.

JESSICA: And now we don't know where people are because there's been so much moving around [due to a lot of smaller Homes being dissolved in the "Restructuring" period, causing people to either find new, bigger Homes to join or drop out. See Melody and Jeff interview below]. Many people have been hurt, because nobody has written to find out how they are. They left and nobody wrote, and they feel hurt about that. People assume that Mama and Peter know everything. They'll write and say, "You probably know my history and background." Often they don't write their Home number, their country, or their age, and it's like, "How in the world am I ever going to find out who this is?" Another problem is that people have a grace period for reporting. So if they haven't sent in their tithe for a month or something, you don't want to send them a letter right away and say, "Oh, we're so thankful for your service." Ha. It could be a computer glitch, and it could maybe offend people that you think that they're leaving. So it's kind of a dilemma. Plus there's a guilt factor. People feel bad. They think that Mama and Peter are going to be mad at them.

MARILYNN: Well, we did have a different kind of mind-set about backsliders before; the older people in the Family especially feel very bad about leaving.[7]

JESSICA: Especially if they've been 20 or 30 years in the Family. That's a big change, and so we do try to encourage them and let them know they're loved and appreciated.

MARILYNN: And they *are*! We're not just trying to make them feel good; they *are* very appreciated and loved. Their contribution to the Family has helped make the Family what it is. Everyone who does write us, with their contact information, and says, "We've decided to leave the Family," we always write them a letter and send them a commendation. Because even if they've only been in the Family a week or have done something for the Lord for a week— and most people have done much more than that—it's just incredible. They need commendation for whatever they've done.

Jessica answered our question of how letters to Family members in the field are actually written.

JESSICA: We have a form letter that we do every month, but only for the beginning and the ending parts of the letter. For the middle part we don't follow a form; we fill in the middle, tailor-made to whatever was written to us. We're in contact a lot during the day, through Voice Chat on our computers; we're always contacting each other and discussing and praying together about things. Then, there is also someone who helps us to polish the prophecies. We don't do that either, because that would really slow us down.

MARILYNN: That would be Veronica. Her main job is to polish the *GN*s, but she also polishes our letters, making them grammatically right, and checking the spelling; she is excellent. She was Dad's [David Berg's] editor. She's "Sally Scribe" [her pen name]. You might know her from reading past *MO Letters,* which she helped edit before they were published.

JESSICA: Every month we do a new one [form letter].

MARILYNN: And then some of those who write in get tailor-made ones, depending on if it's a "Home-going" letter [when a Family member passes away] or if it's a specific problem that we need to really talk to them personally about. All of the letters are actually tailored in some small way. Plus if we know that two or more people are in the same Home, we don't use the same form portions either. Although, it doesn't really matter if they know it's a form, because we can just tell them Mama doesn't have enough time to write.

SHEPHERD: Are all of the letters signed "Mama"?

MARILYNN: No. They are signed "Ashley, on behalf of Mama."

SHEPHERD: Who's Ashley?

JESSICA AND MARILYNN TOGETHER: We're Ashley.

SHEPHERD: So if the two of you left tomorrow, there'd still be an "Ashley."

MARILYNN: Yes, exactly. That way also, if there is anything in the letter that's not right we can take the brunt of blame or criticism.

JESSICA: Ashley gets the blame.

MARILYNN: But there are letters written from Mama herself.

JESSICA: The Home-going letters are, and Mama goes over them.

MARILYNN: And others to whom she wants to send her own personal letters; they're signed Mama. Peter does the same thing.

Jessica and Marilyn confirm that, as noted elsewhere, Maria and Peter's direct involvement in many day-to-day operations, such as letter writing, has decreased through delegation of responsibility to WS staff.

JESSICA: Mama used to be much more intricately involved in all aspects of WS.

MARILYNN: In everything. Approving every single publication, and answering every brushfire in the whole world. Goodness! But the Lord and Mama and Peter have trained us. And also pushed down the responsibilities—it gives them freedom. I'm just so jazzed about the new structure, because it'll free them to do their job of feeding the Family and being able to spend more time on spiritual concerns and what *they* do best.[8] The physical things, the tending of the tables so to speak, are not things they have to take care of anymore. They don't have to know about everything going on. They only have to know what they have to know. They have faith in us, and faith has creative power. I know that that is what helps us to be able to do it. I know that Mama is praying for me. She puts her trust in the Lord, and the Lord will work through me somehow in some miraculous way! She asks us to do things that we don't have the faith for. But we do it because she has faith that the Lord can do it.

INTERVIEW WITH COACHING AND SHEPHERDING BOARD MEMBERS MELODY AND JEFF

The focus of discussion for this interview shifts to more specific organizational strategies developed and implemented by the Family to strengthen Home morale and commitment standards and to facilitate transition from first-generation to second-generation leadership. A major new program in this regard is the Coaching and Shepherding Board, which is chaired by Melody. She leads off with a detailed summary of the history and development of recent Family reform and reorganization.

Further developing the theme of strengthening youth commitment to their parents' faith, we discussed a number of issues related to the organizational development of second-generation leadership in the Family International, with particular emphasis on the new "coaching" program in conjunction with the "restructuring and renewal" reforms instituted in the Family over the past several years. We learned that two-thirds of the old visiting shepherds have been replaced by second-generation (SGA) coaches who, in the new program, must undergo coach training, which is overseen by Melody and her CS Board cochair, Kelsi (whom we did not meet). Once properly trained, it is the coaches' job to monitor Home shepherds in Family field Homes. Under Peter's direction, current WS administrators believe that these restructuring reforms provide more effective organizational mechanisms for effective monitoring and maintenance of disciple standards in Family communal Homes worldwide. We also learned that regional shepherds (formerly continental officers, or COs)—to whom the coaches report—are all appointed by Peter and Maria; and that newly appointed SGA s have equal formal authority with first-generation (FGA) leaders. A certain amount of informal tension between FGA and SGA leaders was acknowledged to exist, especially during the current transition period of restructuring and renewal, but the Family Policy Council is determined to continue cultivating and developing second-generation leadership for the future revitalization and advancement of the Family International and its end-time missionary agenda. This willingness to invest in and promote young people into positions of organizational authority has become a characteristic of the contemporary Family International, setting it apart from more typical modes of religious organization which, over time, lead to the development of relatively rigid and conservative gerontocracies.

MELODY: I'm the International Board Chair of Coaching and Shepherding [CS]. It used to be VS [Visiting Shepherds], and the CS Board used to be called the VS Board. I cochair it with Kelsi. It's the board that is the shepherding ministry in the Family. It's been very active these last two years, because it's very much involved with the Family's restructuring and the Year of Strengthening. The governing of the Homes and the shepherding of the Homes has changed. We used to have Home teamworks consisting of the personnel teamworker, the outreach teamworker, and the finance teamworker. Well, in order to strengthen the spiritual state of the Homes worldwide, we needed to have better shepherding on the Home level. We needed to have the Home Shepherds trained better in how to spiritually shepherd the members of their Home and keep their Homes spiritually on track, and we needed to have a way to monitor the Homes and their shepherding better than the VS Board program was doing. The VS program worked well for what it was, but there came a time when the VS program was ineffective and the Visiting Shepherds themselves were spiritually weakened, because their job was too big; they were called upon so much that they were unable to keep their own spiritual lives strong, and they basically got burned out.

So we were really at quite a crucial time in Family history, the time when the Lord revealed that the Family was very compromised, that the "*Titanic* was sinking" in a very well-known prophecy that has the Word picture of the *Titanic* sinking. The Lord compared the Family to the *Titanic,* and He said, "You're not going to be the Endtime Army if you don't obey and be strengthened and get back to full discipleship." So it was quite an emergency. That was January of 2004. So there was a huge push to strengthen the Family spiritually, which was the Year of Restructuring, and now we're in the Year of Strengthening.

The CS Board is very much involved with this. The way it worked is that we had many brainstorming meetings with the Family Policy Council at the beginning of last year. This was the follow-up to Peter's trips to Brazil. Kelsi and I went with him to Brazil, so we were very involved with the Brazil thing for nine months [Family Homes in Brazil were perceived to be straying from disciple standards and new WS programs]. We went there three times, and we stayed a total of about four months. That's when the whole Brazil membership was put on suspension for six months, and it was a big deal. Well, the Lord indicated that what happened in Brazil and the state of Brazil was basically a microcosm for the whole Family.

We came back from Brazil in the middle of December of 2003. Then in the first months of 2004 there were a lot of meetings and brainstorming here in WS with the Family Policy Council to try to come up with a plan for strengthening the Family worldwide. We met numerous times here, and then Kelsi and Peter and I went to our International Board meeting and spent five weeks at the Champions Training Center in Mexico.

In between the Brazil and the International Board Meeting was the Family Summit in Mexico.[9] So that was a real time to discuss.

The Mexico Summit was where all the Regional Shepherds and most of the Regional Board Chairs of all the boards attended. It was about 100 people, plus about five people from WS, who were not International Board Chairs, and both Mama and Peter. We were there for five weeks, and really talked about the restructuring of Family membership requirements. That's where the Home Reviews came about, and it was agreed upon by all of that body of leadership in the Family. Then coming back from the Summit there were various *GN*s that Peter put out to the Family, explaining to them about the restructuring, about the new Missionary Membership status, Home Reviews, about what was going to be happening.

In the meantime we had the meeting with our Coaching and Shepherding Board, with Peter and a few others, in which we talked about the details of the restructuring of the shepherding of the Family. That's where the concept of the Coaching Program came about. The Coaching Program has taken the place of the Visiting Shepherd Program. That entailed deciding what the Coach Program goals would be; discerning what the problems were with the old VS Program and how to avoid them; what kind of leadership we're looking for; and who would be the people to try to raise up to be in these positions.

Since that time there has been a push to find those coaches and train them. That involved having two seminars. The seminars were made up of videos that were filmed by Peter and Kelsi and myself. The first seminar went for seven days. The Regional Shepherds held seminars in each world region; they would bring in people that they wanted to train as coaches, people from their fields who had leadership potential or were pillars of the work or other Regional Board Chairs that they wanted to train. That took place this year in April.

JEFF: How many P&Ps [recorded prayers and prophecies] so far concerning the coaching program? Five hundred?

MELODY: Oh, thousands. Ha. And right now taking place is the *second* coach training seminar worldwide. It's going on now in all the world regions. The coaches were chosen last month. The first coaching seminar was broad. It was to bring in the people that Regional Shepherds felt they wanted to train. The first seminar was more general leadership training—lots of training on how to avoid the pitfalls of leadership and some of the ongoing problems within our leadership structure that either causes people to burn out or causes them to be weakened spiritually or not be effective. But this second seminar involves a smaller group. It's mostly just the new coaches, the executive secretaries of the Regional Shepherds, and a few other people who are directly involved.

The second seminar is at the CTC [Champion Training Center] in Mexico; it's being held right now. And, yes, they got the roof repaired. Ha. You know how they fixed it last time with plastic? Well, the heat caused the plastic to melt. And, oh, it can rain like it's unbelievable. So they had to postpone their coach training seminar for two days, and they blitzed repairing it for two and half days. Maggie wrote and said, "Oh, it's such a great victory! We're just cleaning up now, and the attendees are going to arrive in two hours!" That was so CTC style! Ha! So thank the Lord. The Lord gave them a good solution. They took all those thousands of tiles off and put them on again with better insulation and adhesion.

Mathias, my son, was very involved in all of this. He's a real man of faith.

He takes risks and he likes to do new things; he has this wild Don Quixote faith.

JEFF: Did you see the photos of the place when they first bought the property? Unbelievable. Maggie told me that when they were considering getting the property and fixing it up, she said, "I didn't have the faith for it. Nobody had the faith for it, except Mathias. And we all said, 'We don't have the faith for it. If you do, then go for it,' but we're going to attach ourselves to your faith, because we don't have it."

MELODY: It was a huge test for him. They got the property, and then they were in the process of fixing it up, which was enormous. So we planned to have this five-and-a-half-week meeting, and we set the dates. And people were coming from all over the world. There were about 35 people coming in.

JEFF: And the place just wasn't ready. Wasn't even close!

MELODY: Kelsi and I arrived two days before everyone else got there, and we were like, "Okay, Jesus!" It was just unbelievable, and Mathias was so calm. Maggie said when I saw her, "Oh, I came a week ago, and I couldn't even sleep! I was so nervous. I just had to get out of here! There were no windows, there were no doors, there were no beds, there was nothing!"

JEFF: No dining tables and chairs.

MELODY: And we arrived just two days before the meeting, and, honestly, it was *so* not ready.

JEFF: And that's when the three tons of glass arrived for the windows: huge, big as this room, this one piece of glass. So they had to take it to a guy who could cut it for them.

MELODY: You can't even take glass like that off of the truck. You have to be a professional. The glass truck arrives, so then they have to go take it to the place that they provisioned [obtained donated labor] to have it taken off the truck and cut.[10] The day before everyone is going to arrive, I'm talking with Mathias, and he's orchestrating this huge handyman team, and a guy comes up and says, "Just wanted to let you know that the stables are flooding." He said, "Oh, really? Which one?" And the guy said, "All of them." He said, "Oh, how much?" He said, "A lot." Mathias replies, "Oh, just a little hiccup." Ha! I was thinking, "Oh, dear Lord!" I was a nervous wreck, but the Lord did it, and we were ready in time. It was a very interesting experience. Anyway, it's a cool place, and the Lord is really using it.

JEFF: Mathias has been a handyman since the age of 12. He got trained by two or three of our best handymen. So I think that's one of the reasons he has the faith. He knows all the aspects of construction and repair work.

MELODY: I don't know how he learned that. He just has a knack. He has a gift for it. Our young people have a lot of faith, and they have a lot of drive; they like to do new things, which is part of the push now in our Board, and that is to expand the mindsets of the Family, to really broaden the way we look at our young people, to raise up a lot more young leadership like Mathias into the higher ranks of the leadership of the Family.

The big picture about training is we need to train leaders in every aspect of the Family, not just spiritual leadership, not just Shepherds, but leaders in every pillar of Family life. The Family is very complex, but what happened over time is that our perspective of leadership has become very narrow; that's one problem, and it has limited opportunities for young people [SGAs] to feel that they are in leadership, that they are doing something important. We, as an organization, and FGAs [first-generation adults] overall, haven't opened it up enough to the things that young people like, or we haven't given them enough recognition, or we haven't had a mechanism in place.

JEFF: Except Mama and Peter here at World Services, promoting SGAs as WS department heads.

MELODY: Well, yes, Mama, Peter, and WS, but that's so few people. We have so many very talented young people in the Family that feel frustrated, or they haven't found the calling, or they feel a little like they are not valued. The young people that we work with are so talented, so brilliant, so led of the Lord, that if Mama and Peter hadn't had the faith, and WS had not put those young people in positions where they have authority, they might not have done as well. They have responsibility, they make decisions, they really do something, and they are exercising change. As a result, they are challenged, and they are very happy, they are growing. And there are a lot of young people like that in the Family.

JEFF: In 1995 we had no young people in WS. Now we have 60 percent young people. The Family Policy Committee here is made up of about half FGAs and half SGAs, and WS department heads are almost all young people now, and they have most of the authority.

SHEPHERD: It's extremely unusual for organizations of any kind to be doing this, especially religious organizations, which tend to develop gerontocracies. So this is very farsighted to make an organizational transition now to accommodate the SGAs and to do it at a time when it is most effective. But there is a balancing issue, because when you're bringing SGAs into leadership positions, it means you're removing a lot of FGAs, who may now suddenly experience a sense of "What am *I* good for? I've lost my place." Some FGAS whom we've talked to actually are happy just being ordinary missionaries. They have a new set of children, in some cases, and say, "Now I get to be with my kids while they are growing up, and I can do what I really love to do, which simply is to witness, and I wouldn't want to be back in leadership." But some aren't in that situation, and they do feel like they've been eased out, just like someone in the secular world who may not only be passed over, but may be discarded by a company to save overhead costs on salaries before they're ready for retirement.

JEFF: There's no unemployment in the Kingdom.

SHEPHERD: Sure, but still there's that letdown feeling for a number of FGAs. So in order to achieve balance, that's the other side of the coin: how to affect that transition and make it a little easier for people?

MELODY: That's a problem that we are facing right now, because on the Home level they elect their Home officers, their Shepherds and managers. It's a very important level, and there are a lot of positions there, and they are very important to the overall success of the Family. The Family will only be as strong as our Homes are. It's not like you can just make your top leadership strong, without strengthening the very core of the Family, which is the Home.

In the Coaching Program, we made a concerted effort to raise up new coaches, young coaches. And that was difficult. It took a lot of explanation to the previous Visiting Shepherds, who are very dedicated people, and who really sacrificed. Some of them sacrificed for years, and some of them really suffered for it—their health, their relationships, and their spiritual lives. They really gave a lot. So it's hard to say, "Well, we really appreciate it, and it was great, and you're great, but actually, you know, we need new coaches. We need fresh blood." But it was prayed about extensively and discussed extensively, and the thing is, in order to keep the Family moving and fresh, and in order to raise up new leadership and train new leadership, and in order to make a break with some of the mindsets of the past that have to change, you have to bring in quite a number of new coaches. There are probably two new coaches to everyone that used to be a Visiting Shepherd. It's a time of change, and the leadership has to be different.

JEFF: But as you know, FGAs have a lot of faith. They have faith for finances, etc. So with some of the old Visiting Shepherds or other leaders now being more involved at the Home leadership level, they really strengthen those Home situations. So it's a transition, but I think they're fitting into those positions now.

SHEPHERD: In some Homes, of course, you have majority voting in the SGA ranks, and that means the Home management tends to be SGAs. So you'll have FGAs who suddenly are being shepherded by their kids.

JEFF: But I think if you talk to some of those SGAs, they'll tell you that "we really need the faith of the FGAs and their experience." They don't want to just take it all on by themselves.

MELODY: And it really depends on the FGAs. Some FGAs are very happy to have the time and be supportive, and they see the need. But it is very difficult, and there is an undercurrent right now where the FGAs feel a little insecure and destabilized and passed over and wanting the training the SGAs are getting. Beginning last year the CS Board prepared actual training programs for training the coaches and for training the Regional Shepherds. So FGAs say, "Hey, I've been in the Family so long, I want that training." I think their battles are legitimate, but it's a time of transition. It's hard on the FGAs. It's hard on us to try to have to make those decisions. It's hard on the Regional Shepherds to have to take flack from people who are saying, "Why didn't I get invited to the Coaching Program? I'm a pillar in the Home." It's very human. But as difficult as it is, we have to go forward to save and strengthen and create the Family of the future; it's all about raising up and training the leadership of the second generation.

Kelsi and I also help Mama and Peter to shepherd the Regional Shepherds, and an extremely interesting thing happened last year at that meeting that we had at the CTC. One of the training topics was on the SGA and FGA Regional Shepherds working as equals. We talked and prayed about it literally for months, because you've got FGA Regional Shepherds who have been in top leadership for 20 years, some for 30 years—absolute seniority. Then you have young Regional Shepherds, who have been in their position for two years. And there was a problem. We were saying, "Well, yeah, you need to work as equals."

But it just wasn't working; the FGAs were limited in their faith because of the lack of experience of the SGAs, and the SGAs were very timid because of their lack of experience. We had to figure, "There's got to be an answer from the Lord." Because otherwise there will never be equality, and the top leadership of the Family will never sync up as the Lord wants it to. You have a status quo, and until the SGAs can balance that out and really come into their position, you will not have the freshness and the change that is needed in the top leadership. If you don't have it in the top leadership, you just lose it. It won't filter down, and our different Family regions won't move forward.

It was clear to us that the coaching program is now one mechanism by which the Family is seeking to change the status quo in Family generational structure and operation. They hope that this program will elevate the SGAs' level of confidence and the FGAs' acceptance of the transition.

MELODY: Regional Shepherd equality is a little different from the Lord's perspective. The Regional Shepherds are all appointed by Mama and Peter, and they all have the same job description, the same authority in the Charter. Each Regional Shepherd is a bona fide, full-blown Regional Shepherd no matter their age, no matter how long they've been in the Family. They are equals. And the reason they can be equals is because those SGAs and FGAs are all on the same page spiritually. They are totally dedicated disciples. They are all loyal. They all believe. As far as their spiritual lives are concerned, they are on par. That may or may not apply to the rest of the Family. There are a lot of people in the Family, and they're going through unique tests, and many are facing difficult times of decision. Some are on board spiritually, some are struggling spiritually. Some are flexible new bottles, others are inflexible old bottles.

JEFF: You know the term "old bottles?"[11]

MELODY: They're stuck in ruts and like things done a certain way. They don't change easily. They run "mom-and-pop" shops. I'm painting with an extremely broad brush here. But that very problem is one of the reasons why the Family had to be restructured: the small Homes and the mom-and-pop shops run by people who had been living a certain way for years. It's not as if all of a sudden Homes are restructured, they get a couple of new people, and they can just change. It takes a long time.

SHEPHERD: In some of the Homes we've visited many of the older members are very good because they do have a lot of experience. And whatever the formal organization of the Home might be in terms of the new Home management structure, there's a tendency to acquiesce to them because it's "their Home."

MELODY: Yeah, they're the ones who signed the contract, who own all the furniture, etc.

SHEPHERD: And sometimes they're literally mom and dad. In Australia there was a father-daughter situation. The daughter had recently been elected to be Shepherding Coach in the Home, and her father was not in the Home management team at all. One morning he was going to drive me somewhere and discovered that the daughter had made another commitment for the vehicle without talking to him about it. And he got upset and was chastising her like a father to a daughter: "That was irresponsible, etc." And you could just hear your old man. It seemed sort of prototypical of some of the tensions. They're living in the same Home, and the formal arrangement is that she has a leadership position; but still, they're father-daughter, and she had done something that was probably a repetition of other incidents over all those years when he was the dad in charge.

MELODY: When we established the new program, we knew that it wasn't going to be perfect. There were going to be some flaws, and we'd have to adjust. But the Lord showed us that we had to do it and do it quickly, because there was a certain momentum established. A lot of momentum came from the Brazil situation. It really caused a lot of waves. We said that the whole field was flattened, because everybody was put on the same level, whether they had been a Charter Member Home or a Fellow Member Home.[12]

They were all flattened, yeah. It was pretty radical, and Mama's "Woe" video was very heavy, and it made a big impact.[13] Then the videos that were created for the Brazil brethren were turned into *GN*s, and they had a very big impact. That was then followed up by the Renewal of Home commitment in the Year of Strengthening. The Homes and people were really getting strengthened and getting back in the fear of the Lord, and their discipleship was getting much stronger. So, we had to move quickly. Because you know in a big movement like this, if things don't keep going, you lose it, and it's so hard to get it going again.

JEFF: But we did it; we had the Renewal.

MELODY: The Renewal was tremendous. We knew there were going to be problems, but the thing is, we believe that we now have mechanisms in place to monitor these changes. We have the Home Shepherds, and they are shepherded by the Coaches. And Kelsi and I shepherd the Coaches through the CS Board and International Board Chairs. In other words, we have Coaches on the ground level, and they are in touch with the Home Shepherds. They each have three to five Homes. The coaches report to their Regional Board Chairs. Every CS Board regional board chair has from three to twelve coaches. Some small regions, like the Middle East, have only two coaches. Big regions like Brazil have twelve coaches. So Home Shepherds are in constant touch with their coaches.

Peter recently made a video that was sent out with the videos for the second coach training program, and that was the video to the Regional Shepherds, explaining to them the importance of training the coaches—that training the coaches is crucial to the successful restructuring and strengthening of the Family. So there are mechanisms. That's where the Family was weak before. We would have revolutions [major policy innovations or revisions], but there was no monitoring. There was no mechanism to follow up to see how the changes were going. So later down the line, you'd find out it went awry, or there were weaknesses, or something would just take on a life of its own, and it takes years until we in WS figure out what happened. So coaches were appointed. They're in their second coach training program seminar. Within a month, the Homes will know who their coaches are, and then it begins.

THOMAS: I was thinking about the transition of SGAs, because we have a lot of SGAs that carry big responsibilities, and the FGAs have had to move over in WS too. We spent a lot of time with our FGAs, getting them behind the program. We sat down with them and talked about it, so they were behind us. It didn't happen (snaps his finger), just like that.

JEFF: The SGAs were 20 and 21 when they came to WS, and they're around 30 now.

THOMAS: So it hasn't been easy for all the FGAs; nevertheless, because of sitting down beforehand, talking about it, communicating, getting their support, telling them "we're going to be doing this transition," that made it a little easier I think. It was a little more proactive.

VIVIAN: Also, we had to experiment. It's not like in WS there's never been training. Years ago, Peter used to come to Sunday Fellowship all the time, give meetings, classes, and things. And most of our FGAs have been there and done that. They've gotten a lot of input over the years; we all have. We just had to explain that as much as we would love to give everybody the Coach training, as much as everybody could probably benefit from it, the time has come to give it to the SGAs. It's not that they are better than anybody else. They need more help. They need more work. They need more training. I'd say for the majority of them, they've dealt really well with it. For some of them, it's been difficult.

THOMAS: Some of the FGAs here at World Services are just content to do their editing, their programming.

VIVIAN: They like their jobs.

MELODY: And they do them well.

THOMAS: Yes, and if they can focus on their job, they're happy to do that. And they're happy to knock off in the evening and not have to worry about all the complexities and responsibilities that the new department heads have. The new WS department heads work many, many hours. They have the energy, and they can do it.

JEFF: And the WS Home managers, they're young now too.

VIVIAN: The Lord said our FGAs were like our skeletal system, whereas the SGAs were everything else. We need that strong skeletal system to keep our structure. We can't do without it.

JEFF: And the SGAs have accepted that all along. "We know we can't do this by ourselves, but we do want to get trained. We want to move forward, but we want to do it with your help." They're not saying, "Get out of the way old man, get out of here, and we'll take over." Which has been nice, as often that can happen.

SHEPHERD: You're old wine.

MELODY: *Vintage* wine. Ha.

INTERVIEW WITH ADMINISTRATION
DEPARTMENT HEADS AVIS AND ANSON

Whereas most WS departments are relatively specialized and focused in their particular organizational missions, the Administration Department must maintain a comprehensive understanding of all WS operations—their interconnectedness and impact on the functioning of the Family International as a whole. Among other things, the Administration Department communicates with all the

Family's world reporting offices, including regional and shepherding "desks" and the international boards, all of which have supervisory responsibilities in the field. While regional officers are authorized to make a number of decisions for their respective world regions (North America, Mexico–Central America, South America, Brazil, Western Europe, Eastern Europe, Africa, the Middle East, India, Southeast Asia, Japan-Korea, and the Pacific), they must funnel reports and occasional queries to World Services headquarters to be scrutinized and responded to by the Administration Department staff.

Regional officials also are authorized to excommunicate members who are in serious violation of Family standard or reinstate excommunicated members who petition to rejoin. If membership reinstatement is denied at the regional level it can be appealed to World Services, in which case it becomes a matter for the Administration Department to dispose of. While a certain amount of latitude is exercised in judging the sincerity of people's motives for wishing to be accepted back into the fold, no leniency can be given to members who have been excommunicated for violations of the Family's contemporary proscription of sexual contact between adults and minors.[14] Adults who have sexual contact with minor children are considered a "danger" to the well-being of the religious community and cannot be readmitted, regardless of the sincerity of their repentance. Thus, the Administration Department has ultimate responsibility for maintaining the Family's strong membership boundaries and strictly enforcing its internal sexuality rules, past violations of which have fueled a tremendous amount of negative publicity and legal strife and constitute the primary grounds for attacks made against the Family by antagonistic former members.[15]

Of central concern to the Administration Department is the Family International's charter legislation—its interpretation in response to local problems, and its periodic revision and ratification. As discussed in chapter 1, the charter, issued in 1995, is the contemporary Family International's basic governing document, defining in comprehensive detail both the rights and responsibilities of individual members and those of Family communal Homes. Subsequent to its original printing, numerous changes have been introduced in the form of amendments and clarifying appendices. At the time of our visit, the Administration Department was involved in the lengthy process of producing an entirely new edition of the charter, which will encompass all of the many changes that have occurred in the Family's institutional structure over the past decade. The ongoing process of revising charter rules reflects the dialectical tension produced for religious groups like the Family that seek to balance the rights of individual members with the larger goals and welfare of the religious community as a whole. Too much emphasis on individual rights weakens community cohesiveness, while too much emphasis on the community strangles individual initiative. For communal religions like the Family International, this basic dilemma of social life predictably results in retrenchment and reassertion of the priority value of community goals over individual concerns.[16] In conjunction with its heretical beliefs and practices, it is this priority that clashes with the larger secular values of economic and political individualism, reinforcing the Family's public image as a deviant "cult."

As discussed previously, changes in the charter are brought about as a result of decisions made by the Family Policy Council (FPC) at summit conferences, convened approximately every two years. These conferences are characterized by considerable grassroots input, discussion and debate. In the end, however, religious unity typically prevails. Backed up by channeled prophecies attributed to Jesus, virtually all of the FPC's final decisions are unanimous. If and when specific changes or amendments to the charter are advocated, the substance of the amendments is forwarded to the WS Administration Department's Charter and Board Handbook Committees, who are charged with the responsibility of drafting the precise language to be used in charter and board handbook revisions. Final approval of the rewrites must then be obtained from Peter, Maria, and the FPC before communicating the final results to the Family International as a whole.

In the new charter, performance accountability has shifted from individual members to Family Homes and world regions. In their annual reviews, regional shepherds now assess and score the performance of Homes (rather than individual worthiness) under their jurisdiction according to a set of discipleship standards and criteria. If particular Homes achieve a substandard score, they face the prospect of being reclassified in the Family's three-tier ranking system. If a region as a whole is substandard, then international board chairs at World Services must work with regional councils to find ways to raise the discipleship performance level. By objectifying oversight of the Family International's communal Homes and missionary endeavors through a standardized scoring system, Family leaders have moved another degree forward in the rationalization of organizational procedures so common to the institutionalization of successful religious movements.[17]

Besides strictly administrative issues, the emerging problems associated with an aging first generation and with child-care concerns are also discussed in this interview. The Family's first-generation adults are approaching retirement age as conventionally defined in Western societies, having forsaken occupational careers to devote their lives to a religious cause without accruing any retirement or senior health benefits. And, inevitably, health concerns attendant to advancing age will increasingly limit their ability to engage in the Family's strenuous day-to-day outreach and witnessing activities. Some of the reciprocal benefits of communal living for grandparents and their children are considered in our discussion, but exactly how Family leaders will come to grips with the looming problem of its aging first generation is not clear.[18] In the meantime, Family leaders also recognize the importance of valuing and rewarding child-care roles in the organization of their communal Homes worldwide. For a religious movement whose first-generation converts were narrowly focused on the any-moment advent of the resurrected Christ and the onslaught of apocalyptic events, current Family leaders have substantially refocused their end-time efforts by investing in and nurturing a second (and now third) generation of missionary disciples.[19]

Our understanding of the Administration Department's operations was obtained from Avis, a 31-year-old SGA who is the department head with five years' experience at WS, and Anson, a 56-year-old FGA with four years of experience in WS. Anson simultaneously serves as an international board chair of public relations. Our interviews with Avis and Anson were conducted during lunch. Joining us for the meal, and also participating in the conversation, were Michael and Clarissa, who are regional public relations officers for North America, and WS shepherds Thomas and Vivian.

AVIS: We take care of Charter legislation, answering any Charter-related or Board questions from the reporting offices, the Regional desks, the Shepherding desks, all those kind of administrative bodies in the Family. That's what takes the majority of my time.

We just set up the Regional desks this year. Previously we had offices in every continental area, but now it's broken down to regions having the equivalent of an office. It's one or two people at each desk, and they handle a lot of the reporting, communications, clearances, and the rejoining process for former members at any level. They handle processing the Home Review, putting it together, giving it to the Board Chairs, and sending out the grades for Family Homes. They're like the secretaries for their administration area.

There is a certain amount of administrative supervision that they handle, and that's the whole point of having the Regional Desks. Most of the people handling the Regional Desks, or at least 50 percent of them, are new at the job. The desks have been set up for about six, seven months. If they don't know how to process something, or there are questions they don't think are within their mandate to handle, they'll send it to us.

Excommunication issues, and how they are handled in the Family, include some of the following scenarios.

AVIS: Say someone, who left as a persona non grata, wants to rejoin the Family. Ha! If someone is *excommunicated*, they need permission to rejoin. And if they don't get permission, well, sometimes people are pretty persistent.

The Regional *Shepherds* have to give the permission, not the Regional Desk. Like I said, the desk is like a secretary for the region. They handle all of the forms and reports. But almost everything they do also has to get approved by the Regional Shepherds—like the rejoining process or the clearance process. So if someone was excommunicated, and they want to rejoin the Family, the Regional Shepherds make that call. As a general rule the Regional Shepherds say no. But if the person who is applying for reinstatement wants to appeal, it becomes an appeals process. The appeal would then come to WS, and that would be in the Administration Department's court. We look to see if they've changed.

CLARISSA: Plus there's the hosting Home that they would be rejoining. The Home would also have prayed and received prophecies and would have requested counsel. The Regional Shepherds would be praying and getting prophecies and counseling. It's a whole process. But it wouldn't be an automatic no-can-do kind of thing.

AVIS: If they're still manifesting the same problems for which they were excommunicated, then it's unlikely they would be readmitted as Family Disciples. Maybe they'd be readmitted as a Fellow Member instead. If someone is given the okay to rejoin the Family, whether it's at the WS level or the Regional level, they have to start pretty much from scratch, just like any other new disciple, and go through a probationary period, including rereading all of the basic material.[20] It depends on why they were excommunicated. There are a variety of things you can get excommunicated for. If they are a danger to the Family, they're not going to get back in.

CLARISSA: Adult sex with minors, that's permanent, depending on the age range.

AVIS: We look at the scope of what occurred. We look at what the age range of those involved was. Sometimes we get borderline age combinations, for instance 21- and 17-year olds having a sexual relation. But that's different. That's close in age.

CLARISSA: But adult-child is nonnegotiable.

AVIS: Yes, adult-child sex is the only category of excommunication for which there is not a second chance; there wouldn't be an exception made, even if the person had undergone a basic change. Otherwise the Family follows the basic rules of repentance, change, and forgiveness. Even somebody who leaves the Family and became a hostile ex-member—attacking the Family on the ex-member Web sites and so on—may subsequently undergo a reconversion, or at least repent and want to rejoin the Family. This person would not be considered a security risk, not if they changed. People would know them, and you'd want to verify. There would probably be fruit or convincing evidence manifested to the fact that they had changed.

MICHAEL: For instance, a member by the name of Beverly did this and then repented of her attacks on the Family. From what I remember, she was offered to rejoin. It was made clear that she could, but she said she felt she could be of more benefit to the Family not being a Family Disciple member. But even though she wasn't FD, she basically was living almost like a FD member. From that point on, she was a very big help to us in a lot of court cases and different things like that. It was left open. She could come back. But it was a decision she made herself. She would come over to a Family Disciple Home and read the GNs and was really all there as far as the Word was concerned.

SHEPHERD: We've hear that occasionally someone may go on "furlough," what seems to us an ambiguous member status.

AVIS: Someone may leave the Family, but say they just want to leave for a short while.

CLARISSA: Angela [Ricky Rodriquez's murder victim], for example, was on a furlough, but technically as far as our categories go, she was an ex-member. She wasn't Fellow Member, Missionary Member, or Family Disciple.

VIVIAN: And that was determined by the amount of time away, right? After a certain time period of not reporting or not being on a Home report.

AVIS: I guess. I don't know. I'm not at all aware of Angela's progression; I just assumed she decided to stop reporting.

THOMAS: I think it depends on the person, too. Angela said, "I'd like to go on a furlough." That meant specifically, "I want a little time away to think, with plans on coming back."

CLARISSA: It's mostly first-generation members who request time off. You won't hear second-generation members saying, "I want a furlough."

AVIS: You're either in or out.

VIVIAN: Furlough is not an official term. The best way to describe it, I guess, is, "I need a break."

CLARISSA: Someone wants a break, but they are not intending to leave; it may eventually evolve that way, however.

MICHAEL: I can't remember the actual name of the Letter, but Dad used the word "furlough" in the title.[21] It was a point in time where people had been in the field a number of years, and if they felt they needed a little break, they could come back to the U.S. if they were U.S. citizens, or to Australia, or wherever, and spend some time off the mission field. But at the same time, they were supposed to be working towards going to another mission field, establishing contacts, still witnessing and still being active. It was like a furlough from the mission field. That is the way it was in the beginning.

AVIS: Full reinstatement into the Family depends. For instance, say someone wants to live on their own for awhile. In order to be a Family Disciple you have to live in a communal Home. But let's say they decide, "I want to be

MM for awhile." So they report as a Missionary Member. If subsequently they wanted to return to Disciple status, they would have to go through just a three-month process compared to a six-month process for new converts. It's not the same as leaving the Family, because they would still be a part of the Family as Missionary Members.

CLARISSA: For example, Lynnetta left from WS and got a secular job and was very happy, very friendly toward the Family. She just wanted to do something different with her life. I think with older members [FGAs] the furlough term is used more because they're still very friendly toward the Family. They really just want a break. They've been doing missionary work for so many years.

It is apparent to us that aging of Family membership will increasingly be an administrative concern, as well as a concern for other areas of Family organization. What longtime Family members are going to do as they get older and hit the age of conventional retirement, begin to have health problems, etc., is a looming issue. What the Family is going to do about this issue is still somewhat of a open question, as shown in our respondents' comments.

AVIS: I don't know. I think that would be a Family Policy Council [FPC] decision. I do think that part of the solution is our communal living. You can carry people, if you're living communally. Then older people can bring something to your Home. Everyone has something to give. So even if they can't pull the same load when they're 65, they can still contribute in some way, and they can benefit from a Home environment. I lived with Leanne Gable. She was 70-something when she passed on, but she was very much a part of our Home. She did secretarial work. She had to have her rest. She was an older woman. We could carry her as a Home, and it wasn't a problem that she was older and couldn't contribute as much. But she was able to contribute some; she read with the children. She did a lot of different things, and it was really nice to have someone like her in the Home.

CLARISSA: There's a 72-year-old in Argentina. He was FFed to the Family years ago [converted through flirty fishing], and he lives with his daughter and his grandkids. He's a blessing in the Home. He goes out two hours every day on outreach. He says, "I have to get exercise anyway." So he goes out and witnesses, and when he's Home, he helps with the kids and does dishes. He needs a lot of rest and he's slowing down. Up til 70, he was totally doing his normal load. It seems to work really well, actually. Of course, the kids love having "grandpa" living at home with them.

AVIS: Like child care here at WS, you try to limit the hours put in by child-care staff in the field, because it's a taxing job. You're pouring out or giving of yourself all day. It's needs to be broken up somewhat.

CLARISSA: Our idea of child care requires a lot of focused attention. I mean, it's not just having kids running around the house while you're doing something else.

AVIS: At least in the field Homes that I lived in, you have child-care workers, but they can also do other things. They can go out witnessing. There's variety in what they can do. Whereas here at WS, if you're on child care, you're on child care. You don't get the inspiration of going outside of the Home. It's a lot easier to get burned out here, because it's every day. So therefore, you try to protect the child-care workers. You have to. I have a daughter, and I want her to have good teachers and everything else in her child care.

MICHAEL: I think, too, in the field there was a shift at one time. We had big "combo Homes," with as many as 100 or more people living together communally, before the Charter, and to be in child care was like a career. That was something everyone wanted to attain to, to be a teen shepherd. But then when the Charter hit, and the big combos melted down to smaller Homes, the child-care career didn't look so good anymore. Some of the young people who had been on child care for a long time were kind of burned out, and there was a shift from the importance of being in child care.

This shift in attitude we're talking about had something to do with a recent *GN* that reemphasized the fact that child care *is* a career, and if this is something the Lord is calling you to do, you shouldn't be thinking, "I don't want to be tied down to that." Now that the Homes are getting bigger again, the emphasis is going to be back on groups and children. Now that the smaller Homes are going to Missionary Member status, and the larger Homes will be Family Disciple, hopefully the pendulum will swing again to the other side.[22]

We understood that the Family charter is currently undergoing needed updates, one of the major preoccupations of the Administration Department.

AVIS: We just finished Charter legislation that goes with the coach program, which caused a lot of other stuff to be changed. The Administration Department communicates directly with the field concerning what's already in the Charter and application of the Charter to particular problem situations. Then we also have a Charter Committee here in WS for when rewrites are needed, Charter amendments, and that kind of stuff. Members include me, Anson, Jeff, and Benjamin. The four of us are also on the Board Handbook Committee. We handle the rewrites; we're working on rewriting the Charter. The last printing was in 1998, so that's been seven years.

But of course, before we start drafting changes, we have to see what else it affects, which is always a lot. You have to figure out, "Okay, if we make this change, that's going to affect this down there," and you have to make sure that everything adds up. In the Administration Department, we have to have an overview of the way all the programs operate and all the inner connections and overlaps.

ANSON: Actually, the new Charter is really close to completion—450 pages.

AVIS: As I said, 1998 was the last printing. In 2003 we had major Charter amendments that went out in a *GN*, but then in the last year or so, there've been three or four appendices.

ANSON: All of these changes, amendments, and more are going out in the new Charter edition. *The Board Handbook* [which defines the organizational structure and procedures of all Family boards] will also be incorporated into it. The original Charter was built both inside and outside of WS.

AVIS: There were Charter meetings. I remember those. I was about sixteen. Ha!

ANSON: A rough draft was presented; the entire membership voted and discussed and suggested and amended and all sorts of things. It's different now. It goes to the Family Policy Council, which consists of the International Board Chairs [IBCs], the Regional Shepherds, Mama and Peter, and the WS Administration Department. Everybody on the FPC goes over all the amendments and approves them. It's made clear in the introduction to the Charter that Homes, or any individual member, if they see something that they question or don't think fits, are welcome to write in, and then that would go through an amendment process to see if it changes or not. But as far as *approving* new amendments, no, it's just the Regional Shepherds, the IBCs, and Mama and Peter—the FPC.

We knew from previous research that the new charter revisions attempt to tighten up standards in some areas of Family life that previously were loosened up too much in the original charter. This conclusion is reinforced below.

AVIS: We've gone through the Charter and looked at it in light of the new Word [channeled prophecies published in *GN*s] and the direction that the Family is going. You look at everything and ask, "Okay, how does that fit?" Are we complementing it? Are we in sync? Basically, we've looked at the whole Charter like that. For instance, we've emphasized the discipleship standard and larger Home size. Or sometimes there are certain things that used to be individual responsibilities but were not the responsibility of the Home—things that are important aspects of discipleship or Family life if you're going to be able to live the way we do.

It's funny, a lot of that stuff, almost all of it really, was there in the original

Charter, but it was a little looser. It wasn't quite so defined or underlined. And now we've tweaked the actual root clauses and explanations to more clearly state that you have to have certain size Homes [a minimum of six voting adults], and there's not as much leeway as there was before. It's all pointing in the direction of raising the discipleship standard. I think a lot of confusion before had to do with Charter interpretation or lack of Charter enforcement. People can find loopholes in almost anything. Even within the new Charter there will be loopholes, it's just that way. And sometimes you leave a little loophole, because you don't want to box yourself in too tight.

CLARISSA: I think, too, a lot of it has to do with the pendulum swings that we talked about earlier. Because we went from very tightly, more controlled, more orchestrated, organized large Homes before the Charter, with an executive body overseeing everything everybody did. The Charter swung it way out to the other side. And, of course, that brought a whole new set of problems. The goal now is to bring it back to the middle, not go to either the authoritarian side or the overly liberal side.

ANSON: Hopefully, by underlining or defining expectations more clearly, some things will simply be more apparent. It's like revising an instruction manual. The first version is very technical and difficult to understand. Then you go through it and say, "Let's simplify this. We don't want to lose the point, but we can express it more clearly, so that it's reader friendly."

MICHAEL: Plus the criteria now help to define what the standard is for each of the Family Boards, spelled out very clearly in layman's terms.

ANSON: The criteria are something like a living document themselves. It's all going to morph and change and be qualified as we go. The Homes will see it and try to figure out what applies and how much and where they stand.

It is apparent that WS has generated a tremendous amount of complicated, organizational change in a relatively short period of time. Ordinary members may take awhile to process it all, but, according to our respondents, some positive responses are already evident.

CLARISSA: I think it's a little hard to casually perceive the new changes with the new Home accountability principle. Our Home Council Meetings have changed 100 percent. We used to have meetings with people that were like, "Come on guys, participate." And others would say, "It's fine with me, whatever." We don't have those kinds of meetings anymore. People are passionately concerned about everything! There is a lot more sense of accountability, that people have to speak up, and they have to pray and to help make decisions. You really see a major change. It's hard to imagine. We even have people who write little notes like, "So and so has got this little thing going on, are they going to sink our Home?" Whereas before, they wouldn't have cared. It was more like, "Whatever, let him do his thing, I'll do mine." Ha! It's changing, and I think we're only seeing the beginning of the change. It's going to play out in many ways. Child care is another example. You'll have parents who say, "Oh well, I'm not into disciplining my kid." What does that mean now when you go to fill out your Child Care Home Review? It means a lot. In our Home we've got two children. So we have to sit down, fifteen adults, and talk about those two children and vote on whether we think they're getting disciplined properly. The dynamics are very different from what they used to be.

We had previously learned that Home Review is a pilot program, but that it's very quickly going to become standard operating procedure. This means that a mass of new information has to be processed, analyzed, and responded to, initially by the Administration Department, but eventually by the international boards.

AVIS: Home Review will be handled by the Boards. The International Board Chairs, they're the ones; it filters up to them. We've been very involved in this pilot study, but I don't see that continuing in the long term. We're not involved in the results of the Home Review program. That's handled on a regional level.

ANSON: But also, I'm on the International Public Relations Board, for example, and if a region scores low or is kind of substandard, then we on the PR Board would hear about it, and we would, in counsel with the Regional Chairs, come up with plans, ways, or activities to try to raise the standard. So in that sense, yes, the International Board Chairs at WS would be involved.

CLARISSA: What about analyzing the overall results? You get in all these results from the Family worldwide, and you've got all your IB chairs here at WS. Would you analyze, "Where is the Family going this year and next year?"

AVIS: Yes. That would be WS.

ANSON: Also, the Regional Shepherds, who are part of the Family Policy Council, are the ones who actually make final judgments on the Home Reviews for the Homes themselves. And if things come up for the FPC to discuss, the Shepherds will make suggestions; feedback goes both ways.

AVIS: And we're working on it. It's a process.

CHAPTER 10

World Services and the Contemporary Family International

Summary and Conclusions

The primary orienting thesis of this book is that the current organizational and administrative structure of the Family International offers an instructive case study for understanding the ways in which the evolving leadership of a heretical religion can guide followers through the transition from an emergent to a mature religious movement. By *mature* we don't mean necessarily civil acceptance by adversarial or mainstream competitor religions, but achievement of a certain level of organizational stability and continuity for new generations of adherents.

Like all new religions, the Family has been embroiled in moral controversies and has suffered serious defections and setbacks over the years. Nonetheless— while still heretical and much maligned—post–David Berg Family leadership has midwifed the emergence of an international religious culture that not only sustains the faith of a significant number of the founding convert generation but also inculcates and nurtures the commitment of a rising second and third generation of young disciples. In the process of organizational maturation, Family leaders have, first, managed the group's moral career by modifying certain practices in response to pressures from outside the boundaries of its own moral community while periodically renewing commitment to core beliefs and values within its community of Family disciples.[1] In doing this they have, second, succeeded in developing an astonishing organizational system for proliferating, rather than curtailing, official prophetic guidance through multiple channels rather than a single prophetic oracle. We see this last point as representing a remarkable achievement in the long history of Western charismatic religion.

The Family's ultrasupernatural beliefs regarding an end-time apocalypse and the second, messianic advent of Jesus Christ generate transcendent goals of witnessing, conversion, and spiritual preparation that, to at least some degree, are widely shared by evangelical Christians both today and in centuries past. It is not these religious goals but the means by which the Family pursues them that has generated its reviled standing as a deviant cult among other evangelical Christians. As demonstrated in our WS interviews, a well-organized and rational administrative system for producing missionary aids and regulating the conformity of an international network of communal Homes to rigorous religious norms is among the principle means employed by contemporary Family leaders in pursuit of their end-time objectives.

Most of the Family's organizational and administrative methods are not, of course, of themselves unusual or objectionable to outsiders. Rather, it is the specifically religious means of channeling verbatim prophecies from spirit entities to guide and justify Family practices and policies that set the group apart as a religious heresy and "deviant" subculture. In a religious subculture that is not only centered in ultrasupernatural beliefs concerning the end-time, but also democratically stimulates the profusion of official revelations, we have the necessary ingredients for the sustained elaboration of heretical beliefs and practices.[2] In the past, flirty-fishing methods of Christian witnessing were justified by God's revealed word. Continuing today, communal living and sexual sharing among consenting adults, obtaining the material necessities of life through "provisioning" rather than gainful employment, the putative sexual passions of Jesus Christ as the Family's husband and lover, and the specification of both demonic spirit adversaries and angelic spirit helpers, are but a few examples of religious heresy promulgated through the social construction of teamwork prophecy in the Family International.

MATURE VERSUS EMERGENT MOVEMENTS

At a certain stage in their development, maturing social movements achieve a level of coherence and organizational structure initially lacking at the outset of their history. The concept of maturation with respect to social movement development—including the development of new religious movements—implies a certain degree of success and continuity in the accomplishment of movement goals through the implementation of a variety of action agendas over time.[3] In contrast to emergent movements, mature movements typically have become more institutionalized and less spontaneous in their modes of action. Leadership and decision-making functions previously entrusted to charismatic leaders or performed by informal groups and ad hoc committees increasingly become the tasks of administrative organizations. As Gary Marx and Doug McAdam have noted, "Over time, the study of social movements begins to shade into the analysis of other more institutionalized forms of behavior. Social movements begin to look more like formal organizations, public-interest lobbies, or even religious or political institutions."[4] This, as documented at length in this book, is precisely what has occurred with the evolutionary development of World Services in the Family International.

Explicitly articulating the same point many years ago, Herbert Blumer proposed a life cycle model of social movement development that described the typical stages through which relatively successful movements pass.[5] In this model the preliminary stages of social unrest and agitation, followed by a popular stage of collective action, are sequential aspects of what Marx and McAdam refer to as emergent movements. In turn, the subsequent stages of formal organization and, ultimately, institutionalization in Blumer's analysis represent different phases of a mature movement. Typical of most stage theories, each phase of development represents a set of necessary conditions for passage to the next stage.

As Ralph H. Turner and Lewis M. Killian point out, however, particular movements frequently suffer setbacks or become arrested at different stages of development as a result of what they call external and internal contingencies.[6] *External contingencies* refer primarily to the way other groups, including government agencies, respond to the movement's activities. *Internal contingencies* refer to the movement's ideology, modes of organized action, and the nature of movement leaders' decisions either to change the group's ways or resist change in response to external contingencies. This is a process approach to the study of movement development that, in the language of organizational theory, is consonant with contemporary open-systems analysis.[7] It is also an approach that dovetails with our comprehension of the moral career of the Family International, which has achieved complexity and organizational coherence while continuing, on ideological grounds supported by group prophecy, to resist mainstream integration in the world's religious economy.[8]

CONVERGENCE OF MOVEMENT AND ORGANIZATIONAL ANALYSIS

Resource mobilization theorists in particular have focused on the importance of understanding the latter stages of social movement development in preference to studying the origins and early phases of emergent movements.[9] They argue that it is the potential impact of mature movements on the larger processes of political and cultural change that most deserves attention, emphasizing that successful movements must develop an effective leadership and administrative structure, incentives for participation, and dependable means for securing resources and support, while simultaneously maintaining ideological commitments to a moral or political cause. All of these criteria for movement maturation have been clearly met by the contemporary Family International.

The convergence between social movement analysis and organizational studies has increasingly attracted the attention of scholars in both fields of study.[10] Not only have social movement scholars turned to organizational studies for conceptual tools to better understand social movement organizations, but organizational theorists reciprocally have begun to incorporate social movement concepts in their work to better understand the dynamics of established organizations that function in environments of constant technological, political, and social change.[11] As resource mobilization theorists and organizational scholars come to more clearly appreciate convergences in their fields of study, it also has been argued—in a manner reminiscent of the older collective behavior tradition's emphasis on emergence, social contingencies, and human agency— that both approaches need to pay greater heed to the cultural and historical contexts in which movements and organizations operate. They both should also "attend more closely to the problem of action in conditions of uncertainty, and to sources of innovation and creativity," as noted by Elizabeth Armstrong.[12] These are all themes we have discerned and emphasized in our analysis of the Family's organizational development, especially leaders' willingness and ability to guide institutional change by making democratic adjustments through teamwork prophecy to emerging problems in changing international environments.

Thus, the analytical distinction between emergent and mature movements provides us with appropriate conceptual language for the ongoing study of new religions like the Family International that, having survived the hazards of their early years, go on to sustain second and third generations of adherents. While groups like the Family still have relatively abbreviated ecclesiastical histories and often continue to be stigmatized as alien and heretical by their mainstream competitors, they also typically have developed fairly complex organizational structures and modes of administration for guiding and regulating their followers' religious commitments.[13] They have made a transition from emergent religious movements to mature religious movements.

At some point in their development, then, the analysis of enduring religious movements like the Family must shift from the dynamics of movement origins and emergence to that of organizational formation and institutional adaptation.[14] This, we would argue, is one of the topic areas on which current scholarship in the sociology of new religions needs to concentrate more systematically.[15] Scholars of relatively mature religious movements must carefully examine the means by which second- and eventually third-generation leaders respond to cultural and historical contingencies, succeeding or failing at effectively framing the group's goals and agenda (for both members and nonmembers) and innovating adaptive organizational changes in the face of new problems over time. This kind of organizational adaptivity is clearly demonstrated in the moral career of the Family International. Early examples include cessation of flirty fishing and institution of child-care and educational reforms. Present and near-future examples of more sweeping changes are discussed in the epilogue section of this chapter.

From its emergence as an evangelical street mission to countercultural youths in Southern California, the Family International has evolved into a transnational religious community. The Family's dedicated disciple membership does not constitute an exceptionally large number of active participants worldwide, but the scope and energy of its various missionary outreach programs are impressive—especially for a group whose real property and capital assets are relatively meager compared to other transnational organizations.[16] The key factor in the Family's maturation has been the development of its World Services headquarters organization, which not only obtains and disseminates what it considers to be God's official Word, but also is responsible for directing and administering the group's worldwide network of communal Homes and associated missionary activities.

Though granted a certain amount of local leeway in their fund-raising and witnessing work, Family Homes are not autonomous units in a "federated" or congregational system of religious organization.[17] Rather, as revealed in our interviews with WS staff, they are subject to the centralized program guidance of national, regional and international boards, the ecclesiastical oversight of regional shepherds, and the authority of doctrinal and policy decisions formulated by the Family Policy Council (FPC). In turn, all of the international board chairs are situated at World Services, as is the FPC Steering Committee. All of these organizational structures are ultimately coordinated through World Services and function to define, guide, and maintain the Family's religious programs and way of life.

PROPHECY AS A RELIGIOUS FRAMING MECHANISM

The development of World Services as a leadership organization has been crucial to the institutional development of the Family International, but the WS departmental structure described in this book is not especially remarkable. One may be appropriately impressed by the interconnected complexity of WS operations carried out by a relatively small staff lacking formal education or training. But the specialization of tasks in separate departments, and their administration and coordination by means of rational procedural rules and a supervision hierarchy, are standard features of formal organizations everywhere, including most organized religions. What is unique about World Services operations, as we argue throughout this book, is the way that teamwork prophecy has become the institutional mechanism for making all organizational decisions.

Institutional mechanisms refer to those social practices by which movements and organizations change, develop, and maintain themselves.[18] "Framing" practices in particular are crucial to a movement's development, involving what John Campbell refers to as "the strategic creation and manipulation of shared understandings and interpretations of the world, its problems, and viable courses of action."[19] A renewed interest by scholars in the ways that social movement organizations frame their agendas and justify their action programs to participants, according to Campbell, has "emerged as a corrective to earlier work that failed to recognize that the interests of movement supporters were not objectively given by their social circumstances, including political opportunity structures, but had to be defined, interpreted, and socially constructed."[20] Prayer and occasionally revelation or prophecy—or more commonly "inspiration"—are standard framing mechanisms employed to some degree in virtually all religious groups that believe in divine guidance. In fact, prayer and some form of revelation or prophecy arguably are the most peculiarly *religious* framing mechanisms by which religious organizations justify either changing or preserving their beliefs, policies, and practices. It is, of course, the supernatural valence attached to communications attributed to a transcendent source that makes prayer and prophecy such potent religious framing mechanisms.[21] It is through various forms of prayer or petition, and subsequently what is interpreted as God's revealed will, that religious communities typically construct their moral careers in interaction with other groups in society.

The unique aspect of the way World Services has instituted the framing mechanisms of prayer and prophecy is found in the mode, scope, and frequency with which it employs these intertwined practices. Following petitioning prayers, verbatim "channeling" is the mode systematically used by all WS organizational staff members, not just charismatically gifted leaders. Furthermore, those channeled messages used to guide group decisions are socially constructed through an interactive process—a process that is routinely and systematically followed for virtually every issue or operation, large or small, in every department of the organization. This process is unique, so far as we know, in the history of prophetic religious movements.

The Family does not merely equate prophecy with inspiration or cite it as evidence of God's favor, personal salvation, or the proclamation of new visions for spiritual crusades in the idiosyncratic preaching of charismatic entrepreneurs. Instead, Family leaders have elaborated and democratically instituted the core Christian belief in divine revelation as a normative, organizational mechanism with multiple functions. These functions include both the formulation and legitimation of group policies and decisions, the welding of shared commitments and reinforcement of social solidarity by actively engaging all adult members in ascertaining God's will, and the stimulation of organizational change while simultaneously exerting social control over the religious lives of its members.

FAMILY DEMOCRATIZATION AND EQUALITY NORMS

A good case can be made that, in contrast to the Family International, most prophetic religions that cohere over time around the canonization of prophetic texts tend to develop professional clergies and centralized ecclesiastical organizations that preserve orthodoxy while squelching innovation, flexibility, and democratic input from lay believers.[22] While World Services constitutes the administrative leadership organization of the Family International, it shares little in common with conventional ecclesiastical hierarchies. Insisting on democratizing the religious framing mechanisms of prayer and prophecy, Family leadership since the death of David Berg has systematically encouraged the active participation of members in the ongoing social construction of new organizational forms, incorporated in such innovations as the Family charter of member rights and responsibilities; the legislative Family Policy Council; the "board vision" of national, regional, and international program boards; and the restructuring of Family membership status to reflect a three-tier level of commitment, as discussed in previous chapters.

All of these organizational innovations expanded democratic decision making and grassroots input, and none was simply imposed in an authoritarian, top-down manner by a handful of upper-echelon WS leaders claiming exclusive oracular authority. Rather, all innovations were the result of extensive discussion and debate among World Services staff and at periodic summits of what is now the Family Policy Council. And all were ultimately confirmed and justified through the collective mechanisms of teamwork prayer and prophecy.

Furthermore, World Services has taken the lead in promoting the empowerment of both women and young people in positions of responsibility and leadership at every level of Family organizational life. This appears to be relatively rare in centralized religious hierarchies, where patriarchal gerontocracies tend to prevail.[23] The Family's organizational development actually seems more in line with the egalitarian ideologies of contemporary environmental and global movements that explicitly function as nonhierarchical alliances based on consensus decision making.[24] At the time of our visit to WS headquarters, all department heads and assistant heads were second-generation members, ranging in age from 23 to 32, and three of the eight international board chairs were also second-generation young people. At the same time, two-thirds of WS department heads and assistant heads were women, as were three of the international board chairs and two of the four WS shepherds. And, of course, Maria and Peter, as a female-male team, exercise approximately equal executive authority at World Services as coleaders and successors to David Berg.

REFLECTIONS ON THE FAMILY INTERNATIONAL'S FUTURE MORAL CAREER

The Family International is administered through a centralized organizational hierarchy, but it is a hierarchy that is oriented to change, innovation, and flexibility through democratic participation, gender equality norms, and the promotion of young people of the second and third generation. To say this is not to minimize the legacy of the Family's past problems and conflicts, nor is it to underestimate the fresh problems that surely lie ahead for a relatively small, apocalyptic, and controversial sect committed to expanding its international agenda of Christian witnessing in what it continues to insist is the end-time of human history. But other heretical religious groups also have weathered delays in millennial expectations and gone on to flourish. Some Jews still await a messianic coming, many Christians a messianic return. Latter-day Saints, Seventh-day Adventists, and Jehovah's Witnesses were all founded on the assumption of a swift apocalyptic end, to name but a few historical examples. It is not at all far-fetched to suppose that the Family International also will succeed in effectively managing the millenarian dilemma of anticipating the any-moment end of human history while simultaneously continuing to formulate and execute an ambitious agenda for future generations of Family missionaries.

Lacking the kind of prophetic powers that the Family International claims and practices, we hesitate to hazard categorical predictions concerning its ultimate successes or relative failures in the years to come. That will continue to depend in the future, as it has in the past, on the ability of its collective leadership to construct adaptive responses to new contingencies, both internal and external to its current organizational structure, in a world context that often changes in unexpected ways. But we can modestly say that, at this point in its developmental career, the Family International has successfully instituted organizational forms and mechanisms for sustaining a religious way of life that is likely to persist for generations to come.

It is conceivable that the Family's current outreach efforts may result in a substantially larger, supportive following worldwide in the future. But, unless fundamental alterations of requirements and practice are instituted, it seems unlikely that there will be significant recruitment increases to its core disciple membership of approximately 5,000 communal-living, full-time missionaries. Family leaders themselves appear to recognize the limits of the group's appeal at the level of commitment currently required by Family disciple status. In periodic retrenchment campaigns against worldly compromise, members who have become lax in their commitment have been urged to rededicate themselves or to relinquish their disciple standing, as previously discussed in chapter 1, 8, and 9. Those who remain steadfast in their compliance with charter requirements typically have been characterized through prophecy as an elect "Gideon band" of spiritual warriors whose sacrificial calling is to lead exemplary lives, save souls through their personal witness of Jesus Christ, and be at the forefront in the war against Satan and his henchmen in the last days.

Much of this resonates, as we previously have observed, with the ultrasupernatural doctrines of various Christian fundamentalist and Pentecostal groups. The Family's communal lifestyle, sexual sharing practices, and insistence on the prolific channeling of prophecies from supernatural entities for guidance rather than reliance on the Bible, however, have been huge barriers to acceptance by most members of established Christian denominations. These and other doctrinal commitments represent the primary obstacles (or "contingencies") that block the Family's transition from its current stage of organizational development to ultimate integration and respectability as an organized religion within the institutional structure of conventional society.

Organized opposition to the Family International by conventional religious denominations, various secular groups, and government agencies may have abated since the 1990s but is still likely to flare up from time to time. The constant charismatic quest for new revelation also persists as a potential source of internal skepticism, conflict, and possible schisms. At the same time, the Family's unique prophetic culture—emphasizing cooperation and teamwork— has functioned for the most part to produce consensus rather than division.[25] The particular content of Family revelations and the institutional procedures that have evolved to generate them are, of course, peculiar to the Family. We would argue, however, that careful historical study and contemporary analysis of other prophetic religions is likely to reveal that most official revelations are not merely the idiosyncratic pronouncements of unusual or gifted individuals but are, to a greater or a lesser degree, also the product of social interaction in response to the contingencies and concerns of human group life.

While proclaimed revelation frequently serves to justify the heretical beliefs and practices of new religions, it may also justify accommodating changes in the quest for greater respectability, acceptance, and—for evangelizing religions—a more universal appeal in the host societies in which they reside. And while long-standing doctrines and traditional practices are always resistant to change, corporate belief in divine guidance through direct revelation to authorized leaders is a powerful and potentially flexible religious mechanism for overriding objections and charting a new course in the moral careers of religious institutions. Flexible adaptation through the mechanism of group prophecy has, of course, been one of the organizational hallmarks of the Family's historical development. Precisely which institutional course Family leaders will determine to pursue at the current juncture in their history remains to be seen. It seems apparent, however, that unless the Family modifies or abandons some of its heretofore distinctive practices, it is likely to remain a sociologically encapsulated group that resists integration into the Christian mainstream.

EPILOGUE

Four years after our visit to World Services in 2005, Maria and Peter made an unusual public appearance at the 2009 meetings of the Center for Study of New Religions in Salt Lake City to present jointly a paper formally announcing what they called the Change Journey.[26] Their summary remarks at this conference represented the public anticipation of what could well become the most comprehensive set of changes in the 40-year history of the Family International. The changes they put forward, and which the Family is beginning to implement, are driven by three principle imperatives: to vastly increase effective evangelization of the world (which is the Family's core mission); to retain the participation and commitment of second- and third-generation Family members; and to care for and sustain an aging first generation. Consideration of these prime needs has led leaders to contemplate modifying or dropping every established Family practice and assumption that does not facilitate the core organizational objectives or constitute a core belief.

Such previous hallmark practices and assumptions include disciple requirements to live communally and homeschool their children. (If communal living is no longer required of disciple members, then commitment to sexual sharing could subsequently be deemphasized and eventually abandoned, thus removing two of the major current obstacles to Family respectability and growth.) Elimination of long-standing distinctions between different levels of membership is also under serious consideration. Vigorous recruitment of new Family members as an outcome of evangelization rather than simply winning souls to Jesus will be emphasized once again. New and old members alike may be allowed to pursue outside jobs and professional careers. Participation in local, non-Family community affairs will be valued. Positive attitudes toward education in general, including advanced, university training, will be encouraged. In conjunction with conventional Christian belief in miracles and the healing efficacy of prayer, positive attitudes toward modern medical practices will be more strongly encouraged, including immunizations for children and resorting to surgery and prescribed medications for all ages whenever appropriate. Members who chose to leave or withdraw their participation in Family missionary work will not be stigmatized but will be assisted in making necessary transitions to full-time secular life. At the same time, those who leave will be encouraged to maintain a positive identification with the Family and maintain friendly relationships with relatives and friends who remain committed.

Certain theological assumptions, including the imminent return of Jesus, also are being modified. Leaders now project at least a potential 30- to 50-year time frame for the Second Coming of Jesus, or even longer. They do not profess to know precisely how long it will be—in their youth, first-generation members once believed the end-time was imminent. But leaders now assume a much longer time frame in order to make responsible, effective plans for future growth and, correspondingly, the continued implementation of necessary institutional programs and organization to support this growth.

These and many other specific changes now being implemented or seriously contemplated are radical for a religious group originally founded as an end-time rebuke to the worldly accommodations of establishment Christianity. Along with many anticipated positive results, the possible negative consequences of these changes—from loss of faith and commitment to secular corruption of Family values and uniqueness—are well understood by Family leaders. Even Family prophets are not now certain what the eventual net balance of consequences will be. But their faith that these changes are what God wants, and that the fruits of these changes will ultimately be good, is steadfast. Through the practice of group prophecy, Family leaders no doubt will continue to emphasize sharp moral contrasts between the conviction of their own divinely sponsored commission and the perceived spiritual shortcomings of mainstream denominations, not to mention the assorted evils of secular society. But they will do so within the pragmatic parameters of an adaptive organization that is simultaneously sensitive to the legal judgments of outside authorities and the personal and relational needs of its international membership. The ongoing moral career of the Family International should therefore continue to be both interesting and instructive for scholars of new religions.

Notes

Preface

1. We capitalize references to Family "Homes" throughout the book. As summarized in chapter 2, the Family International does not own or construct conventional meeting centers. Disciple Family members both live communally and assemble for worship in private residences (usually leased or rented) that they call simply Homes. Family Homes are the basic organizational unit for the Family International worldwide.

2. See for example, Lattin, *Jesus Freaks,* 111–12, for a recent statement of this claim.

3. For recent examples, see K. Jones, C. Jones, and Buhring, *Not without My Sister;* "Murder and Suicide Reviving Claims of Child Abuse in Cult"; "Stabber's Friends Blame Decades of Abuse"; Lattin, "Mixed Memories of the Family"; Lelyvedl, Pringle, and Stammer, "Tragic Legacies of a Sex-Based Religion"; Wilkinson, "Life and Death of the Chosen One."

4. See the following miniscule sampling of the hundreds of news articles produced on this subject: Adams, "ACLU Says Constitutional Rights Threatened"; Hylton, "Future of the Polygamist Kids"; Anthony, "Attorneys Raise Concerns about FLDS Child Custody Cases"; MacCormack, "Sect Is a Legal Nightmare."

5. See Jenkins, *Moral Panic,* for a social historian's analysis of how public attitudes and legal definitions of child sexual abuse have been generated, shaped, and elevated to a high pitch in modern America.

6. "Family Sect Case Collapses"; "Children of God: Released"; "Children of God: The Court."

7. For sociological commentary on the problems that virtually all unconventional religious groups have with negative media portrayals, see McCloud, "From Exotics to Brainwashers"; Beckford, "Mass Media and the New Religious Movements"; and Wright, "Media Coverage of Unconventional Religion."

8. See for example, sociologist Stephen Kent's reported comparisons of the FLDS raids to the Family International's earlier experiences in the 1990s with police raids and the taking of hundreds of their children, alleging that child abuse always did and still continues in the Family, despite the collapse of legal cases against them, in Adams, "Polygamy." See also self-proclaimed "cult expert," Steven Hassan, making the same linkage to the FLDS and accusations about the Family in the Anderson Cooper *360 Show* and later the accompanying blog.

9. For critical assessments of the federal government's siege of the Branch Davidians at Waco, Texas, see Wright, ed., *Armageddon in Waco.* For a more recent history and analysis, see Newport, *Branch Davidians of Waco.*

10. Field observational studies of normal Family home life increase in validity to the extent that multiple Homes in different locations yield similar results. Our first published pieces on the Family in 1994 (Gary Shepherd and Lilliston, "Psychological Assessment of Children in the Family" and "Field Observations of Young People's

Experience in the Family") were exploratory and not based on representative sample results. However, our later studies of the Family have benefited from a larger and more diverse sampling of Family Homes. Most recently, our study of ordinary member prophecies generated in Family Homes drew on results obtained in 22 Family Homes in 16 countries, which constituted a reasonably representative cross-cultural sample on which to base conclusions regarding the way the Family International's culture of prophecy functions around the world (see Shepherd and Shepherd, "Grassroots Prophecy in the Family International"). However, in our present study, World Services constitutes the research universe—there is no other WS organization. Hence the only relevant sample would be constituted by the particular members of WS that we were able to interview. And, we concluded, the most significant members of WS to include in our sample of respondents were, in fact, the organization's leaders—Maria, Peter, and WS department heads.

11. Shepherd and Shepherd, "Accommodation and Reformation in the Family/ Children of God"; Shepherd and Shepherd, "Social Construction of Prophecy in the Family International"; Shepherd and Shepherd, "Family International."

12. For overview summaries and analyses of both the value and limitations of open-ended interviews as a data gathering method, see Lindof and Taylor, *Qualitative Communication Research Methods,* and Rubin and Rubin, *Qualitative Interviewing.*

13. A prevailing stereotype of closed, authoritarian religious groups is that members are so insulated from outside knowledge of the world, and so collectively controlled in thought and action, that they are unable to express independent thoughts in a coherent manner.

Chapter 1. Prophecy and Change

1. For sources on heresy and heretical movements in Christian history, see Christie-Murray, *History of Heresy,* and Evans, *Brief History of Heresy.* See also Henderson, *Construction of Orthodoxy and Heresy.*

2. For a succinct discussion of the theoretical distinction between religious cults and sects, see Stark and Bainbridge, *Future of Religion.* See also Gary Shepherd, "Cults."

3. On the transition of the Jesus Movement as a Jewish sect into a new religious tradition, see Harsley, *Sociology and the Jesus Movement;* Ludemann, *Primitive Christianity;* Meeks, *First Urban Christians;* Stark, *Rise of Christianity.*

4. For analysis of the role played by the mass media in perpetrating cult stereotypes, see Beckford, "Mass Media and New Religious Movements." Explorations of those factors associated with episodes of anti-establishment tension and subsequent violence in certain types of new religions can be found in Bromley and Melton, *Cults, Religion, and Violence,* and Wessinger, *How the Millennium Comes Violently.*

5. For discussions of why many social science researchers have come to prefer the term *new religious movement* in lieu of *cult,* see Barker, *New Religious Movements;* Dawson, *Comprehending Cults;* Richardson, "Definitions of Cult."

6. The concept of a "career" has been widely employed in the analysis of social, occupational, and organizational pursuits, as well as in the study of crime and deviance. See, for example, Colin and Young, *Future of Careers.*

7. The concept of a *moral* career, as applied to typical transitions in selfhood experienced by inmates in total institutions, was introduced by Goffman in *Asylums.*

8. Weber, *Basic Concepts in Sociology*, 29.

9. For historical analyses of 19th-century Mormon accommodation to the demands of secular society, with specific reference to Mormon polygamy and the related issue of Utah statehood, see Gordon, *Mormon Question*, and Lyman, *Political Deliverance*.

10. Social science–inclined theologians Ernst Troeltsch, in *Social Teaching of the Christian Churches*, and H. Richard Niebuhr, in *Social Sources of Denominationalism*, made early contributions to a theoretical framework for describing the process in which dissenting Christian religious groups historically tended to compromise their initial heresies in the direction of greater accommodation with secular institutions and establishment religious organizations. For summaries of subsequent social science criticism and literature on church-sect theory, see numerous entries in the *Encyclopedia of Religion and Society* (ed. Swatos).

11. For relatively recent scholarly assessments of the Amish, Jehovah's Witnesses, and Lubavitch Judaism in relationship to contemporary society, see Kraybill, *Amish and the State*; Holden, *Jehovah's Witnesses*; Feldman, *Lubavitchers as Citizens*.

12. See Goffman, *Stigma*.

13. For a sampling of social science sources emphasizing charisma as a social process, see Bord, "Toward a Social-psychological Theory of Charismatic Social Influence Processes"; Dawson, "Convergent Psychopathologies and the Attribution of Charisma"; P. Smith, "Culture and Charisma."

14. Stark, "Theory of Revelations," 287.

15. Stark and Bainbridge, *Future of Religion*; ibid., *Religion, Deviance, and Social Control*.

16. Stark, "Theory of Revelations," 305.

17. Weber, *Economy and Society*, 246–71, 1111–58.

18. For academic sources on both the contemporary Family and its history, see Bainbridge, *Sociology of Religious Movements*; ibid., *Endtime Family*; Chancellor, *Life in the Family*; R. Davis and Richardson, "Organization and Functioning of the Children of God"; Melton, *Children of God*; Shepherd and Shepherd, "Accommodation and Reformation in the Family/Children of God"; Van Zandt, *Living in the Children of God*; Wallis, "Observations on the Children of God"; ibid., "Yesterday's Children." For a surprisingly candid history produced by the Family itself, see Warner, *History of the Family, 1968–1994*.

19. Both Bainbridge (*Endtime Family*) and Chancellor (*Life in the Family*) also depended on open access to Family Homes for the interview and survey data on which their studies were based.

20. For summaries of and references to the Jesus Movement of the late 1960s and early 1970s, including the Family/Children of God, see DiSabatino, *Jesus People Movement*; Melton and Partridge, *New Religions*; and Miller, *60s Communes*.

21. For discussions of the related issues of "brainwashing" and deprogramming in new religions, see Bromley and Cutchin, "Social Construction of Subversive Evil"; and Zablocki and Robbins, eds., *Misunderstanding Cults*.

22. See Deborah Davis and B. Davis, *Children of God*; K. Jones, C. Jones, and Buhring, *Not without My Sister*; Williams, *Heaven's Harlots*.

23. For an analysis of contemporary modes of Pentecostal spirituality, see Poloma, *Main Street Mystics*. Poloma also has authored *Charismatic Movement* and *Assemblies of God at the Crossroads*. For other general sources on contemporary charismatic religion and Pentecostalism, see Harris, "Holiness and Pentecostal Traditions," and Wacker, *Heaven Below*.

24. See, for example, Bird, "Charisma and Leadership in New Religious Movements"; Hann, "Judaism and Jewish Christianity in Antioch"; Neitz, *Charisma and Christianity*. For analyses of a number of religious movements in contention with traditional and legal authorities in contemporary American society, see Derek Davis and Hankins, eds., *New Religious Movements and Religious Liberty in America*.

25. Colony shepherds were the supervisors of the very large communal Homes (or "colonies") of the early Children of God era. Clusters of colonies in a designated area of the world were in turn supervised and coordinated by regional shepherds.

26. For a concise summary of the collapse of COG, see Melton, *Children of God,* 7–9.

27. One of the family's most controversial former practices, "flirty fishing" (ff-ing) involved using sex as a missionary device for witnessing about Jesus' love to unredeemed sinners in need of salvation. Ffing was practiced for roughly a decade between 1976 and 1987 (see chapter 1). For candid interviews with Family members concerning their former involvement in flirty fishing, see Chancellor, *Life in the Family*. A first-person exposé account is presented in Williams, *Heaven's Harlots*. See also Raine, "Flirty Fishing in the Children of God."

28. Berg, "My Childhood Sex" and "Sex Questions and Answers, Part 1."

29. Melton, *Children of God,* 22–26.

30. In 2008, Family coleaders Maria and Peter issued an "Open Letter of Apology" addressed specifically to current and former second-generation members in which they ask forgiveness from any "who suffered hurt or harm because of the effects of Dad's misapplication of the Law of Love, or mistreatment of any kind" (letter dated January 1, 2008; copy in authors' possession). This apology is accompanied by a candid three-part pamphlet series titled "The Family's History, Policies, and Beliefs Regarding Sex," which has been made required reading in all Family Homes.

31. For accounts of these arrests, see Bainbridge, *Endtime Family*, 1–20; Chancellor, *Life in the Family,* 197–202; and Melton, *Children of God,* 27–47. While all charges were eventually dismissed for lack of credible evidence pertaining to the current cases, these experiences have strongly reinforced current Family members' eschatological beliefs that as God's elect end-time missionaries they will continue to be subject to religious persecution as a test of their faithfulness.

32. After leaving the Family, Ricky developed contacts with other disaffected former members. Family detractors corroborated Ricky's claims of physical, emotional, and sexual abuse to the press, while Family spokespersons emphasized that former child-rearing practices leading to instances of abuse in Family Homes were rectified and abandoned years ago. See "Murder and Suicide Reviving Claims of Child Abuse in Cult"; "Stabber's Friends Blame Decades of Abuse"; Pallack, "Sect Rebuts Claims in Murder." See also Lattin, "Mixed Memories of the Family"; Lelyvedl, Pringle, and Stammer, "Tragic Legacies of a Sex-Based Religion"; Wilkinson, "Life and Death of the Chosen One."

33. Amsterdam, "Family."

34. Amsterdam, "Strengthening Year."

35. Shepherd and Shepherd, "Accommodation and Reformation in the Family/Children of God," 83–85.

36. For a summary of the development of the Family charter, see ibid., 71–72. For expositions of the democratic character of what he calls "responsive communitarianism," see Etzioni, ed., *Essential Communitarian Reader,* and also Etzioni, *Spirit of Community*.

37. For summaries of the Family's board system, see Amsterdam, "Family," 11–13, and Shepherd and Shepherd, "Accommodation and Reformation in the Family/Children of God."

38. We have borrowed the term *ultrasupernaturalism* from Wills, who uses it when describing in *Head and Heart* the Calvinistic and Apocalyptic belief system of 17th-century Puritans. While believing in the indubitable reality of the spirit world that surrounded them, the Puritans—in contrast to the Family International—emphatically rejected the antinomian idea of personal revelation as damnable heresy. At the same time, however, as God's predestined elect, the Puritans were anxiously preoccupied with the task of maintaining a pure, Godly community in the midst of a corrupt, demonic "wilderness" ruled by Satan and his minions. The apocalyptic worldview of the Family International is saturated with very similar demonic imagery. The Family's demonology supports their missionary ideology of "spiritual warfare" with Satan and his legions, who Family members believe are bent on destroying their missionary efforts. While less embellished in their particulars, contemporary Christian fundamentalists and Pentecostals share many of these same beliefs. For a comprehensive history of Protestant fundamentalism and contemporary millenarian beliefs similar to those held by the Family International, see Marsden, *Fundamentalism and American Culture*. For a parallel historical analysis of the American Holiness movement and the rapid emergence of Pentecostalism, especially in the American South, see Stephens, *Fire Spreads*.

39. The explanatory role of this sort of religious "dualism" is analyzed further by Lofland in *Doomsday Cult* and Ammerman in *Bible Believers*.

40. Shepherd and Shepherd, "World Services in the Family International."

Chapter 2. The Practice of Prophecy in the Family

1. The title of the Family organ is represented both as *Good News* and *GN* on the publication itself.

2. See Shepherd and Shepherd, "Social Construction of Prophecy in the Family International" and "Grassroots Prophecy in the Family International."

3. Both "channel" and "local" have dual meanings in the Family. In addition to being a particular person, a channel is also the spiritual mechanism of communication believed to reside within each individual for receiving God's words. Similarly, the term *local* not only refers to someone who reviews and critiques another person's prophecy, but also denotes the critique itself, which is believed to be prophetically derived.

4. Family Christology explicitly sexualizes members' special relationship with Jesus as both their husband and intimate lover. See also note 16 in chapter 6.

5. The gift of prophecy is viewed as a "spiritual weapon" to be used by Family members in the end-time struggle with Satan, his demon legions, and various human agencies who, under satanic influence, seek the destruction of the Family and its work of Christian salvation.

6. The Archangel Michael and the chiefs (Michael's band of angels) are designated "spirit helpers" who aid in channeling prophecies to Family members when they have difficulty "hearing from the Lord."

7. The use of "ha!" at the end of a sentence is a standard rhetorical device used in Family written material to indicate irony or a joke.

8. References to the "field," "field leadership," or "field Homes" are to any missionary areas, organizational leaders, or functioning Family Homes outside of World Services.

9. Family teachings portray Jesus as both having and vicariously delighting in sexual passions achieved through loving sexual encounters enjoyed by Family members who, collectively, are his "Bride." "Sexual sharing" among consenting Family adults is regarded as a form of praise and expression of devotion to Jesus, and is considered to be an important part of the Law of Love incumbent on Family disciple members. "Law of Love battles" among second-generation Family youth are discussed in chapter 8.

Chapter 3. The Role of Prophecy in the Family

1. As part of his initial appeal to the youthful Children of God in Southern California, David Berg appropriated the 1960s student rhetoric of revolution. Subsequently, when major new doctrines or organizational changes were introduced by Berg, they were referred to as *revolutions*.

2. The term *feeding* is often used by Family members in reference to spiritually strengthening people through regular exposure to God's revealed Word.

3. "Runaway prophecies" are said to occur when a prophecy contains a person's personal opinions rather than God's Word, and are considered to be the result of pride and insufficient "yieldedness" to God's spirit.

4. As it turns out, there actually have been a few very small splinter groups from the Family in the years since the death of David Berg, including the self-styled Red Letter Kids, the Jesus Christians, Song of Victory, and a few more. (Personal communication from WS staff member.)

5. In 1992, two former Family members infiltrated a Home in the Philippines and stole a large number of Family music recordings and videos that were in storage there. Some of these videos were "dance videos" of seminaked women and some underage girls who had been taped performing "artistic nude dances" per David Berg's request in the early 1980s. These tapes were subsequently banned from Family Homes as Family leaders began imposing greater constraints on and regulation of the group's liberal sexual mores. The purloined videos from the Philippine's storage facility, however, have been disseminated by former members to mass media agencies, and clips of these videos have occasionally been shown to TV audiences in news programs or documentaries about the Family. These tapes have been used to support charges of sexual licentiousness and child abuse in Family Homes. (For a former member's version of the stolen tapes episode in the Philippines, see exFamily.org/people/Ed Priebe, accessed September 15, 2009.) The current Family leadership has been fairly candid about their earlier practices of sexual openness in front of children, acknowledging that serious indiscretions and mistakes were made in the past but emphasizing that, in response to these mistakes, strict sexual guidelines have been implemented over the past two decades to ensure the healthy development and well-being of children in contemporary Family Homes. These sexual guidelines are specified in the *Love Charter*—the Family's governing document of member rights and responsibilities.

6. See O'Dea's discussion of what he called the "five dilemmas in the institutionalization of religion."

7. "Discipleship standard" refers to the requirements for being a disciple member—the most demanding level of Family membership. Among other things, disciple members must live communally, be full-time missionaries, "provision" their material needs, homeschool their children, and practice the Law of Love through sexual shar-

ing with other consenting adult Family members. These standards are not required of other levels of Family membership (see chapter 1).

8. Disciple members are expected to spend a minimum of one hour daily praying and/or reading God's Word from the Bible or Family prophetic publications, especially the *GN*s. The period set apart for doing this is called Wordtime.

9. Because of security concerns, publication or dissemination of photographs of David Berg and World Services personnel were, for years, prohibited. In 2004, however, the decision was made to post photographs of WS personnel and their activities, including Maria and Peter, on the Family's Web site in an effort to make more transparent the operations of World Services to Family members worldwide. For more on the Family-only Web site, see chapter 7.

Chapter 4. Producing Prophecy for the *Good News*

1. Weber, *Theory of Social and Economic Organization*, 363–92.

2. According to the Family charter, the functioning of all disciple communal Homes (including World Services) must be guided by "Teamworks," consisting of at least three elected Home officers with designated responsibilities in the areas of personnel, outreach, and finances and child care. Recently this basic arrangement has been somewhat altered by substituting the Home Steering Council for the Teamwork. In turn, the steering council now consists of Home managers (whose responsibilities are to take care of the Home's temporal needs) and shepherds (whose responsibilities are to oversee the Home's spiritual needs).

3. In recent years, the position of continental officers, with jurisdictional authority over the functioning of Family Homes in different world areas, has been replaced by regional shepherds, whose duties have been more narrowly defined as monitoring the "spiritual level" of Family homes in different regions worldwide and their compliance with the Family's new Home membership criteria.

4. Summit conferences, at which Peter, international board chairs, and all regional shepherds meet, are periodically held at different locations worldwide to discuss organizational problems and vote on new Family programs and policies.

5. "Pillars" constitute major areas of Family concern, as summarized in chapter 1, including parenting children, guiding teens, homeschooling, church growth and outreach, spiritual supervision of Family Homes, and public relations. Boards are assigned to discuss and recommend appropriate programs for each one of these organizational pillars.

6. See chapter 1 for a summary of the WS work ethic.

7. We infer that experienced, "gifted" channels are individuals who have good writing skills and, who through practice, have skillfully learned to employ the rhetoric of prophecy in their writing.

8. This definition of Family member's religious faith in group prophecy is consistent with Émile Durkheim's functional analysis of religion, in which he theorizes that all religion involves the collective projection of and submission to the norms of the religious community itself as the apotheosis of transcendent power. See Durkheim, *Elementary Forms of the Religious Life*.

9. Shepherd and Shepherd, "Grassroots Prophecy in the Family International."

10. It is the responsibility of WS shepherds to screen candidates for positions at World Services. In doing this they use a standard questionnaire form that emphasizes

applicants' "spiritual qualities" more so than their technical qualifications for performing particular WS assignments (see chapter 7).

11. Under partial excommunication, disciple members are placed on probation and denied full member privileges for a designated time to demonstrate their contrition and repentance.

12. Only a few first-generation adult converts audio record their prophecies. We know of no second-generation adult members who do this. Virtually all SGAs routinely rely on word processing when channeling prophecies. As we note in "Grassroots Prophecy in the Family International": "Clearly, word processing has been incorporated as an important facilitating technology in the Family's culture of prophecy, both in Family communal homes and in the publishing enterprise carried out by WS" (48).

13. A number of first-generation Family members who have worked for years at World Services report "living with Dad" (David Berg) before his death in 1994. Typically their reminiscences affectionately portray a somewhat eccentric man with a kind heart but who could also be irascible on occasion, and who liked to micromanage everyday work projects.

14. Prayer requests are posted on the Family Web site by members suffering from various ailments who petition for organized prayers on their behalf from Family members worldwide.

Chapter 5. Illustrating and Laying Out Prophecy for the *Good News*

1. Examples of graphic Children of God art are the illustrations of nude or seminude women in relatively provocative poses used to adorn the covers of David Berg's 1970s *MO Letter* expositions on the topics of flirty fishing and sexual sharing.

2. Like conventional religious denominations, Family Homes in different regions of the world periodically organize "camps" for young people to attend in order to socialize with their peers while reinforcing their commitment to the Family's missionary cause through Bible study, songfests, inspirational speakers, testimonial meetings, and other activities designed to strengthen their faith.

3. Service centers, like the Heavenly City School (HCS) in Japan, are site locations where various artistic, translating, and distribution activities are undertaken.

4. Key promises for children are phrases children can memorize that involve specific prayer requests and their corresponding blessings. Learning key promises is roughly comparable to Roman Catholic children learning to recite basic catechisms. In the case of Family Children, they also are learning how to use the Family's ultrasupernatural rhetoric for "calling upon the power of the keys."

5. National boards function in designated world regions under the oversight of the Family's international boards to generate policies and programs in the areas of: parenting young children, guiding teenagers, homeschooling for children and teens, missionary and outreach programs, spiritual supervision of Family homes, and public relations. National boards may establish programs or policies for their particular national areas which may or may not apply to or be implemented in other areas of the world. See chapter 1.

6. Family children are socialized into a culture of prophecy in which they learn the rhetoric of prophetic discourse from Family publications that target different age groups and in communal living with others who regularly practice channeling prophecies in the Home. Mothers encourage their children to begin obtaining and recording

prophecies at an early age. One mother we interviewed showed us a journal or logbook she started when her son was three, in which she had recorded dozens of his "prophecies" that she prompted him to verbalize while she wrote them down in response to events like birthday celebrations and gift giving, illnesses, meeting new friends, overcoming problems, and his "spirit helpers." Such statements by children are bound to be somewhat eccentric and incoherent, but they also reflect the values being taught by parents and include elementary religious vocabulary and rhetorical forms that establish the linguistic foundations for the type of religious discourse used in Family prophecy.

Chapter 6. Activating Religious Interest of Nonmembers

1. Shepherd and Shepherd, "Accommodation and Reformation in the Family/Children of God."

2. "Litnessing" is the unique Family term for missionary witnessing to people on the street, in shops or stores, and other public places, through selling of religious pamphlets and other forms of religious literature.

3. "Inspirationalists" are Family members who play musical instruments—usually guitar—and lead the singing in various devotional settings.

4. "Teams" in the Family are any designated units for performing a task or assignment that requires organized teamwork and cooperation to accomplish group objectives.

5. "Board vision" refers to the establishment of regional and international boards for recommending policies in all the major areas of concern for the Family International as a communal missionary organization. See chapter 1 for a summary of Family board structure.

6. *God on God* is classified on the Aurora Productions Web site under the heading Devotional Materials and contains what are presented as verbatim interviews with God (channeled through prophecy by the author) on the subjects of heaven and hell, love and sex, and contemporary social issues concerning the environment, capital punishment, euthanasia, etc.

7. "Activated courses" are framed for the instruction of "outside members" who subscribe to *Activated!* magazine.

8. Periodically, members residing in Family Homes become "road teams" by taking road trips to witness and disseminate Family literature and other products within a certain geographical radius of their Home, sometimes spending several weeks or months on the road, while camping at RV parks along the way.

9. The Aurora Web page itemizes its products for public consumption under the following categories: Children's Videos/DVDs, Videos/DVDs (mostly featuring endtime themes for teenagers and adults), Music, Children's Music, Devotional Materials, Novels (emphasizing apocalyptic storylines for teenagers), For Parents (child-rearing literature), Storybooks for Children, Learning Aids for Children, Children's Devotionals, CD Greeting Cards, and Multimedia products. This products list is dominated by professionally well-done materials for children and reflects the Family International's contemporary emphasis on the care and well-being of their young people.

10. See Shepherd and Shepherd, "Accommodation and Reformation in the Family/Children of God."

11. Both individual sacrifice and communal sharing are important commitment mechanisms analyzed in Kanter's classic study, *Commitment and Community*.

12. The Twelve Foundation Stones course is a required set of scriptural and doctrinal lessons (emphasizing Family teachings found in the *GN*s and original *MO Letters*) that must be completed before a novice recruit can be accepted into full membership.

13. According to the Aurora Productions Web site, "*Treasure Attic* is a live-action, fun-filled educational entertainment series created for an international audience of children from two to eight years of age . . . (it) meets the need for children's educational entertainment . . . most importantly they learn numerous new things like how to get along with others, how to overcome shyness, building self-esteem, showing courtesy, and so on. And on the practical side: travel and home safety tips, cleanliness, nutrition facts, health tips, environmental awareness, new vocabulary words, simple multiplication, how to draw, and much more" (www.auroraproduction.com, accessed September 13, 2009).

14. Deborah Davis and Bill Davis's book is an early exposé of the Family written by David Berg's eldest daughter and her husband. For a more contemporary (and typical) popular-press story of former member grievances and charges of abuse, see "Was the Family Doing God's Work or Unspeakable Harm?"

15. A Web site by and for ex-Family members provides a forum for former members to express their grievances (www.movingon.org). Many who post messages on this site, especially second-generation former members, are deeply bitter about their experience growing up in the Family and attack it and its leaders as a pernicious cult. The Family has countered by mounting a Web site for loyal SGAs to offer testimonials and rebut the charges of abuse alleged by disgruntled former members (www.myconclusion.com).

16. "Loving Jesus" includes sexual love. In this context it refers to the Family's teaching that Jesus has a sexual nature and delights in his followers making vicarious love to him through their own consensual sex with other adult Family members. Sexual sharing among Family adults is one of the many ways in which Family members believe they can express their love for Jesus.

17. Fellow member status is the Family's third-tier membership category, the requirements for which are much less demanding than those for disciple or missionary member categories. See chapter 1 for a description of the requirements for these different levels of Family membership.

Chapter 7. Defending the Faith in the Cyber Age

1. Doctrinal delays in millennial projections constitute a major dilemma for all millenarian religions. The primitive Jesus movement from which Christianity emerged as a world religion was itself an apocalyptic sect. See White, *From Jesus to Christianity*.

2. The Family continues to use David Berg's rhetoric of revolution for designating major organizational or policy changes.

3. The reorganization of World Services into its current departmental structure overlapped with increasing emphasis on delegation of authority, rational reporting procedures, and the cultivation and training of second-generation young people in organizational positions of trust and responsibility.

4. Regional shepherds keep tabs on Family Homes in their designated world regions, making periodic Home visits, reviewing the Homes' monthly reports, and in turn reporting problems and concerns from the field to World Services.

5. TRF stands for Tithing Report Form, which each Family Home submits monthly to World Services via email (rather than by regular mail, as was done in times past), hence the "Tele" designation.

6. Service Homes (or "service people") specialize in administrative, public relations, or various service outreach ministries.

7. The Family's publicly accessible Web site, Family.org, is designed for nonmembers who want to learn more about the Family's missionary message, outreach programs, or religious materials.

8. Ricky is the name Maria's son ("Davidito") took when he left the Family in 2000. Angela is the former WS Family member Ricky murdered in 2005 (see an account of this event in chapter 1). The Web team subsequently created "Ricky" and "Angela" sites so Family members and other acquaintances who had known both of them could post their recollections and impressions of the two from happier times. Among other things, these recollections portrayed Ricky's "sweet side" as a young boy growing up in the Family prior to his departure and growing embitterment against his parents.

9. Myconclusion.com is a Web site created for loyal second-generation Family youth to offer testimonials and rebut the charges of child abuse frequently posted on movingon.org by disgruntled former members.

10. Countdown.org is a Family site that focuses on the "countdown to Armageddon," and features the *Endtime News Digest*.

11. As discussed in chapter 5, Activated ministries, Homes, desks, etc., are references to the distribution and use of *Activated!* magazine to recruit subscribers and financial supporters for disciple members' missionary work.

12. In their daily morning devotionals, Family Home members will often take turns reading aloud from new *GN* issues or from "Word compilations" of Family doctrine or policies culled and assembled from previous *GN*s, or earlier *MO Letters*.

13. For analyses of premillennialist Protestant beliefs concerning the end-time and the anticipated "Great Tribulation" and "Rapture" of those saved in Jesus, see Sandeen, *Roots of Fundamentalism;* Marsden, *Fundamentalism and American Culture;* and Wills, *Head and Heart.*

14. While Family members frequently employ the apocalyptic rhetoric of "spiritual warfare," they—unlike militant apocalyptic groups such as Jim Jones's People's Temple or the Branch Davidians—are nonviolent and have not accumulated or condoned the use of lethal weapons against anyone, including their most vociferous detractors. For detailed case studies and analysis of violent millenarian groups, whose eschatologies contrast sharply with the Family International's essential pacifism, see Wessinger, *How the Millennium Comes Violently.*

15. For a classical analysis of the solidarity consequences of social conflict, see Coser, *Functions of Social Conflict.*

16. We found that most parents at World Services had adult children who had made the decision to leave the Family. Some of these second-generation young adults were still on friendly terms with their parents. Others, like Maria's son, Ricky Rodriguez, had become hostile and adversarial. (Maria also has a daughter, Techi, who has remained in the Family and oversees children's schooling at World Services.)

Chapter 8. Managing the World Services Home

1. Esau was raised in the Mormon Church but was drawn to the 1960s counterculture and was converted by Children of God missionaries. He worked as a handyman for World Services when David Berg was alive and reminisced with us about his conversion, his early days in the Children of God, his initial alienation from his Mormon

relatives, and Berg's inclination to give unsolicited instruction regarding minor building or maintenance projects.

2. Based on allegations of child abuse in the 1990s, police raided Family communal homes in Argentina, Australia, Spain, and France, arresting parents and placing their minor children in state custody, as reported in the preface and chapter 1. Although all charges of abuse were eventually dismissed in court, these earlier experiences no doubt heightened the anxiety of current members about the dangerous potential of negative publicity and the need to take proactive measures.

3. Home managers deal with the temporal concerns of daily life, which include provisioning groceries and household supplies, home maintenance projects, child care, and paying bills.

4. Emphasizing the ideals and positive potential of the Family's sexual norms, the Love Charter declares that, "The 'Law of Love' must govern all sexual activity. The basic tenet of the Law of Love is that what is done is agreed upon by all the parties involved, and precautions are taken so others are not hurt by their activities. . . . The sexual freedoms the Lord has allowed us are a beautiful and fruitful part of our faith. Having the opportunity to share sexually within our Homes brings about a unity and love that is not present in other churches. It is especially helpful in our communal lifestyle as it draws us closer together and to the Lord" (273). This statement is followed by a 34-page section titled "Sex and Affection Rules," which details the kinds of sexual activity that may begin at what ages and with whom. Thus, for example, 12- to 13-year-olds may date with their parents' permission, but only "non-sexual affection" is allowed. Junior teens (ages 14 and 15) may date others within their own age range and have physical contact with other teens that their parents deem appropriate, though not sexual intercourse. Teens (ages 16–17) may engage in sexual intercourse with other teens ages 16–20 with their parents' consent in those areas of the world that define the age of consent as 16 or 17. See discussion of parallel marriage rules in chapter 9, note 14. Young people between the ages of 18 and 20 may engage in sexual intercourse with consenting partners up to seven years older than themselves. Adult members, 21 years of age or older, may only engage in sexual intercourse with other adult members, unless they are married to a younger sexual partners (adult members who are 21 or older may not marry teens under the age of 18).

5. For an exposition of democratic values in what he calls "responsive communitarianism," see Etzioni, ed., *Essential Communitarian Reader*. See also Etzioni, *Spirit of Community*.

6. For a collection of articles that discuss, among other things, the construction of "apostasy narratives" that are used in mobilizing anticult campaigns, see Bromley, ed., *Politics of Religious Apostasy*.

7. While the Family is a strongly pronatal religion that discourages the use of contraceptives, many SGAs—though sexually active—are waiting longer to pair off and become parents than did FGAs. The shepherd's counseling advice to SGAs at World Services reflects a degree of modification from earlier Family marriage and birth control norms. Having a baby and being a "single mom" is not stigmatized in the Family and, in the past, was not terribly uncommon. (The children of single mothers grow up in a supportive communal environment where they are homeschooled and communally socialized along with other Family children.) Today, however, many SGA females seem less eager to begin having babies at an early age, especially in the absence of a

father who will assume coparenting responsibilities. These trends reflect some of the important ways in which Family leadership is having to make institutional adjustments to the coming of age of second- (and third-) generation disciple members.

8. Kanter, *Commitment and Community.*

9. Stark, "Normal Revelations."

10. When children who are born into heretical religions like the Family International ultimately reject their parents' religious values and decide to leave the community in which they were raised, they typically enjoy the sympathy of outsiders, who view their leaving as a sign of intellectual maturity and moral strength. Such sympathy rarely is extended to their religiously devout parents, who grieve over the loss of their children's affection and loyalty in the same way that other parents often do when their children make life choices that violate their core values.

11. For an overview of World Services' turn-of-the-millennium retrenchment campaign to more strictly enforce disciple standards in Family Homes worldwide, see Shepherd and Shepherd, "Accommodation and Reformation in the Family/Children of God."

12. The Year of Strengthening was a designation used in 2004 when all Family International Homes were placed on probation in a collective effort to renew members' commitment and compliance with charter rules and to determine their Home level classification for the following Year of Restructuring. For an overview of this organizational renewal movement, see Amsterdam, "Family."

Chapter 9. Managing the International Flock

1. Individual Family members in field Homes as well as WS staff can and do set up personal email accounts for private correspondence.

2. The Elerian horses, identified from a 2004 symbolic vision that was validated and elaborated on by WS channels, are believed to be angels (not actual horses) of mental freedom who are available to assist Family members in changing worldly modes of thinking and old mindsets and also to strengthen Family members' faith to love and follow Jesus in newly revealed ways.

3. Prayer vigils in behalf of Family members, whose names are on the "prayer list," are also held daily in Family communal Homes around the world.

4. Family disciple members are part of a highly mobile religious community in which individuals frequently move from one communal residence to another or "pioneer" new ministries, for which they experience a "burden" (inspiration from God) to undertake, necessitating a move to a new location. Family members (especially new converts) also typically assume new names or nicknames by which they become familiarly known to other members. But FGAs and SGAs also can and do change their first names from time to time if they feel inspired to do so.

5. Former visiting shepherds (mostly FGAs), who previously were assigned to periodically visit and supervise Family Homes, have largely been replaced by SGAs and are now called coaches. Newly appointed coaches must undergo coach training where, among other things, personnel management skills are taught. Once trained, a coach's job is to subsequently train and supervise Home shepherds in monitoring and maintaining disciple standards in Family Homes. For a discussion of the new coaching program, see the second interview in this chapter.

6. "New moves of the Spirit" is a phrase used in reference to new policies, pro-

grams, or doctrinal innovations that are introduced to Family members' *GN* publications in the form of newly channeled revelations from God.

7. In recent years Family leaders have greatly softened their earlier moral condemnation of individuals who lost their faith or abandoned their commitment to the Family. Increasingly it has been acknowledged that not all their members can sustain the level of faith and sacrifice required of full-time missionary work. This has been accompanied by an attitude of greater reconciliation with those who chose to leave.

8. "New structure" refers to the organizational changes taking place in the Family in recent years, from the development of an integrated department organization at WS to the institutionalization of Family boards, the restructuring of membership requirements at different levels of missionary commitment, and the instigation of the new coaching program.

9. In effect, summits are the Family's "congress," meeting every 12 to 18 months and attended by WS leaders and regional shepherds, who, utilizing the same prayer and prophecy procedures described elsewhere in this book, debate Family issues and formulate official Family policies. Summit meetings demonstrate the democratization of Family governance at the international level, just as the decision-making procedures instituted at World Services do at the headquarters organization and the steering councils do at the grassroots level of Family field Homes.

10. "Provisioning," or obtaining goods and services as missionary donations, is the basic way that most Family members have learned to support themselves and their various outreach programs.

11. The phrase "old bottles"—an allusion to the biblical adage concerning the inadvisability of putting new wine into old bottles—is commonly used in Family rhetoric to refer to people who are unreceptive to the "new wine" of God's Word, as channeled through contemporary prophecy.

12. This Family-wide action was an extension of the crackdown in Brazil. Disciple member privileges were suspended for a year, during which time every Family Home had to make a decision to choose the new level of member commitment—disciple, member missionary, or fellow member—whose standards they were able and willing to live collectively.

13. Maria, costumed in sackcloth and ashes, videotaped a dramatic recitation—referred to as "The Woe video"—of Family Home shortcomings and failures to comply with disciple standards, which was sent to and viewed by all Family members worldwide to justify and inaugurate the "Strengthening" and Restructuring" campaigns of 2004 through 2006.

14. For legal purposes, adults are defined by the charter as 21 years of age or older. Adults are not permitted to have sexual contact with anyone under the age of 21, unless the parties involved are married to each other. Otherwise, if discovered, the adult member will be immediately excommunicated. Furthermore, members who are 21 or older may not marry anyone under the age of 18. Teen members ages 16–17 may marry those who are ages 16–20, providing they have parental consent. See note 4 in chapter 8 for parallel rules regarding sexual contact. Other excommunicable sex offenses for disciple members are engaging in sexual activity with non-Family members; "sodomy" (male-with-male sexual activity); and engaging in sexual activity with new or rejoining members who have been in the Family for less than six months.

15. Maintaining strong boundaries that separate members from nonmembers through enforcement of strict commitment rules is one of the chief characteristics

of successful communal organizations identified in Kanter's study, *Commitment and Community*.

16. See Shepherd and Shepherd, "Accommodation and Reformation in the Family/Children of God."

17. For an analysis of the effects that religious competition in pluralistic societies have on the increasing rationality of administrative procedures in contemporary religious organizations, see Berger, *Sacred Canopy*.

18. One potential transitional role for aging first-generation disciples has been created by the Family's Activated program, discussed in chapter 6. People who become interested in Family teachings, subscribe to *Activated!* magazine, and seek additional instruction without becoming missionaries themselves may be compared to the members of conventional Christian churches in which paid clergy minister to their congregants' spiritual needs. The Activated program is a potential vehicle for every disciple Home to build a supporting congregation or "church" consisting of Activated members who tithe to the local Family Home. Adopting conventional Christianity's model of a quasi-salaried ministry provides an opportunity for older, first-generation disciples to assume pastoral roles to their Activated members. Many FGAs are secondary- (MM) or tertiary-level (FM) members and are not considered "full disciples," i.e., one who is a member of a Family Disciple (FD) Home.

19. One comparison religion is the Church of Jesus Christ of Latter-day Saints (Mormons). Like the Family International, the 19th-century LDS Church was instituted in the belief that the end-time was at hand, but it had to modify its urgent millennial expectations to accommodate the religious upbringing of subsequent generations. Like the Family, contemporary Latter-day Saints continue to imbue their youth with a missionary ethos and groom them to render two years of missionary service. Large numbers of LDS youth conform to the missionary expectations of their religion, but an even larger number do not. Retention problems are an important issue for the LDS Church and, as in the Family, finding ways to sustain the fidelity of its youth is a major priority. See Shepherd and Shepherd, *Mormon Passage*.

20. Charter requirements for becoming a Family disciple member and being accepted into a disciple Home are stringent and include the following: 1) Receive Jesus as one's personal savior and be filled with the Holy Spirit; 2) Be of legal age or have notarized parental permission; 3) Have a basic understanding of the Family, its goals, way of life, and believe that David was God's end-time Prophet, and that Maria is God's chosen and anointed successor (this set of requirements is accompanied by a list of required reading materials); 4) Show a sincere interest in reading God's Word and a desire to engage in evangelism; 5) Have a sincere desire to dedicate life to serving Jesus; 6) Live in a disciple Home for a minimum of 20 days; 7) Be free of substance abuse and illegal drugs; 8) Be free of contagious disease; 9) Test negative for AIDS before moving into the Home and test negative again after a six-month period; 10) Take a test for sexually transmitted diseases; 11) Have no financial debts; 12) Have no legal or military obligations that would prevent being a full-time member of a disciple Home.

21. The reference is to Berg, "Furlougher, Backslider—or Supporter?"

22. According to Peter, "At the time the Charter was drafted, the main concern was that Homes would be too large, as opposed to too small. The ideal Home size proposed in the Charter was between twenty-five to thirty members, which would generally be a Home of ten-fifteen adults, depending on the number of their children.

However, over time, the average number of members per Home continued to drop until the present. In a number of cases, Charter Homes have over time come to consist of nuclear families, rather than communal households. . . . To reverse this trend, the minimum number of members required for a Family discipleship Home will be raised, effective January 2005. In order to ensure that Homes are able to form well-rounded mission works, the minimum Home size will be set at six members eighteen years of age and older, in contrast to the present four members sixteen years of age and older. Our recommendation is that Homes increase their size to over eight adults (aged eighteen and older). We will maintain the current limitation on maximum Home size at thirty-five members (of all ages) so as to ensure that Homes are manageable in size." Amsterdam, "Family."

Chapter 10. World Services and the Contemporary Family International

1. In stating his famous argument that all religions posit a categorical distinction between the sacred and profane, Émile Durkheim concluded that every religion must be sustained by a moral community of like-minded believers who share the same moral meanings (or "collective conscience"), however strange or repugnant they might seem to outsiders. The empirical sources for Durkheim's universal generalizations about religion were not, in fact, contemporary Christian denominations but were based in 19th- and early-20th-century ethnographies of Aboriginal clan societies in Australia. See Durkheim, *Elementary Forms of the Religious Life.*

2. See our more theoretical analysis of heresy in relation to prophecy, based on comparisons between the Family International and the Church of Jesus Christ of Latter-day Saints: Shepherd and Shepherd, "Prophecy Channels and Prophetic Modalities."

3. For a summary of different types of contemporary political and religious movements in historical context, see Garner, *Contemporary Movements and Ideologies.*

4. Marx and McAdam, *Collective Behavior and Social Movements,* 93.

5. Blumer, "Collective Behavior."

6. Turner and Killian, *Collective Behavior,* 254–55.

7. On open-systems analysis in organizational studies, see Scott, *Organizations,* and "Reflections on a Half-century of Organizational Sociology"; Thompson, *Organizations in Action.*

8. By "religious economy" we mean a marketplace of competing faiths in which individuals have the freedom to exercise personal preferences in making decisions about religious affiliation. For applications of the concept of religious economies, see Berger, *Sacred Canopy;* Finke and Stark, *Churching of America;* Sherkat and Wilson, "Preferences, Constraints, and Choices in Religious Markets."

9. For reviews and analyses of the resource mobilization approach to the study of social movements, see McAdam, McCarthy, and Zald, eds., *Comparative Perspectives on Social Movements;* McCarthy and Zald, "Enduring Vitality of the Resource Mobilization Theory of Social Movements."

10. See, for example, Clemens and Minkoff, "Beyond the Iron Law"; G. Davis, McAdam, Scott, and Zald, eds., *Social Movements and Organization Theory.*

11. For an overview of the heuristic value of scholarly exchange between students of organizations and social movements, see McAdam and Scott, "Organizations and Movements."

12. Armstrong, "From Struggle to Settlement," 186.

13. For analyses of a number of relatively mature religious movements in contention with traditional and legal authorities in contemporary American society, see Derek Davis and Hankins, eds., *New Religious Movements and Religious Liberty in America.*

14. The transition from emergent to more institutionalized forms of religious organization has, of course, long been a major theme in the sociology of religion, particularly within the theoretical framework of church-sect analysis. See, for example, Johnson, "Church-Sect Revisited"; ibid., "On Founders and Followers"; Miller, ed., *When Prophets Die.* For sample analyses of the institutionalization of particular religious movements, see Beckford, *Trumpet of Prophecy;* Lawson, "Broadening the Boundaries of Church-Sect Theory"; Shepherd and Shepherd, *Kingdom Transformed.*

15. In a somewhat similar vein, Lorne Dawson, reflecting on the contemporary study of new religions, comments that, "Until recently, the study of new religions was driven by the public need to replace ignorance and misinformation, and the fear they evoke, with accurate information and judicious assessments of the problems posed by new religions . . . [now] attention must turn more squarely to the demands of another reference group: other scholars engaged in the study of religion and their interests, whether in sociology, history, anthropology or psychology of religion, or religious studies, political science, or even theology. If the study of the fringe cannot be made to speak more directly to the interests of the mainstream, the study of new religious movements will lapse into relative obscurity, along with the cult scare that provided so much of its impetus" ("New Religion Studies—Whither and Why?").

16. For an analysis of contemporary transnational movements, see J. Smith, "Globalization and Transnational Social Movement Organizations."

17. For a number of hypotheses concerning the organizational behavior of federated social movements, see McCarthy, "Persistence and Change among Federated Social Movement Organizations."

18. For a systematic analysis of group mechanisms for building and maintaining commitment, particularly in religious organizations, see Kanter, *Commitment and Community.* For a statistical analysis and refinement of Kanter's work, see Hall, "Social Organization and Pathways."

19. Campbell, "Where Do We Stand?" 49. See also Snow, "Master Frames and Cycles of Protest."

20. Campbell, "Where Do We Stand?" 49.

21. For a succinct analysis of the ultimacy of supernatural convictions, see O'Dea and O'Dea, *Sociology of Religion,* 32–37.

22. For a sociological analysis of the emergence and development of professional priesthood organizations, see Weber, *Sociology of Religion,* 60–79.

23. There is a substantial literature on religious patriarchies and women's issues. For a small but diverse sampling, see Bamforth and Richards, *Patriarchal Religion, Sexuality, and Gender;* Bennion, *Desert Patriarchy;* Cantor, *Jewish Women/Jewish Men;* Grangoli, *Indian Feminisms.*

24. Clemens, "Two Kinds of Stuff."

25. Shepherd and Shepherd, "Grassroots Prophecy in the Family International."

26. An international organization of scholars based in Torino, Italy, CESNUR (Center for Study of New Religions) sponsors and reports research on new religious movements around the world; see www.cesnur.org. Zerby and Kelly, "Future of the Family International."

Bibliography

Adams, Brook. "ACLU Says Constitutional Rights Threatened in Texas FLDS Child Custody Proceedings." *Salt Lake Tribune,* April 20, 2008.

———. "Polygamy: Where Religious Liberty Ends." *Salt Lake Tribune,* April 13, 2008.

Ammerman, Nancy Tatom. *Bible Believers: Fundamentalists in the Modern World.* New Brunswick, N.J.: Rutgers University Press, 1987.

Amsterdam, Peter. "The Family—Restructuring and Renewal: An Overview of Organizational Changes, 1994–2006." Paper presented at the annual Center for Study of New Religions (CESNUR) conference, Waco, Tex., June 19, 2004.

———. "A Strengthening Year: A Review of 2005." *Good News* 1163 (2006), 1–7.

Anthony, Paul A. "Attorneys Raise Concerns about FLDS Child Custody Cases." *San Angelo Standard Times,* April 14, 2008.

Armstrong, Elizabeth A. "From Struggle to Settlement: The Crystallization of a Field of Lesbian/Gay Organization in San Francisco, 1969–1973." In *Social Movements and Organization Theory,* edited by G. Davis et al., 161–87.

Bainbridge, William Sims. *The Endtime Family: Children of God.* Albany: State University of New York Press, 2002.

———. *The Sociology of Religious Movements.* New York: Routledge, 1997.

Bamforth, Nicholas, and David A. Richards. *Patriarchal Religion, Sexuality, and Gender: A Critique of New Natural Law.* New York: Cambridge University Press, 2007.

Barker, Eileen. *New Religious Movements: A Practical Introduction.* London: Her Majesty's Stationery Office, 1989.

Beckford, James A. "The Mass Media and New Religious Movements." In *New Religious Movements: Challenge and Response,* edited by Bryan Wilson and James Cresswell, 103–20. London: Routledge, 1999.

———. *The Trumpet of Prophecy: A Sociological Study of Jehovah's Witnesses.* New York: John Wiley and Sons, 1976.

Bennion, Janet. *Desert Patriarchy: Mormon and Mennonite Communities in the Chihuahua Valley.* Tucson: University of Arizona Press, 2004.

Berg, David. "Furlougher, Backslider—or Supporter?" In *MO Letter* 810, no. 1 (January 1979).

———. "My Childhood Sex—Doin' What Comes Naturally." In *MO Letter* 779, no. 6 (June 1977).

———. "Sex Questions and Answers, Part 1—Children and Sex." In *MO Letter* 815, no. 7 (September 1979).

Berger, Peter. *The Sacred Canopy: Elements of a Sociological Theory of Religion.* New York: Doubleday, 1969.

Bird, F. B. "Charisma and Leadership in New Religious Movements." In *Handbook of Cults and Sects in America,* Vol. B, edited by David G. Bromley and Jeffery K. Hadden, 75–92. Greenwich, Conn.: JAI, 1993.

Blumer, Herbert. "Collective Behavior." In *An Outline of the Principles of Sociology*, edited by Robert E. Park, 219–80. New York: Barnes and Noble, 1939.

Bord, Richard J. "Toward a Social-psychological Theory of Charismatic Social Influence Processes." *Social Forces* 53 (1975): 485–97.

Bromley, David. *The Politics of Religious Apostasy: The Role of Apostates in the Transformation of Religious Movements*. Westport, Conn.: Praeger, 1998.

Bromley, David, and Diana Gay Cutchin. "The Social Construction of Subversive Evil: The Contemporary Anti-cult and Anti-Satanism Movements." In *Waves of Protest: Social Movements since the Sixties*, edited by Jo Freeman and Victoria Johnson, 195–218. Lanham, Md.: Rowman and Littlefield, 1999.

Bromley, David, and J. Gordon Melton. *Cults, Religion, and Violence*. Cambridge, England: Cambridge University Press, 2002.

Campbell, John L. "Where Do We Stand? Common Mechanisms in Organizations and Social Movements Research." In *Social Movements and Organization Theory*, edited by G. Davis et al., 41–68. New York: Cambridge University Press, 2005.

Cantor, Aviva. *Jewish Women/Jewish Men: The Legacy of Patriarchy in Jewish Life*. San Francisco: HarperOne, 1999.

Chancellor, James D. *Life in the Family: An Oral History of the Children of God*. Syracuse, N.Y.: Syracuse University Press, 2000.

"Children of God: Released Members Accuse Judge Marquevich; The Return of Their Houses Is Ordered." *El Clarín* (Buenos Aires), December 15, 1993.

"Children of God: The Court Finally Returns 130 Children to Their Parents." *El Clarín* (Buenos Aires), December 24, 1993.

Christie-Murray, David. *A History of Heresy*. Oxford: Oxford University Press, 1989.

Clemens, Elisabeth S. "Invention, Innovation, Proliferation: Explaining Organizational Growth and Change." In *Research in the Sociology of Organizations*, edited by Michael Lounsbury and Marc J. Ventresca, 397–411. Oxford: Elsevier Science, 2002.

———. "Organizational Repertoires and Institutional Change: Women's Groups and the Transformation of U.S. Politics, 1890–1920." *American Journal of Sociology* 98, no. 4 (1993): 755–98.

———. "Two Kinds of Stuff: The Current Encounter of Social Movements and Organizations." In *Social Movements and Organization Theory*, edited by G. Davis et al., 351–425.

Clemens, Elisabeth S., and Debra C. Minkoff. "Beyond the Iron Law: Rethinking the Place of Organizations in Social Movement Research." In *The Blackwell Companion to Social Movements*, edited by David A. Snow, Sara Anne Soule, and Hanspeter Kriesi, 155–70. Malden, Mass.: Blackwell, 2004.

Colin, A., and R. A. Young. *The Future of Careers*. Cambridge: Cambridge University Press, 2000.

Cooper, Anderson. *360 Show and Blog* for CNN, April 10, 2008.

Coser, Lewis A. *The Functions of Social Conflict*. New York: Free Press, 1954.

Davis, Deborah, and Bill Davis. *The Children of God: The Inside Story*. Grand Rapids, Mich.: Zondervan, 1984.

Davis, Derek, and Barry Hankins, eds. *New Religious Movements and Religious Liberty in America*. Waco, Tex.: Baylor University Press, 2003.

Davis, Gerald F., Doug McAdam, W. Richard Scott, and Mayer N. Zald. *Social Movements and Organization Theory*. New York: Cambridge University Press, 2005.

Davis, Rex, and James T. Richardson. "The Organization and Functioning of the Children of God." *Sociological Analysis* 37 (1976): 321–39.

Dawson, Lorne L. *Comprehending Cults: The Sociology of New Religious Movements.* New York: Oxford University Press, 1998.

———. "Convergent Psychopathologies and the Attribution of Charisma: A Brief Critical Introduction to the Psychology of Charisma." Paper presented at the annual meeting of the Society for the Scientific Study of Religion, Columbus, Ohio, 2001.

———. "New Religion Studies—Whither and Why?" Paper presented at the annual meeting of the American Academy of Religion, Washington, D.C., 2006.

DiSabatino, David. *The Jesus People Movement: An Annotated Bibliography and General Resource.* Westport, Conn.: Greenwood Press, 1999.

Durkheim, Émile. *The Elementary Forms of the Religious Life.* Glencoe, Ill.: Free Press, 1965.

Etzioni, Amitai. *The Essential Communitarian Reader.* Lanham, Md.: Rowman and Littlefield, 1998.

———. *The Spirit of Community: Rights, Responsibilities, and the Communitarian Agenda.* New York: Crown, 1994.

Evans, G. R. *A Brief History of Heresy.* London: Blackwell Publishers, 2003.

Family International. *The Love Charter.* Zurich, Switzerland: Aurora Productions, 1995.

"The Family Sect Case Collapses." *Sidney Sun-Herald,* November 2, 1992, 1.

"The Family's History, Policies, and Beliefs Regarding Sex," 3-part series. *Good News* 1234–36 (2007).

Feldman, Jan. *Lubavitchers as Citizens: A Paradox of Liberal Democracy.* Ithaca, N.Y.: Cornell University Press, 2003.

Finke, Roger, and Rodney Stark. *The Churching of America: Winners and Losers in Our Religious Economy.* New Brunswick, N.J.: Rutgers University Press, 1992.

Finzel, Han. *The Top Ten Mistakes Leaders Make.* Colorado Springs: David C. Cook Distribution, 2004.

Garner, Roberta. *Contemporary Movements and Ideologies.* New York: McGraw-Hill, 1996.

Goffman, Erving. *Asylums: Essays on the Social Situations of Patients and Other Inmates.* Garden City, N.Y.: Doubleday Anchor, 1961.

———. *Stigma: Notes on the Management of Spoiled Identity.* Englewood Cliffs, N.J.: Spectrum/Prentice-Hall, 1963.

Gordon, Sarah Barringer. *The Mormon Question: Polygamy and Constitutional Conflict in Nineteenth-Century America.* Chapel Hill: University of North Carolina Press, 2001.

Grangoli, Geetanjali. *Indian Feminisms: Law Patriarchies and Feminism in India.* Burlington, Vt.: Ashgate Publishing, 2007.

Hall, John R. "Social Organization and Pathways: Types of Communal Groups, Rational Choice Theory and the Kanter Thesis." *American Sociological Review* 53 (October 1988): 679–92.

Hann, Robert R., "Judaism and Jewish Christianity in Antioch: Charisma and Conflict in the First Century," *Journal of Religious History* 14 (1987): 341–60.

Harris, Jane. "Holiness and Pentecostal Traditions: Making the Spirit Count." In *Religion and Public Life in the Southern Crossroads,* edited by William Lindsey and Mark Silk, 79–102. Walnut Creek, Calif.: AltaMira Press, 2005.

Harsley, Richard A. *Sociology and the Jesus Movement.* New York: Continuum, 1994.

Henderson, John B. *The Construction of Orthodoxy and Heresy: Neo-Confucian, Islamic, Jewish, and Early Christian Patterns.* Albany: State University of New York Press, 1998.

Holden, Andrew. *Jehovah's Witnesses: Portrait of a Contemporary Religious Movement.* London: Routledge, 2002.

Hylton, Hilary. "The Future of the Polygamist Kids." *Time,* April 15, 2008.

Jenkins, Philip. *Moral Panic: Changing Conceptions of the Child Molester in Modern America.* New Haven, Conn.: Yale University Press, 1998.

Johnson, Benton. "Church-Sect Revisited." *Journal for the Scientific Study of Religion* 10, no. 2 (1971): 124–37.

———. "On Founders and Followers: Some Factors in the Development of New Religious Movements." *Sociological Analysis* 53 (Supplement S, 1992): 1–13.

Jones, Kristina, Celeste Jones, and Juliana Buhring. *Not without My Sister.* London: HarperElement, 2008.

Kanter, Rosabeth Moss. *Commitment and Community: Communes and Utopias in Sociological Perspective.* Cambridge, Mass.: Harvard University Press, 1972.

Kraybill, Donald B. *The Amish and the State.* Baltimore: Johns Hopkins University Press, 2003.

Lattin, Don. *Jesus Freaks: A True Story of Murder and Madness on the Evangelical Edge.* New York: HarperOne, 2007.

———. "Mixed Memories of the Family." *San Francisco Chronicle,* February 27, 2005.

Lawson, Ronald. "Broadening the Boundaries of Church-Sect Theory: Insights from the Evolution of the Nonschismatic Mission Churches of Seventh-day Adventism." *Journal for the Scientific Study of Religion* 37, no. 4 (1998): 652–72.

Lelyvedl, Nita, Paul Pringle, and Larry B. Stammer. "Tragic Legacies of a Sex-Based Religion: Murder and Suicide." *Los Angeles Times,* March 12, 2005.

Lindof, Thomas R., and Bryan C. Taylor. *Qualitative Communication Research Methods.* Thousand Oaks, Calif.: Sage Publications, 2002.

Lofland, John. *Doomsday Cult: A Study of Conversion, Proselytization, and Maintenance of Faith.* New York: Irvington, 1977.

Ludemann, Gerd. *Primitive Christianity: A Survey of Recent Studies and New Proposals.* Edinburgh, Scotland: T & T Clark Publishers, 2004.

Lyman, Leo. *Political Deliverance: The Mormon Quest for Utah Statehood.* Urbana: University of Illinois Press, 1986.

MacCormack, John. "Sect Is a Legal Nightmare." *San Antonio Express-News,* April 14, 2008.

MacGregor, Scott. *God on God.* Zurich, Switzerland: Aurora Productions, 2002.

Marsden, George M. *Fundamentalism and American Culture,* 2nd ed. New York: Oxford University Press, 2006.

Marx, Gary T., and Doug McAdam. *Collective Behavior and Social Movements: Process and Structure.* Englewood Cliffs, N.J.: Prentice Hall. 1994.

McAdam, Doug, and W. Richard Scott. "Organizations and Movements." In *Social Movements and Organization Theory,* edited by G. Davis et al., 4–40.

McAdam, Doug, John D. McCarthy, and Mayer N. Zald, eds. *Comparative Perspectives on Social Movements: Political Opportunities, Mobilizing Structures, and Cultural Framings.* New York: Cambridge University Press, 1996.

McCarthy, John D. "Persistence and Change among Federated Social Movement Organizations." In *Social Movements and Organization Theory,* edited by G. Davis et al., 193–225.

McCarthy, John D., and Mayer N. Zald. "The Enduring Vitality of the Resource Mobilization Theory of Social Movements." In *Handbook of Sociological Theory,* edited by Jonathon H. Turner, 533–65. New York: Kluwer Academic/Plenum, 2001.

———. "Resource Mobilization and Social Movements: A Partial Theory." *American Journal of Sociology* 82, no. 6 (1977): 1212–41.

McCloud, Sean. "From Exotics to Brainwashers: Portraying New Religions in the Mass Media." *Religion Compass* 1, no. 3 (2006): 1–15.

Meeks, Wayne. *The First Urban Christians: The Urban World of the Apostle Paul.* New Haven, Conn.: Yale University Press, 2003.

Melton, J. Gordon. *The Children of God: "The Family."* Salt Lake City, Utah: Signature Press, 2004.

Melton, J. Gordon, and Christopher Partridge. *New Religions: A Guide: New Religious Movements, Sects, and New Spiritualities.* New York: Oxford University Press, 2004.

Miller, Timothy. *The 60s Communes: Hippies and Beyond.* Syracuse, N.Y.: Syracuse University Press, 1999.

———, ed. *When Prophets Die: The Post-charismatic Fate of New Religious Movements.* Albany: State University of New York Press, 1991.

"Murder and Suicide Reviving Claims of Child Abuse in Cult." *New York Times,* January 15, 2005.

Neitz, Mary Jo. *Charisma and Christianity.* New Brunswick, N.J.: Transaction, 1987.

Newport, Kenneth C. *The Branch Davidians of Waco: The History and Beliefs of an Apocalyptic Sect.* New York: Oxford University Press, 2006.

Niebuhr, H. Richard. *The Social Sources of Denominationalism.* New York: Henry Holt, 1929.

O'Dea, Thomas F. "Five Dilemmas in the Institutionalization of Religion." *Journal for the Scientific Study of Religion* 1, no. 1 (1961): 30–41.

O'Dea, Thomas F., and Janet O'Dea Aviad. *The Sociology of Religion,* 2nd ed. Englewood Cliffs, N.J.: Prentice-Hall, 1983.

Pallack, Becky. "Sect Rebuts Claims in Murder." *Arizona Daily Star,* January 13, 2005.

Poloma, Margaret M. *The Assemblies of God at the Crossroads: Charisma and Institutional Dilemmas.* Knoxville: University of Tennessee Press, 1989.

———. *The Charismatic Movement: Is There a New Pentecost?* Boston: Twayne Publishers, 1982.

———. *Main Street Mystics: The Toronto Blessing and Reviving Pentecostalism.* Walnut Creek, Calif.: AltaMira Press, 2003.

Raine, Susan. "Flirty Fishing in the Children of God: The Sexual Body as a Site of Proselytization and Salvation." *Marburg Journal of Religion* 12 (2007): 1–18.

Richardson, James. "Definitions of Cult: From Sociological-Technical to Popular-Negative." *Review of Religious Research* 34 (1993): 348–56.

Rubin, Herbert J., and Irene S. Rubin. *Qualitative Interviewing : The Art of Hearing Data.* Thousand Oaks, Calif.: Sage Publications, 1995.

Sandeeen, Ernest. *The Roots of Fundamentalism: British and American Millenarianism, 1800–1930.* Grand Rapids, Mich.: Baker Book House, 1978.

Scott, W. Richard. *Organizations: Rational, Natural, and Open Systems,* 5th ed. Upper Saddle River, N.J.: Prentice Hall, 2003.

———. "Reflections on a Half-century of Organizational Sociology." *Annual Review of Sociology* 30 (August 2004): 1–21.

Shepherd, Gary. "Cults: Social Psychological Aspects." In *The Encyclopedia of Sociology*, Vol. 2 edited by George Ritzer, 884–87. London: Blackwell Publishers, 2007.

Shepherd, Gary, and Gordon Shepherd. "Accommodation and Reformation in the Family/Children of God." *Nova Religio* 9, no. 1 (2005): 67–92.

———. "The Family International: A Case Study in the Management of Change in New Religious Movements." *Religion Compass* 1, no. 1 (2006): 1–16.

———. "Grassroots Prophecy in the Family International." *Nova Religio* 10, no. 14 (2007): 38–71.

———. *Mormon Passage: A Missionary Chronicle*. Urbana and Chicago: University of Illinois Press, 1998.

Shepherd, Gary, and Lawrence Lilliston. "Psychological Assessment of Children in the Family," and "Field Observations of Young People's Experience and Role in the Family." In *Sex, Slander, and Salvation: Investigating the Family/Children of God*, edited by James R. Lewis and J. Gordon Melton, 47–70. Center for Academic Publication: Stanford, Calif., 1994.

Shepherd, Gordon, and Gary Shepherd. "Evolution of the Family International/Children of God in the Direction of a Responsive Communitarian Religion." *Communal Societies* 28, no. 1 (2008): 27–54.

———. *A Kingdom Transformed: Themes in the Development of Mormonism*. Salt Lake City: University of Utah Press, 1984.

———. "Prophecy Channels and Prophetic Modalities: A Comparison of Revelation in the Family International and the LDS Church." *Journal for the Scientific Study of Religion* 48, no. 4 (2009): 734–55.

———. "The Social Construction of Prophecy in the Family International." *Nova Religio* 10, no. 2 (2006): 29–56.

———. "World Services in the Family International: The Administrative Organization of a Mature Religious Movement." *Nova Religio* 12, no. 3 (2009): 5–39.

Sherkat, Darren, and John Wilson. "Preferences, Constraints, and Choices in Religious Markets: An Examination of Religious Switching and Apostasy." *Social Forces* 73 (1995): 993–1026.

Smith, Jackie. "Globalization and Transnational Social Movement Organizations." In *Social Movements and Organization Theory*, edited by G. Davis et al., 226–48.

Smith, Philip. "Culture and Charisma: Outline of a Theory." *Acta Sociolgica* 43 (2000): 101–11.

Snow, David A. "Master Frames and Cycles of Protest." In *Frontiers in Social Movement Theory*, edited by Aldon Morris and Carol McClurg Mueller, 456–72. New Haven, Conn.: Yale University Press, 1992.

"Stabber's Friends Blame Decades of Abuse." *Arizona Daily Star*, Janaury 12, 2005.

Stark, Rodney. "Normal Revelations: A Rational Model of Mystical Experiences." In *Religion and the Social Order*, Vol. 1, edited by David Bromley, 225–38. Greenwich, Conn.: JAI Press, 1991.

———. *The Rise of Christianity: A Sociologist Reconsiders History*. Princeton, N.J.: Princeton University Press, 1996.

———. "A Theory of Revelations." *Journal for the Scientific Study of Religion* 38, no. 2 (1999): 287–308.

Stark, Rodney, and William Sims Bainbridge. *The Future of Religion: Secularization, Revival, and Cult Formation*. Berkeley: University of California Press, 1985.

———. *Religion, Deviance, and Social Control*. New York: Routledge, 1997.

Stephens, Randall J. *The Fire Spreads: Holiness and Pentecostalism in the American South.* Cambridge, Mass.: Harvard University Press, 200.

Swatos, William H. *Encyclopedia of Religion and Society.* Lanham, Md.: AltaMira Press, 1998.

Thompson, James D. *Organizations in Action.* New Brunswick, N.J.: Transaction, 2003.

Troeltsch, Ernst. *The Social Teaching of the Christian Churches.* Translated by Olive Wyon. New York: MacMillan, 1931.

Turner, Ralph H., and Lewis M. Killian. *Collective Behavior.* Englewood Cliffs, N.J.: Prentice-Hall, 1987.

Van Zandt, David E. *Living in the Children of God.* Albany: State University of New York Press, 2002.

Wacker, Grant. *Heaven Below: Early Pentecostals and American Culture.* Cambridge, Mass.: Harvard University Press, 2001.

Wallis, Roy. "Observations on the Children of God." *Sociological Review* 24 (1976): 807–29.

———. "Yesterday's Children: Cultural and Structural Changes in a New Religious Movement." In *Social Impact of New Religious Movements,* edited by Bryan Wilson, 97–133. New York: Rose of Sharon Press, 1981.

Warner, Samson. *The History of the Family, 1968–1994.* Zurich, Switzerland: World Services, 1995.

"Was the Family Doing God's Work or Unspeakable Harm?" *People,* July 18, 2005, 87–89.

Weber, Max. *Basic Concepts in Sociology.* New York: Citadel Press, 1964.

———. *Economy and Society: An Outline of Interpretive Sociology.* Edited by Guenther Roth and Claus Wittich. Berkeley: University of California Press, 1978.

———. *The Sociology of Religion.* Translated by Ephraim Fischoff. Boston: Beacon Press, 1993.

———. *The Theory of Social and Economic Organization.* New York: Oxford University Press, 1947.

Wessinger, Catherine. *How the Millennium Comes Violently: From Jonestown to Heaven's Gate.* New York: Seven Bridges Press, 2000.

White, L. Michael. *From Jesus to Christianity: How Four Generations of Visionaries and Story-tellers Created the New Testament and Christian Faith.* San Francisco: HarperOne, 2004.

Wilkinson, Peter. "The Life and Death of the Chosen One." *Rolling Stone,* June 30, 2005.

Williams, Miriam. *Heaven's Harlots: My Fifteen Years as a Sacred Prostitute in The Children of God.* New York: William Morrow & Company, 1999.

Wills, Gary. *Head and Heart: American Christianities.* New York: Penguin Press, 2007.

Wilson, Bryan. *The Social Dimensions of Sectarianism: Sects and New Religious Movements in Contemporary Society.* Oxford: Clarendon Press, 1990.

Wright, Stuart A. "Media Coverage of Unconventional Religion: Any Good News for Minority Faiths?" *Review of Religious Research* 39 (Special Issue: Mass Media and Unconventional Religion, 1997): 101–15.

———, ed. *Armageddon in Waco: Critical Perspectives on the Branch Davidian Conflict.* Chicago: University of Chicago Press, 1995.

Zablocki, Benjamin, and Thomas Robbins, eds. *Misunderstanding Cults: Searching for Objectivity in a Controversial Field.* Toronto: University of Toronto Press, 2001.

Zald, Mayer N. "The Future of Social Movements." In *Social Movements in an Orga-*

nizational Society: Collected Essays, edited by Mayer N. Zald and John D. McCarthy, 319–36. New Brunswick, N.J.: Transaction, 1987.

Zerby, Karen ("Maria"), and Kelly, Stephen ("Peter"). "The Future of the Family International." Paper presented at the annual Center for Study of New Religions (CESNUR) conference, Salt Lake City, Utah, June 11–13, 2009.

Index

ments of, 33, 39, 47, 49, 51–52, 55,
120–23, 125, 127–30
Becker, Slim, 127
Beeper, 39–40. *See also* voice chat
Bekka, 103; interview of, 103–6
Berg, David, vii, 16, 18, 143, 148, 167,
181, 203, 209, 220n4, 222n13;
autocratic style of, 9, 71; charismatic
quality of, xi, 8; children of, 6, 8; as
Endtime prophet, 14–15, 51, 133; his-
tory of, 6–11, 133–34, 220n1, 221n9;
messages from as a spirit, 12, 21, 26,
33; teachings of, 8, 36, 42, 47, 52, 55,
93, 102, 113, 140, 145, 157–59, 165,
197, 224n2, 225n1
Berg, Jane Miller, 9
Bible: Family emphasis on, 21, 43–44,
108, 114, 126, 148, 152; prophecy
in, 53
Bible Basics, 126
Blade, 75
Blumer, Herbert, 205
Board Handbook/Committee, 199–200
Board Vision, 112, 209, 223n5
brainwashing controversy, 217n21
Branch Davidians, xi, 215n9
Brazil problem, 184, 190–91, 228n12
burden, 111, 113, 150, 227n4

Campbell, John, 208
career, 1–2, 216n6. *See also* moral career
Cassandra, 111–12
Celestial Manor, 155–56, 160, 166, 171
Center for Study of New Religions
(CESNUR), 231n26
Champion Training Center, 184–86
Change Journey, 212
channeled messages, 3, 7, 24–25, 228n6;
frequency of, 15, 58
channel(s), 32, 144, 204, 208, 219n3;
characteristics of gifted, 221n7;
clearing of, 54, 59; difficulty of being,
59–60; exercising of, 33, 36, 41–42,
58, 75–76, 80, 83, 118, 172; faith in,
43, 54; humility needed for, 54, 58,
61–62, 79; lacking/losing faith in,
62, 74; multiple, 5–6, 16, 22, 46, 51,
55, 58, 64, 74–76, 203; polluting of,
62–63, 79; requirements for being,
23, 61–63 221n7; types of, 34–36,
177; weekly, 74–75. *See also* locals

charisma: routinization of, 4; as a social
process, 217n13; as type of authority/
leadership, 1, 3–4, 204
Charter, Family, 32, 189; amendment of,
13, 193–94, 199–201, 209; content
of 194, 200–201, 220n7, 226n4,
229n20, 229n22; creation of, 200,
218n36; legislation of, 195
child abuse, 215n5; accusations of,
against Family, ix–x, 10–11, 57, 117,
196, 123, 220n5, 225n9, 226n2;
acknowledgment of early, by Family,
220n5; repudiation of, by Family,
218n32, 225n9
childcare: early, in Family, 10; importance of, 195, 198–99, 201–2, 206,
223n9; responsibilities for, 155–56. *See
also* children, Family
Childcare and Parenting Board, 149, 169
children, Family: child custody battles in
Family, 164–65; prophetic socializa-
tion of, 222n6; sexuality of, 10. *See also*
child abuse; childcare
Children of God (COG), vii, 88, 160;
colonies of, 6, 218n25; founding of,
6; history of, 6–14, 218n25, 220n1;
name change of, 9; transition of, 6, 9,
14, 16. *See also* Family International,
The
Christianity: charismatic, 7, 27, 203; early
practices of, 4, 126, 216n3, 224n1;
Family relationship to, xvi, 6, 204; fundamentalist, 15, 48, 144; opposition
to Family by traditional, 48–50, 204,
211; orthodox, schisms in, 1; revelation in, 4, 208. *See also* Christians;
Churchianity
Christian living, 15, 126, 161
Christian Missionary Alliance, 7
Christian publishers/bookstores,
122–24
Christians: beliefs of, 21, 47–48, 119,
140–41; fundamentalist, 210; opposition of Family to established, 15, 48,
59, 213. *See also* Christianity
Chuck, 24, 141; interview comments of,
37, 48, 55
Churchianity, 15, 59
church-sect theory, 217n9, 231n14
Clarissa, 145–47, 168, 195–99, 201–2
coaching program, 20, 160, 188, 199,

227n5; training seminars for, 167, 179, 183–85, 191–92
commitment mechanisms, 167, 223n11, 228n15, 231n18; in Family Homes, 13, 133, 144
communal living, 15, 53, 172; benefits of, 194, 198; requirements of, 18, 52, 58, 118, 126, 160–61, 167, 193–94, 200, 212; responsive characteristics of, 218n36, 226n5
Continental Officers, 13, 72, 151, 168, 221n3; replacement of, 166, 183
Cooper, Anderson 360 Show, 215n8
Corrine, 94; interview of, 95, 98–102
cult(s), 1–2, 216n2; labeling of, x, xii, 6, 10, 216n4. *See also* new religious movements (NRMs)
Cynthia, 131–32; interview of, 134–43

Dad. *See* Berg, David
dance videos, 57, 220n5
David, 109, 122; interview of, 110–16
Davidito, 148–49. *See also* Rodriquez, Ricky
Davis, Deborah, 122, 224n14
Dawson, Lorne, 231n15
Densel, 131–32, 142; interview of, 133–38, 140–43
Devil, 14–15; comic portrayal of, 97; opposition of to Family, 16, 31, 52, 79, 83, 114, 144, 147–48, 179, 211, 219n38
devotionals, 225n12
disciple, Family. *See under* Family membership—categories of
discipleship standard(s), 220n7, 221n8, 229n20
Discovering Truth, 126
Disney, 124, 127
divorce, 159, 161–65
Don, 153–54; interview of, 154–59
Durkheim, Emile, 221n8, 230n1

ecclesiastical hierarchies, 209–10
Elerian Horses, 176, 227n2
emotionalism, 65–68
Endtime: delayed coming of, 140, 210, 224n1; Family beliefs concerning, xi, 8, 14–16, 46–47, 49, 88, 108, 112, 140–41, 167, 195, 203–4, 211, 218n31, 219n38; presentation of on

Family Web page, 136–37, 140–41; waiting for, 110. *See also* Millenarianism
Endtime Army, 10, 14, 184
End Time News Digest, 24, 37, 225n10
Endtime News Digest, 141
Endtime witnesses, 63–64, 210
Enemy, The. *See* Devil
Esau, 154, 225n1
evangelization: Family commitment to, xii, 1, 8, 11–12, 68, 72, 110, 117, 153, 210, 212; methods of, 10, 110, 112. *See also* missionaries, Family
excommunication: appeal of, 193, 195–97; partial, 80, 222n11; reasons for, 10, 171, 193, 196, 228n14; reinstatement following, 196–98
ex-Family members: attacks of, ix, xii, 10–11, 117, 122–24, 127, 138–39, 147–49, 162, 164–65, 193, 224n15; communications with, 164–65, 180, 195; reconciliation of, 146, 196–97, 228n7; transition of to secular life of, 149–50, 180–81, 212; Web sites of, 124, 138, 224n15, 225n9. *See also* apostasy

Faithworks, 123
Family. *See* Family International, The
Family Boards, 209, 219n37, 221n5; Church Growth and Outreach, 112; GP Productions, 130; Jett/Teen, 92–93; national/regional, 143, 222n5; PR, 149. *See also* International Boards
Family core beliefs, 14–16, 79, 88, 117, 212–13
Family culture, 27–28, 37, 52
Family Homes, viii, 9–10, 18, 20–21, 116, 118–19, 215n1; in the field, 219n8; governance in, 183, 188, 190–91, 201–2, 221n2; managers in, 18–19, 190–91, 221n2, 226n3; missionary work of, 130; prophecy in, 26, 63, 196; raids of by authorities 10–11, 218n31; reports from, 132, 150, 173, 174, 197, 226n2; revenue sources for, 124–25, 126–27, 174; reviews of, 185, 194–95, 202; service types, 225n6; sexual deviance alleged in, 10; size of, 199–201, 229n22; standards of disciple, 200–202, 210, 229n20
Family International, The, viii; adaptive

changes of, xi, 3, 14, 26–27, 36, 110, 133, 145, 201–3, 206–7, 210, 212–13; appeal of to outsiders, 48–50, 113–14, 212; business practices of, 116, 118, 121, 124–25, 128–29; core beliefs of, 14–16, 212–13; comparison of to other religions, xvi, 68, 99, 109–10, 183, 204, 207, 209–11, 219n38, 225n14, 229n19, 230n2; conversion to, 198, 210, 212, 224n12; critics of, 20, 48; cult stereotypes concerning, xi, 160, 194, 204; culture of, xii, 160, 215–16n10; democratizing trends in, 10, 13, 55, 143–44, 189, 200–202, 204, 205, 208–10, 228n9; former members of, 55–56, 122–23, 144–48; history of, 6–14, 166, 207; institutionalization of, 5, 203–7; leaving of by members, 149–50, 180–81, 212; mature movement characteristics of, 206–7; media coverage of, 144, 146–48; mission of, 151–52, 157, 183, 203–4, 212–13; name change to, 11; persecution of, 10–11, 144, 146–47, 218n31; publications of, 14, 108–30; responsive communitarian characteristics of, 13–14, 126, 160; skills gained by members in, 150, 154–55; sociological significance of, xvi, 2, 5, 13, 27, 203; study of by social scientists, ix, 5, 213, 217nn13–14; teamwork commitment of, 156–57, 204; transnational characteristics of, 27–28, 203, 207, 211; world spread of, xiv, 11, 112, 139

Family membership: current number, 11–12; education of, 206, 212; growth of, 109–10, 115, 130

—categories of, 209, 229n18; Family disciple (FD), 11, 13, 18, 20, 58, 104, 109, 119, 135, 197, 199, 210; Fellow Members (FM), 12, 58, 127, 135, 196–97, 224n17; Member Missionaries (MM), 12, 197–99. *See also* Activated ministry/program: membership

Family of Love, The. *See* Family International, The

Family Policy Council, 183–84, 194, 207, 209; composition of, 20, 143, 200

Family Policy Council Steering Committee, 20, 22, 207

Family Special Magazine, 72

Family theology, 140, 172, 213, 219n4

FARs, 104

Father David. *See* Berg, David

Feed My Lambs, 124

Fellow Members. *See under* Family membership—categories of

First Generation Adults (FGAs), 27, 59, 65, 213; aging of, 12–13, 109, 194–95, 198, 212; furloughs taken by, 197–98; potential alienation of, 179–80, 187–86, 189; retirement plans for, 194, 110, 198, 229n18; virtues of, 154, 158, 169, 172, 188, 190–91, 198

flirty fishing (FFing), 123, 198, 204, 222n1; abandonment of, 206; reasons for, 9–10, 204, 218n27

Folks, The. *See* Maria and Peter

Frank, 24, 118, 141; interview comments of, 28–29, 33–35, 37–38, 40–42, 45–48, 50–53, 55–58, 61–62, 67, 118–30

free choice/will, 166

Friends of The Family, 12

From Jesus with Love books, 122, 124

Fundamentalist Church of Jesus Christ of Latter-day Saints (FLDS), 215n4; abuse charges against, x; comparison of Family to, 215n8; removal of children from, ix. *See also* Mormons

furloughs, 197–98

gender equality, 14, 209

General Public Department, 24, 109, 112, 116–30

Gen-Up, 104

Gideon band, 211

God on God, 112, 126, 141, 223n6

Good News (GN), xv, 70–86, 199, 219n1, 224n12; department of, 21–22, 70, 174, 176; editing of, 23–24, 28; Family Disciple Home receipt of, 70; impact on Family members of, 41–44, 225n12; meaning of, 21; printing of, 104; prophecies published in, 22, 25–26, 32, 41, 43, 51; prophecy team for, 24; translations of, 106–7

gospel, 47–48

Grandpa. *See* Berg, David

Grapevine, 104, 112
Great Tribulation, 47, 49, 144, 225n13.
    See also Endtime

handyman role, 153–57
Heavenly City School, 222n3
heretical religion, 1–2, 4, 7, 117, 203–4,
    210–11, 216n1, 227n10, 230n2
holy families, 104
Home(s). *See* Family Homes
home-schooling, 11, 121–22, 212

Infostore, 109, 113. *See also* products/
    publications, Family
inspirationalist, 110, 223n3
International Board Chairs, 29, 73,
    136, 141, 200, 202, 221n4; residence
    of at World Services, 143, 209
International Boards, 73–74, 207,
    222n5, 223n5; Church Growth and
    Outreach, 78, 117, 129; Coaching
    and Shepherding, 183–85, 189, 191;
    Family Education, 149; General Public
    Production, 117, 129–30; JETT/Teen,
    92–93; Public Relations, 149, 168, 202
International Society for Krishna Con-
    sciousness (Hare Krishnas), 6
Internet, 131–32. *See also* Web sites, Fam-
    ily
interpretation of tongues, 66
interviewing methods, 216n12
Islam, 4–5

Jack, 24; interview comments of, 32–33,
    35–36, 47–48, 55, 58, 60, 66
Jason, 30, 169
Jeff, 143–44, 199; interview of, 145–52,
    185–92
Jehovah's Witnesses, 3, 115, 210, 217n11
Jesse, 33; interview of, 77–78, 80–82,
    84–86
Jessica, 103, 106, 173–75; interview of,
    175–82
Jesus, 1; atonement of, 21; faith in, 8–9;
    as husband and lover, 25, 204, 219n4;
    love of, 15; pictures of, 17; prophetic
    messages from, 12, 14, 21; second
    coming of, 14, 133, 195, 210–11, 213;
    sexual nature of, 15, 36, 204, 220n9,
    224n16. *See also* Lord, the

Jesus People Movement, 6, 217n20
JETTs, 35, 92–93
Jews, 3–4, 210, 216n3, 217n11
Julie, 24; interview comments of, 40–41,
    53–54, 68

Kanter, Rosabeth, 167
Kelly, Steven. *See* Peter (Steven Kelly)
Kelsi, 183–86, 189, 191
Keri, 24; interview comments of, 32, 34,
    39, 52, 60–61
keys (spiritual): calling upon, 26, 45, 69,
    78; democratic access of, 22; key prom-
    ises for children, 92, 222n4; power of,
    viii, 16, 22, 47; protection of, 83
Keys to Happier Living, 126
Kiddie Viddies, 119–20, 127
Kidland, 104
Killian, Lewis M., 205

Latter-Day Saints (LDS), 4, 210, 229n19,
    230n2. *See also* Mormons
Law of Love, 9, 15, 172, 226n4
Law of Love battles, 167, 172, 220n9
Lem, 160, 171; interview of, 161–66
Life with Grandpa series, 95, 148–49
Link, 104, 118–19, 130
litnessing, 110, 223n2
locals, 219n3; as editorial channeler 22,
    24, 94, 100–102, 129, 132, 136, 174;
    as editorial critique, 76, 87, 112, 141.
    See also channel(s)
Lord, the: dependency on, 77, 81, 89;
    hearing from, 47, 51–52, 67, 76,
    85–86, 111, 124, 126, 147, 158,
    164–65, 167, 172; help of, viii, 25,
    30–31; love of, 37; questions to,
    28–29, 32, 34–43, 53–54, 86, 162,
    170; relationship with, 61, 67; seeking
    will of, 76; serving of, 58, 150–51. *See
    also* Jesus
loving Jesus words, 35, 224n16
Lutherans, 3

MacGregor, Scott, 112, 127, 141
Maggie, 156, 185–86
Mama. *See* Maria
Mama and Peter. *See* Maria and Peter
Mama's and Peter's Letters Ministry
    (MPL), 25, 32, 103, 173–82

Mama's Personal Letters: assignments of responses to, 72–73, 75, 173–82; filing of, 174–75, 178; Maria listening/responding to, 175–76, 178, 182; monitoring of, for issues, 174–75, 178–80

Mama's secretaries, 24, 73, 77–79, 83–84, 106, 173–82

management skills/styles, 156–58

Maria (Karen Zerby, Mama), 25–27, 113, 143; cartoons of, 98; childhood of, 41; emphasis on prophecy by, 15–17, 47, 53–54, 71, 84–85, 165; eye problem of, 139, 173; faith in, by WS staff, 23, 41–43, 76, 182; faith of, in WS staff, 23, 41–43, 71, 76, 80, 86, 182; illustrations of, in Family publications, 98; interview comments by, 25–47, 50, 54–60, 63–68; interviews with, 21, 24; memory of, 40, 84; parents of, 7, 40; relationship with David Berg, 9, 38, 133; as successor to David Berg, vii, 12; "Woe" video by, 190–91, 229n13. *See also* Maria and Peter
—gifts of: anointing, 23, 43, 46, 51; asking questions, 22, 28, 31–32; gift of prophecy, lacking of, 23, 32, 41
—responsibilities of: assignment of prophecies by, 22, 31, 34, 40–41, 72, 74–76, 81, 84, 176; publishing GNs, 21–22, 70–71, 73–76, 87, 94, 132; reading of personal prophecies by, 85, 171; spiritual role of, 22, 31, 54; training of staff by, 38–34, 41–43, 182; as "wine taster" of GN prophecies, 23, 42–43, 78–79, 84, 176

Maria and Peter: attacks against, 11, 148; attitudes of members toward, 180; corrections given to staff by, 62, 170–71; delegation of authority by, 73, 86, 150–51, 181; faith of, in leadership of young people by, 183, 187; interactions between, 56, 65, 73, 78, 85, 95, 146; interviews with, x, xiii, 26; joint leadership responsibilities of, 16–17, 28, 30–31, 41–42, 51, 60, 71, 74–75, 136, 141–42, 166–67, 171, 181–83, 189, 194, 200, 209, 215–16n10; letter of apology by, 218n30; photograph of, xiii, 64, 221n9; presentation at CENSUR conference by, 212; training of staff by, 73, 182

Marilyn, 173–75; interview of, 175–82

marriage: in The Family, 159, 161–62, 165–66; book of, 166

Marx, Gary, 204–5

Mathias, 145, 185–87

McAdam, Doug, 204–5

medical attitudes of Family, 212

Meditation Moments, 113

Melody: 24, 143–44; GN roundtable comments of, 28–32, 36, 38–41, 49–50, 59–63, 65; interview of, 145–52, 182–92

Melton, Gordon J., 10

Member Missionaries. *See under* Family membership—categories of

Methodists, 3

Michael, 145–47, 195, 197, 199, 201

Millenarianism, 14–15, 133, 210, 224n1, 225n13; violent expressions of, 225n14. *See also* Endtime

miracles, 49, 133

missionaries, Family: commitment requirements for, 150–52, 184–85; efforts of, 108–10; methods of, 88, 93, 115–18, 223n8. *See also* evangelization

Mo. *See* Berg, David

MO Letters, 92–93, 135, 158, 181; content of, 197, 222n1, 224n12, 225n12; function of, 7–8, 13–14

moral career, 2, 216n7; of Family, 3–4, 6, 13–14, 109, 203, 205–6, 210, 213

Mormons, 3, 217n9, 225n1. *See also* Fundamentalist Church of Jesus Christ of Latter-day Saints (FLDS); Latter-Day Saints (LDS)

Mother Eve, 9

Mottos for Success, 119, 125

MP3 files, 85, 175

musicians, 126–28

Muslim. *See* Islam

names, 227n4

National Book Network, 123

National Broadcasting Corporation (NBC), 141

new religious movements (NRMs), 2, 216n5; adaptive change of, 3, 26, 50, 117, 203, 211; characteristics of successful, 25, 50, 194; conflicts of with authorities, 218n24, 231n13; mature vs. emergent, 231n14; negative media portrayals of, 215n7, 216n13; scholarly study of, 206, 213, 231n15, 231n26. *See also* cult(s)

Newsweek Magazine, 114–15

Niebuhr, H. Richard, 217n10

Ohio State University, 109–10

old bottles, 190, 228n11

One Wife doctrine, 9

organizational analysis, 205–10

outreach programs, 12, 112–13, 116

Passion, The, 115

Pentecostalism/charismatic revival, 6–7, 15, 23, 217n23, 219n38

People's Temple, 6

Peter (Steven Kelly), 11, 103, 113, 134, 146, 160; administrative role of, 17–18, 20, 22, 29, 72, 132, 138–39, 161, 167, 183–85, 192, 22n4; as co-leader with Maria, 12, 16–17; contributions to prophecy by, 32, 43, 85–86; letters to, 175, 178, 182; making of training videos by 175, 191; secretaries for, 72; trips to Brazil of, 183–84, 191

pillars, 143, 221n5

Policy Council. *See* Family Policy Council

prayer and prophecy (P & P), 61–62, 155, 185; as a framing mechanism, 208–9; requests for, 54, 59, 146, 222n14; solving problems with, 96, 105, 136

prayer mornings, 59, 62, 75, 81, 84

prayer vigils, 227n3

Presbyterians, 3

products/publications, Family, 37, 72, 75, 113, 120, 124, 126, 141; compatibility of, with different cultures, 106; for children, 87, 92, 94, 95, 102, 104–5, 119, 130, 148–49; for Christians, 130; portrayal of sexuality in, 92; translations of from English, 103, 106. *See also* Aurora Productions; Good News (GN); *Xn; and entries for other specific products and publications*

prophecy: culture of in Family, 222n6, 222n13; Dad's comments on, 42; Dad's style of giving, 46; discernment of, 63; dramatic increase of in Family, 45–46, 71, 78, 84, 111, 203–4; early expressions of in Family, 27, 34–35,

42, 46; gender differences in giving, 33–36; language correlations with, 78, 82; limitations of, 56; Maria's comments on, 41–42; need for in Endtime, 47–49; personal biasing of, 62, 83; pitfalls of, 23, 54–55; practical results of, 61, 65–66, 68, 77; study of, 5; taken-for-granted nature of in Family, 58–62, 82; uniqueness of in Family, 34, 46, 48–51, 59, 76, 203, 208, 211. *See also* revelation, divine

—processes of receiving: channeling of, 21; clarification of, 81–82, 94, 175–76; confirmation of, 30, 37, 43, 49, 64, 80, 103, 174, 176; how received, 36–37, 46, 49, 82–83, 222n12; praying to receive, 28–29, 61; social construction of, xi, 21, 28, 204, 208, 211; as a social process, 52, 54–55, 95

—received from: departed spirits, 48–50, 60, 175–76; field, 32, 63–64, 174; Jesus, 14, 21; spirit helpers, 31, 56, 95, 99

—requirements for receiving: faith, 35–36, 41–42, 54, 64, 81, 84; praying to receive, 28–29, 61

—social functions of, 34, 46–49, 55, 79, 208; consensus vs. conflict in, 23, 51–56, 64, 211; democratization of, 16, 24, 34, 55; as a framing mechanism, 207–9

—types of, 33–34, 37, 40, 60; complete vs. incomplete, 22, 31, 39, 43–44, 76, 175; different gifts of, 23, 33, 79; encouragement, 34, 37, 79, 84–85, 174–75, 178–79; home coming, 175–76, 181; at home level, 51–56; levels of, 25–27, 65; personal guidance of, 26, 30, 38, 47, 51, 55, 60, 68, 78–79, 84–85, 168, 175; runaway, 56, 220n3; styles of giving, 23, 34, 37, 78–79; unsolicited, 85

—World Services production of: assignments of, 33, 41, 62, 74–76, 78–79, 83–84; balancing of, 38, 46, 75–76; burden of for whole Family, 41–44, 65; confirmation of, 30, 37, 43, 49, 64, 105–6, 111; controls on, 50–51; corporate, 16, 103; editing of, 22, 30, 38, 76, 93, 181; electronic filing of, 78, 84–86, 177–78; norms of

producing, 27, 41, 53; publication of, x; teamwork, 23, 49, 53, 95; work, 60, 84–85
prophets, ancient, 43
Protestants, xvi
provisioning, 18, 186, 204, 228n10
publications. *See* products/publications
Publications Final Approval Committee, 87–88, 93

Rachael, 24, 79, 83; GN roundtable comments of, 31–32, 38, 40, 42, 44, 48–49, 53, 68–69; interview of, 70–77
Readers' Digest, 113
regional desks, 194–96
relationship problems, 159, 165, 167, 171–72; learning lessons from, 161–62
religious accommodation, 3, 210–13, 217n10
religious dualism, 219n39
religious economy, 230n8
religious scholars, 1, 3
Restructuring and Renewal, 180, 183–85, 191, 227n12
retrenchment campaigns, 14, 117, 194, 200, 203, 210, 227n11
revelation, divine, 3–4; curtailment of, 4–5; guidance of Family by, 5, 15, 43, 211; normal, 168; sociological study of, 4–5. *See also* prophecy
revolutions, in the Family, 46, 159, 191, 220n1, 224n2
Ricky-Angela case: impact of, on Family, 138–39, 144–48, 225n8; *Rolling Stone* article concerning, 146–47. *See also* Rodriquez, Ricky; Smith, Angela
road teams, 223n8
Roberta, 87, 95, 103, 106, 154; interview of, 88–94
Rodriquez, Ricky, 11, 57, 135–36, 139, 148, 178, 197; claims of abuse by, 218n32, 225n16; Web site concerning, 225n8. *See also* Davidito; Ricky-Angela case
R3 support group, 162–63

sacred, routinization of the, 58–61
sacrifice, 52, 58, 151–52, 154
Sally Scribe, 181

Satan. *See* Devil
Savannah, 94, 118, 132; interview of, 96–97, 99–100, 102
schism, 1, 211
school of the prophets, 26, 38, 63
Second Generation Adults (SGAs), 10, 12, 27, 58, 65, 203, 206, 212; anger toward parents of, 162–63, 169, 225n16; capabilities of, 113, 158, 186–87; defending faith by, 144, 147; leadership opportunities for, 14, 132, 154, 158, 167, 183, 186–87, 189, 191–92, 195, 209–10; loss of faith by, 133, 144, 149–50, 162, 165, 179–80, 225n16, 227n10; rebelliousness of, 13; technical training of, 133, 142–43, 168, 179; transitioning from Family of, 133, 139–40, 144, 149–52. *See also* young people, Family
sects, 1, 216n1
secular world: accommodation of Family to, 117–18, 150; attitudes of Family toward, 117, 213; education in, 150, 212; values of, 194. *See also* System, the
Servilla, 158–59
sex: Family regulation of, 13, 193, 196, 218n30, 220n5, 226n4, 228n14; Family teachings concerning, 9–10
sexual sharing, 9–10, 15, 163, 220n9, 222n1, 224n16; SGA problems with, 164, 167
SGAs. *See* Second Generation Adults (SGAs)
Shane, 158–59
sheep, 127
Shepherd, Gary and Gordon, vii, 26, 44–45; cartoon of, 102–3; interview methods of, xiii–xv, 44, 175; research on Family of, viii, xi–xii, 26, 28, 65, 68, 145, 215n10
shepherd(s): skills required by, 167–68, 170
—Field Home, 18–19, 160, 171, 221n2, 227n5
—Regional, 30, 60, 143, 166, 183–85, 189, 193–96, 200, 202, 207, 221n4, 224n4, 227n5
—Visiting, 183–85, 188, 227n5
—World Services, 79, 153, 156, 159–72, 170; confidentiality questions with,

for, 135. *See also* ex-Family members, Web sites of; Internet

Wilkinson, Peter, 146

Wills, Gary, 219

witchcraft, 100

witnessing, 9, 14, 18, 93, 110, 204. *See also* evangelization; missionaries, Family

Word, The, 14–15, 20–24, 220n2

wordtime, 62–63, 155, 222n8

World Services, 10; access to, xii–xiii; channels at, 21, 23, 63, 77–78, 174, 208; childcare at, 92; communal lifestyle at, 153–57, 160, 171; department head revolution in, 134, 187, 192, 224n3; evolution of, 16, 71–73; expenditures at, 141–42; Final Approval Committee at, 103, 105–6; as headquarter organization, xi, 12, 16–20, 207; importance of computer technology for, 103–5; leadership training in, 154, 191; living arrangements at, 17–18, 153; organizational chart of, 19; organizational complexity of, 17–20, 175, 207; oversight committees at, 18, 20; personnel management in, 89, 95, 154–58; pillars of, 161; products provided by, 12, 17, 70, 104, 116–17; prophecy at, xiv, 65; publication work of, x–xi, 11, 22, 25, 93–94, 103–6, 131, 161, 176, 207; responsibility burden of, 41–44, 65, 68, 76, 80, 101, 191, 207; secret location of, xii, 11, 20; security concerns at, xii, 65, 69, 133, 142, 221n9; teamwork approach of, xvi, 65–66, 103, 158; want ads for, 142; work ethic of, 17–18, 74, 157, 221n6; youthful leadership at, 158, 167, 187, 191–92, 209. *See also* shepherd(s)—World Services
—departments of, 18–20, 73–74; Administration, 192–202; Art and Text, 87–88, 103, 105–6, 154; Child Care, 24, 153–56; Church Growth and Outreach, 24, 112, 118, 129; Coaching and Shepherding, 24, 144, 182–92; General Public, 24, 109, 112, 116–30; Home Care and Maintenance, 153–59; Layout, 103, 105; Public Relations, 143–52; Web, 131–52. *See also* Aurora Productions; Good News (GN); Mama's secretaries
—staff of, vii, 13; candor of, x, xvi; competency of, xvi, 17, 105; dedication of, 160, 171; disclaiming of personal ability by, 77–79, 88–89, 104–5, 109–10, 122, 155, 158; gender composition of, 36, 209; interviews with, x, 16–17; 20, 24; qualifications of, 71, 87–89, 95, 117–18, 121, 133–34, 142, 155, 187, 207; training of, 32, 38–39, 42, 71–73, 87–89, 103, 131–32, 134, 139, 155, 167, 192; youthfulness of, x, xvi, 41, 148, 167, 187, 191, 224n3

Xn, 35, 75, 89, 91, 96, 104, 138

Year of Strengthening, 146–47, 172, 183–84, 191, 227n12

yieldedness, 23, 53, 58, 61–62, 220n3

young people, Family, 59; discouragement of, 180, 187–88; leaving Family of, 56–57, 149–52, 169; maintaining commitment of, 222n2, 226n7; publications for, 35; sexual conservatism of, 165; talent of, 159; teens, 35, 93. *See also* Second Generation Adults (SGAs)

Zerby, Karen, xiii, 7. *See also* Maria

Zine, 72

Zondervan Publishers, 122–23

GORDON SHEPHERD is a professor of sociology at the University of Central Arkansas. GARY SHEPHERD is a professor of sociology at Oakland University. They are the coauthors of *Mormon Passage: A Missionary Chronicle.*

The University of Illinois Press
is a founding member of the
Association of American University Presses.

Designed by Kelly Gray
Composed in 9.5/13 ITC New Baskerville
by Celia Shapland
at the University of Illinois Press
Manufactured by Thomson-Shore, Inc.

University of Illinois Press
1325 South Oak Street
Champaign, IL 61820-6903
www.press.uillinois.edu